Writing
for Magazines

Writing
for Magazines

Second Edition

Myrick E. Land

Reynolds School of Journalism
University of Nevada, Reno

PRENTICE HALL
Englewood Cliffs, New Jersey 07632

Library of Congress Cataloging-in-Publication Data

Land, Myrick, (date)
    Writing for magazines / Myrick E. Land. — 2nd ed.
      p. cm.
    Includes index.
    ISBN 0–13–971193–7
    1. Authorship. I. Title.
    PN147.L32   1993
    808′.02—dc20   91–42883
                                       CIP

Credit lines appear on pp. 191–192.

Acquisitions editor: Steve Dalphin
Editorial/production supervision and
   interior design: Colby Stong
Copy editor: Patricia Daly
Cover design: Karen Salzbach
Prepress buyer: Kelly Behr
Manufacturing buyer: Mary Ann Gloriande
Editorial assistant: Caffie Risher Barfield

© 1993, 1987 by Prentice-Hall, Inc.
A Simon & Schuster Company
Englewood Cliffs, New Jersey 07632

Printed in the United States of America
10 9 8 7 6 5 4 3 2 1

ISBN 0-13-971193-7

Prentice-Hall International (UK) Limited, *London*
Prentice-Hall of Australia Pty. Limited, *Sydney*
Prentice-Hall Canada Inc., *Toronto*
Prentice-Hall Hispanoamericana, S.A., *Mexico*
Prentice-Hall of India Private Limited, *New Delhi*
Prentice-Hall of Japan, Inc., *Tokyo*
Simon & Schuster Asia Pte. Ltd., *Singapore*
Editora Prentice-Hall do Brasil, Ltda., *Rio de Janeiro*

To Barbara, Robert, and Jacquelyn

Contents

7 Developing Your Skill as an Interviewer 60

8 Organizing Your Material and Writing a First Draft 71

9 The First Hundred Words 77

10 How to Hold a Reader's Interest   86

11 Developing Your Own Style   94

12 Discovering the Right Structure for Your Article 101

13 The Writer and the Law 113

14 Free-Lancing: Occasionally, Part-Time, or Full-Time 126

15   Joining a Magazine Staff   137

Advice from Eight Editors   146

Experiments in Magazine Writing   162

A Look at the New Journalism   171

Appendix A: Checklist for a Magazine Article   179

Appendix B: Information on Mechanics 183

Preface

This book is for anyone who wants to write for magazines. It outlines a method that many students in magazine courses at universities across the country have used successfully.

Writing for Magazines is based partly on what I have learned about magazine writing as a free-lancer, as a magazine editor, and as a teacher of magazine writing courses at universities in Wisconsin, Nevada, Venezuela, Australia, and Great Britain. More importantly, in this second edition I have had the assistance of at least 100 other people—free-lance writers, staff writers, magazine editors, and teachers of magazine writing—who have shared their experiences and generously offered their advice to those who are entering the field. The names of many of these contributors appear in the chapters that follow.

This book is directed also at those who have experimented briefly and unsuccessfully with magazine writing and have been baffled by the chilly reception from distant, unseen editors. Each year thousands of writers type out a few magazine articles, rush them off to the largest national magazines, receive printed rejection slips, and then give up. This discouraging experience convinces most of them that the field of magazine writing is dominated by writers who are already widely known, or that there is some secret formula for success that only a few privileged people know.

The errors made by those unsuccessful writers are easy to identify and easy to avoid. The most common cause of failure in magazine writing is the writer's lack of understanding of the publication he or she wishes to write for. In the opening chapters I have emphasized the importance of making a close, analytical study of any magazine before offering ideas to the editors. You should be able to answer six basic questions about the publication and its readers before making a submission, and these are listed and discussed in Chapter 4, "How to Analyze a Magazine."

Very few editors will read completed manuscripts sent in by free-lancers who have not previously written for them. They prefer to receive brief query letters or article memos that give a clear idea of your article proposal. You will find a suggested form for a query letter or an article memo and examples of each in Chapter 5, "How to Offer Ideas to Magazines."

Chapters 6 through 12 offer specific advice on researching, writing, and revising magazine articles. One of these chapters focuses on the most important words in any article—The First Hundred Words. Another tells you how to develop your own writing style. Each of these chapters also includes many illustrations drawn from the work of successful magazine free-lancers and staff writers.

Chapter 13, "The Writer and the Law," offers advice on the most important legal questions that writers must keep in mind.

The closing chapters discuss the advantages and disadvantages of full-time magazine free-lancing or of working on a magazine staff as a writer or an editor. Here you will find specific suggestions about how to get started as a free-lancer and how to find a job on a magazine staff.

A special section brings you "Advice from Eight Editors." Editors of eight magazines tell you exactly what *they* would do if they were beginning free-lancers and wanted to write for their own magazines. This advice was specially prepared for this book.

Perhaps the most important new feature of this second edition is another special section. "Experiments in Magazine Writing." Here you will find *most* of the information you need to write three magazine articles—a health article, a general interest article about counterfeiting and counterfeiters, and an article offering readers advice on what to do after an automobile accident. By testing your skill in carrying out the necessary additional research, organizing your material, and writing articles based on one or two of these topics, you may discover whether this is a field of writing you would like to enter.

A NOTE OF THANKS

The names of many of those who helped me with *Writing for Magazines* appear in the chapters that follow. I would like to add this special note of appreciation to Steve Dalphin, my editor at Prentice Hall, who offered valuable advice and encouragement on both editions of this book; Caffie Risher Barfield, his capable and enthusiastic assistant; Colby Stong, for his editorial supervision and interior design; and these teachers of magazine writing across the country who contributed substantially to the development of the manuscript:

Professor Rob Phillips, Oregon State University; Professor Louis Alexander, University of Houston; Professor Stephen E. Emerine, University of Arizona; Professor William A. Emerson, Jr., University of South Carolina; Professor Miriam G. Hill, University of Alabama; Professor Milton Hollstein, University of Utah; Professor Marcia L. Hurlow, Asbury College; Professor Carol Reuss, University of North Carolina; Professor William B. Toran, Ohio State University; Sammye Johnson, Trinity University; Carolyn D. Scott, Lindenwood College; Karen Hammond, State University of New York at Binghamton; and Sharon M. W. Bass, University of Kansas.

I am also grateful to the faculty members of the Reynolds School of Journalism for their strong interest and help with both editions, and to the writers whose articles I have quoted as models for those who want to become free-lancers or staff writers. My special thanks to Robert Laxalt, John Frook, James K. Gentry, Jake Highton, Warren Lerude, Theodore Conover, Phillip Padellford, Philip Barry Osborne, and Roberta Ashley for their valuable contributions to this book.

Myrick E. Land

Biographical Note

Myrick Land sold his first magazine article while taking a magazine writing course at the Graduate School of Journalism at Columbia University.

In the decades since, he has written more than 200 articles for 35 national magazines, including *The New York Times Magazine, Look, Parade, McCall's, This Week, Coronet, Saturday Review/World, Cosmopolitan, Junior Scholastic, World Week, Toronto Star Weekly,* and *The Listener.*

Land spent five years as an editor of *This Week* and twelve years on the staff of *Look* magazine, including four years as assistant managing editor. He is author or coauthor of eleven books. One was nominated as Best First Mystery of the Year by Mystery Writers of America, and another was offered as a dividend to members of the Book-of-the-Month Club. He and his wife Barbara collaborated on *A Short History of Reno,* published in the spring of 1992.

Land helped establish the first school of journalism in Venezuela and has taught courses in magazine writing at universities in Australia, Great Britain, Wisconsin, and Nevada. He is now Professor of Journalism at the Reynolds School of Journalism, University of Nevada, Reno.

1

Entering the Magazine World

What chance does a beginner have of achieving early publication in magazines? Here you will find seven suggestions that could shorten your period of apprenticeship.

While studying magazine writing at the University of Nevada, Reno, Connie Denham sold "The Myth of Instant Love" to a very small publication, the *Stepfamily Bulletin*.

Encouraged by the *Bulletin*'s quick response to that article (which offered advice to new stepparents), Denham submitted carefully written article proposals to several larger magazines. *Our Family* accepted "Helping Families with a Handicapped Child," and *Family Journal* bought "Breast Feeding and Working—Several Women Tell How You Can Do Both." *Ladycom* paid $350 for "The Parental Divide—After Divorce, It's Up to You to Share Your Children's Lives," and *Dynamic Years* paid $800 for "Grandparenting After a Divorce."

Because she concentrated her efforts, Denham saw four of her articles in print in three months.

This is an unusual record, but it is not unique. Another University of Nevada student, Diane Banegas, made her way from the university's alumni magazine, the *UNR Times,* to *Growing Parent,* and to *Cosmopolitan* while completing graduate work at the university.

Similar achievements have been recorded in magazine classes at universities across the country. The first articles by most of these students have appeared in specialized publications, such as *American Collector, The Quarterhorse Journal, International Coaching,* and *Bridal Trends,* or in one of the thousands of trade or professional journals. But others have seen their work in *Seventeen, Mother Jones, Esquire, The New York Times,* and *The Nation* while still in college.

It would be misleading to promise you instant success in this field. Many free-lancers who later achieve wide publication go through months of submitting articles before they see their first pieces in print. But if you have considerable writing talent and if you are ready to approach this field intelligently, you should be able to write articles that will satisfy the editors of some of the 17,000 or more magazines now being published in the United States. And you should see your first article in print within a reasonable period of time. Of course, there are no guarantees. Your success depends entirely on your readiness to give adequate imagination, time, thought, skill, and energy to this new undertaking.

TWO MYTHS ABOUT MAGAZINE WRITING

Many talented students are handicapped from the beginning because they take seriously two widely circulated statements about magazine writing:

"National magazines will not buy an article from you unless you are a famous writer."

"It takes years to learn to write magazine articles. You must expect to receive hundreds of rejection slips before you have any chance of having an article pub-lished."

These two assertions are endlessly repeated—and they are demonstrably false.

Many people will tell you that you are wasting your time trying to write for magazines unless you are already as well known as James A. Michener, Tom Wolfe, Gloria Steinem, Norman Mailer, or Gore Vidal.

A simple test will reveal the baselessness of this widely held belief. Examine the current issues of a dozen of the most popular magazines now being published—for example, *People, Reader's Digest, Playboy, TV Guide, Sports Illustrated, Esquire, Seventeen, The New Yorker, National Geographic,* and *The New York Times Magazine.* You will be surprised to discover how *few* of the writers' names you recognize.

Although most magazines would welcome articles from famous writers, relatively few famous writers devote much of their time to writing for magazines. They are much more likely to concentrate on writing books or plays or television series.

But even if every famous writer in America devoted most of his or her time to magazine writing, the articles these authors produced could not begin to fill one-tenth of the pages of the thousands of magazines published in the United States month after month.

Bylines are less important to most magazine editors than many outsiders believe. Because these editors have discovered that they cannot count on featuring famous writers issue after issue, they instead watch for promising writers who come up with carefully thought-out ideas, research their articles thoroughly, and present them with skill.

The second myth—about the inevitability of years of rejection before the first acceptance—is based on the experiences of those writers who do not approach the field analytically or systematically.

Many of these discouraged writers *invited* rejection, although they do not recognize this. They casually dashed off pieces about subjects that happened to interest them but were of little or no interest to the readers of the magazines they approached. They settled on the magazine without much thought, sent the editors a rough, unfinished manuscript, and settled back complacently, waiting for an enthusiastic telephone call or letter of acceptance.

This is the mark of the amateur, and it naturally leads to a series of rejections. Disappointed by their own lack of success, these writers then warn other beginners to stay away from magazines.

While it would be misleading to promise you quick acceptance by magazine editors, the experiences of many hundreds of talented writers over the years prove that publication is possible within a year or a year and a half after you begin submitting ideas regularly to magazines. This will not happen if you are lazy in your approach or if you are easily discouraged. "Persistence is as important as talent," one successful free-lancer observes.

One directory (*The Working Press of the Nation*) lists just over 5,400 magazines as "principal publications." There are many thousands of other magazines that are too small, too obscure, or too new to be included in that listing. For example, one expert estimates that there are at least *17,000* company publications that could be classified as magazines.

The field you are entering is obviously enormous. But unless you have made a special study of magazines, you are probably familiar with only a minute fraction of the thousands of publications now in existence. Most readers are aware of only the 200 or 300 magazines visible on large newsstands and may in fact know very little about most of them.

About 55 of those visible magazines have circulations ranging from 1 million to 18 million copies per issue. For many decades, these mass-circulation magazines dominated the field. The success of a magazine was gauged chiefly by its circulation. When a publication began selling at least 1 million copies weekly or monthly, advertisers were attracted by the size of the publication's audience.

This single test of a magazine's vitality no longer applies. Thousands of magazines are now edited with the special interests of smaller audiences in mind. Skiers look for copies of *Ski,* bypassing the latest issues of *TV Guide, Reader's Digest, Modern Maturity,* and *National Geographic*—the four most widely read magazines in the 1990s. Other readers will reach for *Sunset* or *Travel and Leisure* or *Parent's Magazine* or one of the publications directed to coin collectors or owners of personal computers or sports fans.

Chapter 2—entitled "Magazines Many Writers Overlook"—discusses the range and diversity of magazines. Chapter 4—"How to Analyze a Magazine"—offers suggestions that will help you discover what subjects are most likely to interest readers of the magazines for whom you choose to write.

WHY WRITE FOR MAGAZINES?

Many writers are attracted to magazine free-lancing as a possible career because of these advantages:

You can choose the magazines you wish to write for.

You can select the subjects you wish to write about.

You can specialize in an area of special interest to you, such as health or personal finance or gardening or media personalities.

You can range widely over a variety of subjects, writing first about a major political figure, then about a sports star, moving on to an article about proposed changes in high school courses, then collaborating with someone on a dramatic first-person experience.

You can set your own writing schedule, as long as you are realistic about spending enough hours at the typewriter or word processor.

If you are successful, you may be able to travel freely in search of ideas and in carrying out your research.

You can live wherever you wish.

Although these advantages make magazine free-lancing unusually appealing to many thousands of writers, it is important to recognize early that there is one major problem in this field: the lack of security. You will find a candid, detailed examination of both the rewards and the perils of full-time magazine free-lancing in Chapter 14.

Chapter 15 offers information about two alternatives you might wish to consider: staff-writing for magazines, or working as a member of an editorial staff. There are hundreds of staff-writing jobs and thousands of editorial positions on a wide range of magazines, including the smaller publications few journalism students know much about. You will receive specific suggestions about the best ways to discover these jobs in the closing chapter.

HOW TO BEGIN

There are many ways to enter the magazine world, but experienced free-lancers and magazine editors have suggested that the following eight steps will increase your chance for early success:

1. Choose a few magazines to concentrate on during your early months as a free-lancer. Many beginners scatter their work widely during this early period, sending off one idea to *The New Yorker,* another to *Sports Illustrated,* a third to *Popular Mechanics,* a fourth to *Travel/Holiday,* a fifth to *Reader's Digest.* This is apparently based on the same theory followed by those gamblers who go down the line, dropping a dollar in every accessible slot machine, certain that one of them is ready to pay a $50,000 jackpot.

Your chances will be greater if you focus your effort on a few publications at first. After you have gained a great deal of skill you may be able to satisfy the editors of a wide range of magazines. But it is usually unrealistic for apprentice writers to hope to impress both the editors of *The Nation* and the editors of *Mechanix Illustrated.*

Experienced free-lancers suggest that beginning magazine writers include both small, specialized publications and one or two mass-circulation magazines in their early list of likely publications.

2. Study those few magazines closely. There is little resemblance between an article in *People* and one in *The Atlantic.* There is no resemblance at all between a piece about Tahiti in *The National Geographic* and an article on the same subject in *Parade.*

You need to spend some time studying a magazine closely before you try to write for it. Yet editors are frequently astonished by the tendency of many writers to send their work off to any publication they happen to notice on a newsstand. Many inexperienced writers seem to be completely unaware of the differences in the subjects dealt with by various magazines, in variations in the tone of writing, or even the differences in the lengths of articles.

Even if you have read a magazine for years, you should analyze it carefully before trying to write for it. (See suggestions in Chapter 4.)

3. Learn to focus your article ideas sharply. Rather than offering to write an article on such a broad subject as "divorce," you should instead propose an article on one aspect of that topic. You might suggest a piece entitled "How to Survive a Divorce," or perhaps one called "The Hidden Costs of Divorce." Rather than proposing a general piece about "children's health problems," you could first locate an expert to collaborate with on "What Your Child's Headache Means—and What to Do About It." Instead of suggesting an article about the rising crime rate, you could write an article on "Five Ways to Burglar-Proof Your Home."

Many beginners do not recognize the importance of focusing on a single aspect of a subject. You will find many examples of how this is done in the early chapters of this book.

4. Learn to distinguish between a fairly good idea and an excellent one. Editors receive many suggestions for articles that would be all right—but no more than that. Lazy editors sometimes settle for such material—but lazy editors rarely last long. As a beginning free-lancer, competing against thousands of other free-lancers, you should learn early to discard any idea you do not feel enthusiastic about.

This rigid testing of article ideas is very important. Some beginners waste weeks on manuscripts that are doomed in advance because the central idea is trite or routine or uninspired.

You will find it useful to spend some time at a newsstand or two, or in the periodicals room of a large library, making notes of the titles of the articles featured on the covers of the magazines you would like to write for. The editors obviously believe those subjects are most likely to appeal to their readers—including those browsing at the newsstand.

It would be overambitious to limit yourself to ideas that merit cover blurbs, but you should be aware of the editors' eternal search for something exceptional. Free-lancers who are capable of discovering and developing such topics will be received cordially in any magazine office. Payments for such articles at a few of the major magazines could range from $2,500 to $5,000 or more.

In general, you will be using your time more wisely if you concentrate on the search for strong ideas and set aside those that seem to you only mildly interesting.

5. Learn to present your ideas briefly and effectively. If you take three or four pages to describe your article idea, many editors will be irritated by your wordiness, and some will not bother to finish reading your article proposal.

Most editors—but not all—emphasize the importance of keeping query letters or article memos brief. Some prefer one or two paragraphs; most indicate that the most effective article descriptions run no more than a single page. Yet they expect you to pack a great deal of information in the 200 or 250 words.

You will find many examples of successful query letters and article memos in Chapter 5.

6. Develop the ability to carry out research in depth. Even though you come up with a strong idea and offer it to the appropriate magazine, you will run into difficulties if you then skim over the surface while conducting your research.

If your work up to now has consisted of writing news stories, you may have concentrated chiefly on gathering facts. This is *part* of the work of the magazine writer, but only the most obvious part.

You will need to develop the ability to carry out research *in depth* for most magazine articles. You will probably need to do far more intensive library research than you are accustomed to, and your interviews must be carefully planned and skillfully conducted.

You will find many specific suggestions about magazine research in Chapter 6— "Finding the Facts You Need"—and Chapter 7—"Developing Your Skill as an Interviewer."

7. Develop your writing skill. If the first hundred words of a magazine article are not presented with imagination and skill, there is little chance that the manuscript will be published. If the writer fails to hold the reader's attention through to the end of an article, a demanding editor will consider the work unpublishable.

A skillfully written magazine article may appear simple and easy to write to the casual reader. Actually, most successful free-lancers and staff writers make subtle use of a variety of techniques to gain and hold the reader's interest. You will find five chapters in this book devoted chiefly to the development of your writing skill.

8. Learn to recheck every fact, every quote, every name, every date, every detail. This elementary precaution is often omitted by beginning writers. When a magazine editor discovers a single error in a manuscript—an incorrect date, a misspelling of a name, an error in the use of statistics—this immediately raises questions in the editor's mind about the writer's reliability. If you let something so easily verifiable as the spelling of a name go through uncorrected, how can the magazine have confidence in the accuracy of the direct quotes you have used? Editors who begin to doubt your attention to detail will probably reject the complete manuscript. You will not be considered a valuable reporter and contributor.

AN ALTERNATIVE WAY TO BEGIN

Some beginning writers prefer to start with ideas that appeal to them, research and write the manuscript, and then look around for publications that are likely to be receptive.

This method works occasionally, if the writer is imaginative enough to come up with *many* ideas and is also ruthless in discarding all but the strongest ones. The writer must also be very familiar with a wide variety of magazines, which makes it possible to match each of the strong ideas with an appropriate publication.

Few full-time magazine free-lancers follow this approach to article writing, and for a good reason. There is a major risk in writing an article and then testing it on possible publishers. If no editor shares the writer's enthusiasm for the already-completed manuscript, the weeks spent in researching and writing it have obviously been wasted. And even if the idea appeals to an editor, he or she might prefer an entirely different treatment of the subject or might want an article half the length or twice the length the writer settled on.

In the chapters that follow, you will find specific suggestions from many successful free-lancers and staff writers about the steps that can lead to early publication. In "Advice from Eight Editors" you will also find invitations for submission of your work from the editors of a wide range of national magazines.

2

Magazines Many Writers Overlook

Some writers begin by submitting articles successfully to major magazines. Others find they are not yet ready for *The New Yorker* or *Reader's Digest*. Here you will find a description of the thousands of smaller specialized magazines you might want to concentrate on during your early days as a free-lancer.

"If you decided to become a doctor, you wouldn't expect to start by doing brain surgery on the President," said free-lancer Roselyn Edwards, who is also an experienced magazine editor. "You'd expect to go through medical school first, then spend some time as an intern."

Edwards suggests that free-lancers should also be ready to settle at the beginning of their magazine writing careers for something less than a cover story in *Cosmopolitan*, a lead article in *Reader's Digest*, or a profile in *The New Yorker*.

She reached that conclusion after observing the experience of a friend who kept submitting article after article to *McCall's, Ladies' Home Journal*, and *Cosmopolitan*— and built up an impressive collection of rejection slips.

"I decided I would start at the bottom of the ladder and work my way up," Edwards said. She was familiar with a magazine then called *Junior Guide* (now called *Guide*), which her children brought home from church. She wrote a piece about a little girl who tried to earn enough money to pay her own way to summer camp, submitted it, and sold it. Encouraged by that initial success, she began submitting articles regularly to both *Junior*

Guide and to other magazines for children, then to religious magazines, camping magazines, and other publications she had studied closely—and sold them all.

Ambitious students sometimes resist the advice offered by Edwards and many other editors that they begin with smaller magazines. But those who follow that suggestion often are the first in any magazine writing class to achieve national publication.

Two examples:

At the University of Nevada–Reno, a student named Dan Small heard about a woman who had an unusually impressive collection of buttons. He obtained copies of a magazine called *American Collector,* studied it, and then submitted a piece based on long, detailed interviews with the button collector. He was the first student in my magazine class to make a sale that semester, and the article was given major display and space in the magazine.

At the University of Wisconsin–Oshkosh, a journalism major and gymnast named Alan Hobson realized that his coach had an exceptional record in training gymnasts who had won national and international recognition. He offered a profile of coach Ken Allen to *International Gymnast,* and that article also was featured in the magazine.

Teachers in many university magazine writing classes have observed that students who focus on smaller, more specialized magazines are often the first to receive assignments from editors.

DIFFERENT MAGAZINES, DIFFERENT SUBJECTS

Before you make a choice of two or three of these publications for your early submissions, it might be useful to note the extraordinary range of subjects they cover. Descriptions offered in writer's magazines and in books listing the current requirements of magazines will give you some idea of the entirely different audiences various editors have in mind when they open the morning mail, looking for prospective features.

Five examples chosen at random demonstrate the wide range of audiences and subjects:

Scott Stamp Monthly, Box 828, Sydney, Ohio 45365, buys about 60 unsolicited manuscripts a year.

"We are in the market for articles, written in engaging fashion, concerning the remote byways and often overlooked aspects of stamp collecting," editor Richard L. Stine told *Writer's Market.* "Writing should be clear and concise, and subjects must be well-researched and documented. . . . We do not want stories about the picture on the stamp taken from a history book or an encyclopedia and dressed up to look like research. . . . Illustrative material should also accompany articles whenever possible."

Payment is "about $100," and the magazine works with a few new, unpublished writers each year.

Aquarium Fish Magazine, Fancy Publications, Box 6050, Mission Viejo, California 92690, depends entirely on free-lance writers.

Editor Edward Bauman asks for "well-written feature articles, dealing with all aspects of the hobby and directed toward novices and experienced hobbyists." He requests that you also submit color transparencies. He pays from $100 to $300 for articles ranging in length from 1,500 to 3,000 words. Please query first.

To obtain a copy of the magazine, send $3.50 and a self-addressed, stamped envelope. The magazine offers free guidelines to writers.

Entrepreneur Magazine, 2392 Morse Avenue, Box 19787, Irvine, California 92714-6234, is "eager to work with any writer who takes the time to see *Entrepreneur*'s special 'angle' and who turns in copy on time." The magazine needs articles that offer tips to people looking for opportunities in small business as owners or franchisees. The editor emphasizes the importance of reading and analyzing the magazine before submitting ideas.

Skin Diver, Petersen Publishing Co., 8490 Sunset Boulevard, Los Angeles, California 90069, "offers broad coverage of all significant aspects of underwater activity in the areas of foreign and domestic travel, recreation, ocean exploration, scientific research, commercial diving, and technological developments."

The magazine buys 200 manuscripts a year, and 85 percent of those are from free-lancers. Payment is $50 for each published page.

American West, American West Management Corporation, Suite 30, 7000 E. Tanque Verde Road, Tucson, Arizona 85715, is about 60 percent free-lance written. "We look for relevant subject matter skillfully written to interest our readers who travel or want to travel in the West," the editors say.

The magazine pays from $200 to $800 for articles ranging in length from 1,000 to 2,500 words.

This list could go on and on. There are at least 33 health and fitness magazines now being published, 73 hobby and craft publications, and 44 business and finance magazines.

Each of these has its own focus and must be examined closely by any writer who wishes to contribute to it. In the hobby and craft category, for example, you will find magazines aimed specifically at collectors of books, ceramics, antiques, knives, coins, stamps, dolls, model trains, needlework, miniatures, bottles, classic cars, and sports memorabilia.

To begin your research on current requirements of these publications, you will want to consult the latest edition of *Writer's Market.* As a second essential step you must obtain copies of the magazines you wish to write for. I recommend that you read at least three issues analytically before you send out your first article proposal.

Because some magazines cease publication each year, it is important to consult the most recent edition of *Writer's Market* (Writer's Digest Books, Cincinnati, Ohio) when you begin surveying the field. If you cannot find a copy of the magazine you've chosen in a library or on a newsstand, the editor will often send you a sample copy or two and may include a useful Writer's Guide for potential contributors.

A reminder: When you request a sample copy of a magazine, *always* send along a stamped, self-addressed envelope of the appropriate size. (A 9 × 12 envelope may be best if you are unsure of the magazine's size, and be certain to put on enough postage.) In some cases there will be a moderate charge for a sample issue—$1 or $2, occasionally more.

SAVING A BUSY EDITOR'S TIME

If you receive an assignment from one of the small magazines, you should research and write the article with special care because many of these publications have very small staffs—sometimes a single editor. If the editor feels that your work will require a substantial amount of his or her limited editorial time, you will probably not be encouraged to continue as a contributor. Editors must have confidence in your reliability as a researcher, because they will not have time to double-check the details in your manuscript.

When editors of these smaller magazines discover that a beginning writer is offering good ideas and then submitting carefully crafted articles, they are often ready to give specific advice to the contributor. Some experienced free-lancers have said that they get their greatest pleasure from working with editors of magazines that can pay them only $500 or $750 for an article.

MAKING A CHOICE

More than 2,500 of these smaller magazines are listed in *Writer's Market,* and some beginning writers find the 500 or more pages of listings a little overwhelming.

Fortunately, the publishers of *Writer's Market* group the various magazines under some headings that are clear-cut. For example,

Aviation
Business and Finance
Detective and Crime
Food and Drink
Health and Fitness
Literary and "Little"
Music
Religious
Science
Theatre, Movie, TV, and Entertainment
Women's

Rather than reading hundreds of descriptions one after another, many students find it useful to begin by looking for perhaps eight or ten groups of magazines that are of particular interest to them. One might choose Aviation, Hobby and Craft, Military, Photography, Science, and Sports, for example, while another might begin with Art, Child Care and Parental Guidance, General Interest, History, and Literary and "Little."

You will probably find this selective approach more satisfactory if you have not previously used *Writer's Market.*

BUSINESS, TRADE, AND PROFESSIONAL MAGAZINES

Many students begin by writing for the consumer magazines—the ones seen on newsstands —since these are the only magazines they read regularly.

But as a beginning free-lancer, you might want to consider another very large group of publications that can be particularly receptive to beginning writers: business, trade, and professional journals. One researcher estimates that these magazines and journals reach an audience of at least 60 million.

James K. Gentry, dean of the Reynolds School of Journalism at the University of Nevada, Reno, offers this description of the trade press: "In these journals and house organs, you will find grocers talking with grocers, undertakers talking with undertakers, and bankers talking with bankers. You will learn the important issues in a field, how an industry markets its products and services, and what legislation it fears and favors. . . . When Chris Welles wrote a piece on the health hazards of modern cosmetics, much of his best information came from trade magazines."

Gentry, former director of the Business Journalism Program at the University of Missouri, adds, "To find trade publications, consult the *Standard Periodical Directory, Ulrich's International Periodicals Directory, Standard Rate & Data Service: Business Publications Rate and Data,* and the *Ayer Directory of Publications.*"

The Writer and *Writer's Digest* also offer selected lists of magazines in these fields. These six recent listings give some idea of the variety of these publications:

Across the Board—845 Third Avenue, New York, New York 10022. Justin Martin, Assistant Articles Editor. Articles, to 5,000 words on a variety of topics of interest to business executives; straight business angle not required. Pays $100 to $750 on publication.

American Coin-Op—500 N. Dearborn Street, Chicago, Illinois 60610. Ben Russell, Editor. Articles, to 2,500 words, with photos, on successful coin-operated laundries: management, promotion, decor, maintenance, etc. Pays from 8 cents a word, $8 per black and white photo, two weeks prior to publication. Query. Send Self Addressed, Stamped Envelope (SASE) for guidelines.

California Lawyer—1390 Market Street, Suite 1016, San Francisco, California 94102. Thomas Brom, Managing Editor. Articles, 2,500 to 3,000 words, for attorneys in California, on legal subjects (or the legal aspects of a given political or social issue); how-tos on improving legal skills and law office technology. Pays $300 to $1,200, on acceptance. Query.

Dental Economics—P.O. Box 3408, Tulsa, Oklahoma 74101. Dick Hale, Editor. Articles, 1,200 to 3,500 words, on the business side of dental practice, patient and staff communication, personal investments, etc. Pays $100 to $400, on acceptance.

Entrepreneurial Woman—2392 Morse Avenue, Irvine, California 92714. Rieva Lesonsky, Editor. Profiles, 1,800 words, of female entrepreneurs; how-tos on running a business, and pieces on coping as a woman owning a business. Payment varies, on acceptance.

Restaurants, USA—1200 17th Street, N.W., Washington, D.C. Sylvia Rivchun-Somerville, Editor. Publication of the National Restaurant Association. Articles, 1,500 to 3,500 words, on the food service and restaurant business. Pays $350 to $750, on acceptance. Query.

As this brief sampling indicates, the range of business, trade, and professional publications is very wide. A quick look at the headings in the "Trade, Technical and Professional Journals" section of *Writer's Market* demonstrates just how broad this field is. Looking first at the A's, B's, and C's, you will discover these headings:

Advertising, Marketing and PR
Art, Design and Collectibles
Aviation and Space
Beverages and Bottling
Books and Bookstores
Brick, Glass and Ceramic
Church Administration and Ministry
Confectionery and Snack Foods
Construction and Contracting

and so on through the alphabet to

Toy, Novelty and Hobby
Transportation
Travel
Veterinary

Writers who choose this as the place to begin sometimes stay with these magazines. They discover that editors of these publications can be particularly helpful to beginners who show promise of becoming reliable contributors. Dependable income from several of these magazines can become the base for a free-lancer's livelihood.

MAKING YOUR OWN LOCAL SURVEY

You can supplement the magazine listings in *Writer's Market* by looking around for publications in your own area that make use of free-lance submissions.

Some beginning writers first achieve publication on the "Op-Ed" pages of the major newspapers in their region. Others write travel articles for the weekend editions of those papers.

Because no single directory covers all existing publications, you might wish to look for copies of local and regional company, trade, and public relations magazines. Some of these are probably entirely staff written, but others may be especially receptive to contributions from free-lancers. As with other magazines, you will want to analyze these publications closely before offering the editors your article proposals.

FOCUSING ON A FEW MAGAZINES

In choosing which local, regional, or national magazines to try during your first few months of free-lancing, consider each of these questions:

1. How receptive is this magazine to free-lancers? (Some indicate clearly their reliance on free-lancers: "Buys 80 mss (manuscripts)/year" or "Buys 10 mss/issue" or "75% free-lance written." Others are far more guarded.)
2. What does the magazine pay? (Some omit this important information in their *Writer's Market* listing. Others are very specific: "Pays $50–$250" or "Pays $500 minimum.")
3. Does the magazine promise quick decisions on submissions? (Some do: "Reports in 2–3 weeks." Others indicate that you should be ready to wait 6 to 8 weeks, and many do not make any statement at all about the time required for an editorial decision.)
4. When does the magazine pay for the manuscripts it accepts? (Obviously, magazines should pay "on acceptance." If one says it "Pays on publication," you should be aware that that can mean a wait of many months—or even years.)
5. Does the magazine recognize the writer's right to offer the same article to another publication at the same time? (Some are now very specific about this: "Simultaneous and photocopied submissions OK." If you do not see such a statement in the listing, the editors probably expect exclusive submissions only.)
6. Should the writer supply photos?
7. Does the magazine promise bylines to contributors? (Most do.)

Most writers look for magazines that indicate heavy reliance on free-lancers, offer a reasonable rate of pay (certainly more than the $10 to $50 that some mention), promise quick decisions (2 to 4 weeks), and also promise payment on acceptance.

It is worth reemphasizing: There are more than 2,500 publications that make some use of free-lance material. They cover almost every activity or field of interest you could name.

Isn't it a mistake to overlook them during your early months as a free-lancer?

3

Finding Article Ideas

Where do experienced free-lancers find their article ideas? Here some veteran free-lancers list the most useful sources and also retrace the origin of some of their published pieces.

John M. Allen, a retired vice president of *Reader's Digest,* sometimes tells beginning free-lancers about an experienced magazine writer who received one firm assignment and ended up with five published articles.

The writer's assignment was from an outdoors magazine, which sent him to Wyoming to do a fishing story. He immediately began thinking of ideas that might be appealing to the editors of other magazines.

What if he went to Wyoming by trailer and took along his teenage son? Would the story of the trip itself have possibilities for some magazine? The answer was yes: When he queried the editor of a trade magazine that focused on trailers, he received his second assignment.

Rather than following the interstate highways, he decided to travel along the byways. When he suggested a piece based on this more leisurely journey, one of the automobile magazines encouraged him to go ahead with that idea.

He had chosen a new kind of coupling to attach the trailer to his car. He discovered a highly specialized magazine that carried stories about trailer couplings; the magazine was receptive to his proposal for a piece based on his experiences with the new coupling.

Finally, he wrote an article about cooking a variety of meals in the limited space available in a trailer kitchen; he sold that one, too.

That extraordinarily imaginative use of material growing out of a single, limited journey is unusual, even for a writer who has free-lanced for decades. But it demonstrates one essential talent in magazine writing: the ability to *recognize* potential subjects for articles.

From a more ambitious trip, the New York free-lancer Linda Stewart also developed five magazine articles for a wide range of publications.

She had decided to take a leisurely journey along the Caledonian Canal in Scotland, and to pause along the way to visit some luxurious guest houses she had heard about.

One obvious possibility was a general travel piece about Scotland, telling readers who had never been there what they would want to include in their first visit. She wrote this article and sold it to *Adventure/Travel.*

For *Modern Bride,* she offered suggestions for readers who were thinking of choosing Scotland for their honeymoon trips.

"The editor told me that I should not offer the readers 'gourmet living at McDonald's prices,'" she recalls. "Although not a sophisticated audience, the readers of *Modern Bride* save up their money and often spend more on their honeymoon trips than other travelers might."

She had also decided to write a piece for *Cosmopolitan,* and she recognized that it should have an entirely different approach. For the editors of *Cosmopolitan* she wrote "A Swinger's Guide to Scotland."

She assumed that many of the readers of *Harper's Bazaar* would have traveled through Scotland before, and in writing for that magazine she did not touch on the popular tourist attractions. Instead, she focused on the guest houses "run by Lord and Lady Ha-Ha."

And for *The New York Times Magazine* she wrote about her journey through the Caledonian Canal.

These two extreme examples illustrate the ability of many free-lancers to make full use of everything they experience and everything they observe. This is essential for anyone who hopes to make a living from magazine writing.

When asked to list the sources of most of their article ideas, 20 free-lancers agreed that these four were of major importance:

Reading (newspapers, magazines, and books)
Personal experience
Observation
Conversations

Other sources they mentioned included:

Imagination
Library research
Bulletin boards
Conventions
The Yellow Pages
Old magazines

Professional journals
Ph.D. dissertations
Congressional Record

This list is not exhaustive, but it does begin to indicate the wide range of sources available. One writer said that the principal difference between the successful free-lancer and the unsuccessful one is the ability to see article possibilities in ordinary, everyday life.

Here are a few specific examples of this discovery of article ideas by successful free-lancers:

SOURCE: A NEW MAGAZINE

Reno free-lancer Connie Emerson, author of a valuable book entitled *Write On Target,* noticed a new magazine, *Cruise Travel,* during one of her frequent visits to newsstands.

Connie knew that editors of new publications are especially hospitable to free-lancers (because they have not had time to build up a dependable stable of regular contributors), so she was interested immediately.

She picked up a copy of *Cruise Travel* and noted that the editors had introduced a regular feature, "Port of the Month."

"That seemed promising to me," Emerson says. "I know some of the Caribbean ports very well. I have visited St. Thomas, for example, but I saw that the magazine carried an announcement that it would be covering that port in the next issue, so obviously that one was out.

"I queried the editor about two other ports I know, and received an assignment to do San Juan, Puerto Rico."

"I wouldn't have queried an established magazine about San Juan, because I would have considered the idea too obvious. But in this case I guessed—correctly, as it turned out—that there would be a chance at *Cruise Travel* because San Juan would fit naturally into that ongoing series."

SOURCE: PERSONAL EXPERIENCE—
AND SPECIAL KNOWLEDGE

Celia Scully, a prolific free-lancer, and her husband, Dr. Thomas Scully, a professor of pediatrics, often travel with their five children. They know how disturbing it can be for parents when a child develops a temperature or suffers from diarrhea while the family is visiting Tokyo or Athens.

Dr. Scully, a former medical school dean, was also fully qualified to offer expert advice on what parents should do if their children suffered from motion sickness, stomachache, upper respiratory infection, or flu while traveling.

Drawing from their own experiences, observation, and Dr. Scully's knowledge, they proposed a service article: "What to Do when a Child Gets Sick Away from Home." The editors of *Odyssey,* a leisure and travel magazine, featured it in an issue distributed at a time when families would be planning their vacation trips.

SOURCE: CLOSE OBSERVATION

When Linda Stewart was living in Paoli, Pennsylvania, she often played tennis at the YMCA. On her way to the courts, she sometimes noticed 3- and 4-year-old children fearlessly swimming in the Y's outdoor pool.

She contacted the swimming coach and asked him, "Why do so many very young children come here to swim? And why do they swim so well?"

"It's because of an accidental discovery we made a few years ago," the coach said. "Before we built this pool, we used to use pools that belonged to wealthy families to teach kids to swim. It happened that one of the pool owners had arthritis and kept the water heated to 90 degrees. The kids who learned to swim in that pool were streaks ahead of the others, and we soon discovered why. Most 3-year-olds are tense in cold water. But if you put them into a warm, comfortable pool, they relax, and they quickly learn to swim."

Stewart knew that millions of parents would be interested in this discovery. She also knew that an article about using a warm-water pool for beginning swimmers would be strengthened if the theory were endorsed by an authority. She consulted Dr. Howard Rusk, a nationally recognized health expert, and he gave the idea his full backing.

Result: a featured article in *Family Circle*.

ONE SOURCE—THREE ARTICLES

Free-lancer Richard Rothschild's brother and sister-in-law live on Shelter Island, New York, where the Lyme tick has caused infections that can lead to nerve damage, miscarriages, and birth defects.

Because of his familiarity with the effects of Lyme disease, Rothschild developed a strong interest in attempts to control the Lyme tick and methods used in diagnosing and treating the disease. This led to three articles for *American Health:* "The Lyme Ticks Are Coming!," "AIDS Test Aids Lyme Test—Diagnostic Assays Do Double Duty," and "Lyme Facts: Epidemiologists Have a Field Day."

The leads in each article indicate Rothschild's success in finding different focuses for the three articles:

"Front-line reports show Lyme disease is on the march. The tick that spreads the infection has infiltrated 41 states, according to the CDC."

"Scientists are devising quicker, more accurate diagnostic tests for Lyme disease—by borrowing from AIDS research."

"Your risk of coming down with Lyme disease this past summer was about one in 30,000, according to the CDC. In fact, you were about 30 times more likely to get injured in a bicycle collision. . . ."

SOURCE: AN ANALYSIS OF OTHER MAGAZINE ARTICLES

All of the experienced free-lance magazine writers I know spend a great deal of time reading and *studying* the magazines they wish to write for. As a result of this analysis, some of them periodically come up with ideas for what one of these writers calls "parallel articles."

For example, if you notice that a magazine gives major space to a piece called "What to Do About Your Aching Back," you might consider offering a piece dealing with some other troublesome physical problem that many of the magazine's readers are likely to experience. Several parallel problems will come to your mind immediately in this case: headaches, strained muscles, aching feet. You will, of course, check back issues to make certain that the publication has not already carried pieces on these common physical problems.

As another obvious example, you might observe that a magazine such as *Seventeen* demonstrates a special interest in emerging young television stars. Here you would want to do some research before offering a parallel article. If all of these pieces were staff written, you would be wasting your time to offer such a suggestion from the outside. But if the articles come from a variety of free-lance writers, you could explore the possibility of contributing to the series.

A parallel article is not a *duplicate* of the published piece. It grows out of your recognition that the editor believes the magazine's readers have a strong interest in a certain *kind* of article—pieces about marriage problems, for example, or do-it-yourself home repairs, or gardening—and is depending on outside writers for these pieces. Your parallel article should be at least as good—preferably better—than the piece that suggested this possibility to you.

RECYCLING SOME TRADITIONAL ARTICLE SUBJECTS

Month after month, all over the world, the most popular magazines offer their readers articles that deal with these 21 subjects:

1. Diets
2. Health
3. Sex
4. Money
5. Celebrities
6. How-to
7. Self-help
8. First-person experiences
9. Human behavior
10. Marriage
11. Children
12. Travel
13. Fashion
14. Home furnishing
15. Cooking
16. Trends
17. Sports
18. Hobbies
19. Animals
20. National problems
21. Foreign news

This list is not exhaustive, of course, and some writers (and editors) might suggest that two or three of these categories be eliminated and others included. But you could use this list as a starting point for your own analysis of current magazines.

Recognizing the broad subjects of greatest interest to millions of readers is only the beginning, of course. For an editor to be intrigued by your suggestion of a piece about dieting, or sex, or money, or travel, you need to come up with a fresh treatment of a traditional subject.

This checklist may help you determine whether you have come up with a likely possibility:

Checklist for an Article Idea

1. **Is this topic fresh enough to attract an editor's attention?** A magazine article idea does not have to be absolutely original, but it is a mistake to waste time on ideas that will seem too familiar to editors.
2. **Is the angle intriguing?** An imaginative writer can find a new way to deal with subjects that have been written about by many earlier writers. Later in this chapter you will find examples of treatments of such general subjects as dieting, human behavior, marriage problems, health, and money by writers who understood the importance of a new and imaginative angle.
3. **Will the subject be of interest to a wide audience, or is it too limited?** Ordinarily, a health magazine would not devote space to a detailed piece about a disease that is likely to affect only one person out of every half-million. A travel magazine editor would probably hesitate before featuring a major article about traveling in Albania. Magazine editors concentrate on a search for skillful treatments of subjects that are likely to arouse the immediate interest of *most* of their readers.
4. **Is the article idea tightly focused?** A very common error is to try to tell the reader too much about a broad subject. As a result, the piece sounds like an encyclopedia article, packed with many facts and details. Your article proposal should convince an editor that you have already chosen an *aspect* of the subject that will give your article a sharp focus. The examples given later in this chapter indicate how other writers narrowed their focus and selected a single aspect of various broad topics.
5. **Can the research be carried out in reasonable time and at reasonable cost?** Some beginning writers come up with very ambitious ideas requiring expensive trips for research, and they hope that magazines will bear the cost. One free-lancer spent months going from one magazine to another, requesting a $6,000 advance to finance a two-month trip to Russia that might—or might not—produce a single magazine article. A writer in Texas offered a proposal that required research in Alaska—and hoped the magazine would foot the cost. Although you should not limit yourself to articles that can be researched at almost no cost, you should be realistic about choosing subjects you yourself can afford to research, perhaps recovering the costs when you sell the piece.
6. **Do you yourself feel a strong interest in this idea?** One editor said she could always tell when a writer was "just batting out ideas." The lack of commitment on the part of the writer would affect his or her work, she said, and readers would be equally indifferent to a piece that was written mechanically, without any purpose beyond the receipt of a check.

FRESH ANGLES FOR TRADITIONAL SUBJECTS

Almost all magazine articles offer *specific* treatments of *general* subjects. The writer carves out a part of the subject and focuses tightly on that aspect. Professional magazine writers understand this, but many beginners do not.

To begin to comprehend this, you should read analytically at least 25 or 30 articles from magazines that have special appeal to you. Notice both what the writers do in those articles and what they do *not* do. If it is a sports article, the author almost always chooses a single sport—perhaps football—and then will choose a single team. Often the writer will concentrate on a single season or a single player.

You might make a comparison with the choices made by a skillful photographer. He or she will not try to give you an impression of the Grand Canyon by photographing it from a great distance but by focusing on one chasm or one waterfall or one sheer wall. The photographer might even show a single tourist riding along a narrow, treacherous path thousands of feet above the canyon floor.

A scattered sampling of the titles and front-cover blurbs of articles that fit into the categories favored for decades by editors of popular magazines will give you a clearer idea of the methods followed by successful free-lancers (and staff writers) in catching the reader's attention once again even though they are writing about old, old general subjects.

Diets

"10 Minutes a Day to a Flat Tummy (Tiny Waist Too)"

—Woman's Day

"In Search of the Perfect Diet"—Our guide to shedding pounds and staying healthy

—Harper's Bazaar

"Born to Be Fat?"—How to fight back

—Family Circle

Health

"Back Pain: Why Women Suffer More"

—Redbook

"After the Operation: What Doctors Don't Tell You"

—New Choices

"Faster Test for Breast Cancer"—New screening may replace breast biopsy

—McCall's

Sex

"Sex and the Prom"—What really happens on the big night

—Seventeen

"Exercise and Sex: Strange Bedfellows"—Working out is the new sexual turn on. Here's why

—Beauty

Money

"Sending Cash in a Flash"—There are more ways to do it than you might think

—Changing Times

"When It's Smart to Borrow"—Shake off the notion that debt is always bad if you have the cash on hand

—Kiplinger's Personal Finance Magazine

"Smart Money Moves You Can Make Today"—Whether you have $500, $5,000, or more to invest, here are the answers to our reader's most asked financial questions

—Black Enterprise

Celebrities

"Diana and Charles' 10th—1981–1991"

—Good Housekeeping

"Oprah: How Success Has Changed Her"

—Ladies' Home Journal

"Honestly (We Think) the Real Milli Vanilli Turns Up with a New LP and, This Time, No Video Stand-Ins"

—People

How-to

"Easy to Build Log Homes"

—Popular Mechanics

Self-Help
> "You Call All the Shots with a 'Lawyer in a Box'"
>
> > —*PC Computing*
>
> "Make Smarter Financial Decisions"
>
> > —*Home Office Computing*

First-Person Experiences
> "My Heart Was Killing Me"
>
> > —*Philadelphia Inquirer Magazine*
>
> "How I Survived a Tax Audit"
>
> > —*Changing Times*

Human Behavior
> "Employee Conflicts? Try Trading Places"
>
> > —*Working Woman*
>
> "Why Are Siblings So Different?"
>
> > —*In Health*

Marriage
> "Love? Or Money? What Are You Really Fighting About?"
>
> > —*Family Circle*
>
> "Can This Marriage Be Saved?" (Series)
>
> > —*Ladies' Home Journal*

Children
> "But All the Other Kids Are Doing It . . ."—How to deal with peer pressure
>
> > —*Family Circle*

"Mothers and Daughters: Handling the Need to Grow Apart While Staying Close"

—McCall's

"Far, Far from Home"—Summer camp can be a scary prospect—if you've never been away from Mom and Dad before

—Life

Travel

"The Greatest Drive"—4,300 miles across America with the top down

—Condé Nast Traveler

"Roughing It Gently"—Since the 1880s, the AMC huts have been easing people into New England's high country

—Backpacker

"Kids on Trips: How to Keep Them Happy"

—Family Circle

Fashion

"Scenic Attractions: Weekend Styles That Look Splendid in the Grass"

—Mademoiselle

"TV's Top Model Forecasts Summer's Most Dazzling Fashions"

—TV Guide

Home Furnishings

"Pre-School Activity Center"

—Workbench

Cooking

"French Minus the Fats"—A three-star chef shares his secrets

—Self

"Health Mex: Lost Treasures of an Ancient Cuisine"

—American Health

Trends

"The Changing Face of Ambition"—A lot of ex-hard chargers are discovering a taste for life in the middle lane

—Gentlemen's Quarterly

Sports

"A Season in the Minors"

—National Geographic

"Wanna Buy a Baseball Team?"

—Sports Illustrated

Hobbies

"Bimini Bound"—Heading across the Gulf Stream in five of the most power-packed performance boats on the market today

—Motor Boating & Sailing

"The Trials and Triumphs of Outdoor Painting"—The struggle inherent in outdoor painting can actually inspire you to create better paintings

—American Artist

Animals

"Guilty or Not Guilty?"—Your dog may look ashamed, but he knows no moral values

—Dog World

"The Marvelous Spadefoot Toad"—Like all true desert dwellers, it's found a way to escape the worst of summer's heat—until love starts to bloom

—Arizona Highways

National Problems

"A Cure for What Ails Medical Care"—Call it the American disease. The symptoms: unchecked health care spending and too many uninsured. The remedy: introducing more market logic into the system.

—Fortune

"How Do We Measure the Deficit? Let Us Count the Ways"

—Business Week

Foreign News

"South Africa Today: Living on the Edge"—A Country in Crisis

—Vogue

"Gorbachev's Time of Trouble"

—U.S. News & World Report

If you look up several of these articles—or choose other examples of fresh treatments of familiar general topics—you will have a clearer idea of the need for a new angle when dealing with any of the 21 subjects listed earlier.

IF THESE SUBJECTS DO NOT INTEREST YOU . . .

Some beginning writers are reluctant to join in the exploitation of these familiar subjects. Why not concentrate on the discovery of *new* subjects? they ask. Why pander to the reader's preoccupation with his aching back or her failing marriage? Why waste time writing about someone destined for instant fame on a television sitcom, to be followed by instant obscurity?

These are legitimate questions. One of the greatest attractions of magazine writing is that you have a choice. You may prefer to write for *The Nation* or *The Atlantic* or *Mother Jones,* and to ignore *People, Money,* and *Travel/Holiday.*

If you find the prospect of writing an article called "10 Minutes a Day to a Flat Tummy" or "Oprah: How Success Has Changed Her" or "Can This Marriage Be Saved?" boring, you should not attempt to sell such pieces. Your contempt for what you are doing will be obvious to editors.

But if you find at least some of these popular topics interesting, you might want to experiment with writing them. The field is open to you, because editors realize that millions of readers respond to skillful presentations of such subjects as "Sex and the Prom" or "Why Are Siblings So Different?" or "TV's Top Model Forecasts Summer's Most Dazzling Fashions."

How to Analyze a Magazine

Before you try to write for a magazine, you should know who reads the publication and what subjects interest those readers. If you can answer six questions about a magazine, your chances for a successful submission will be substantially increased.

"You know what a writer sent me yesterday?" a travel magazine editor asked. "A 5,000-word piece on how to repair a truck transmission."

At *Nevada* magazine—which focuses entirely on that state—an editor received a carefully researched, skillfully written piece about a desert-trek through New Mexico.

A very bland Sunday magazine, distributed with the most conservative newspapers in the United States, was offered a detailed, vivid account of the daily lives of male prostitutes written by a widely known novelist.

Hundreds of magazine editors have spoken or written about this puzzling behavior by writers. Articles that might interest the editors of *Playboy* are sent to *Esquire* and are rejected immediately. Long, thoughtful essays on world affairs that could impress the editor of a scholarly magazine are casually submitted to a publication that devotes all of its space to gossipy reports about the lives of celebrities. A magazine devoted entirely to bowling receives an article about stamp collecting. And year after year fat manuscripts—some of them 10,000 to 20,000 words in length—are sent to magazines that have *never* run an article longer than 2,500 or 3,000 words.

The solution to this basic problem is simple.

"If you want to *write* for magazines, you must read magazines," a *Reader's Digest* editor said. "I know that has been said a hundred thousand times, but an astonishing number of writers ignore that advice. You must read magazines, study them, analyze them. You must try to understand why an editor selects the articles he features, and why he gives special emphasis to some of them on the front cover. You must begin to realize why a reader buys that particular magazine, and what he expects from it."

WHAT DO ADVERTISEMENTS TELL YOU?

Before we focus on six questions that could be helpful to anyone who wishes to study a magazine closely, it might be wise to deal with one piece of advice that is often given to beginning magazine writers.

"Study the advertisements in the magazines you want to write for," writers are told. "That will tell you a great deal about the readers, and on the basis of that information you can choose subjects that will be of greatest interest to those readers."

Even though you should include an examination of the advertisements in your study of a magazine, I would caution you not to rely heavily on this single source of information.

For example, suppose you studied three issues of a magazine and found that it carried these ads in a fairly typical issue:

International hotels (Expensive)	12 ads
Travel (U.S. and international)	11 ads
Men's clothes (Expensive— including one ad for a $5,000 tie)	11 ads
Women's clothes (Expensive)	9 ads
Watches (Expensive)	9 ads
Other gifts (Expensive)	9 ads
Restaurants (Expensive)	6 ads
Automobiles (Expensive)	8 ads

Would this give you the impression that this magazine is read only by a wealthy, frivolous, overprivileged elite with little interest in anything except conspicuous consumption?

If you came to that conclusion and concentrated on offering articles that were written with such an audience in mind, I doubt that you would interest the editors of that magazine.

The magazine, as you may have guessed, is *The New Yorker*. It has published decade after decade some of the most thoughtful and impressive work appearing in any magazine in the world. The readers do not limit their interests to luxury goods and $5,000 ties.

I am not suggesting that you ignore the advertising when you examine a magazine. I do suggest that you consider an examination of the advertising as no more than a preliminary step toward an in-depth study of the editorial content.

The relationship between the advertising columns and the editorial columns is often exaggerated. Although it is true that there have been instances in which short-sighted publishers have "traded off" editorial space for advertising contracts, my impression is that the practice is now fairly rare. Most of the editors I have known over the past 40 years were quick to resist advertising pressures. They spent far more time thinking about readers than about advertisers.

HOW EDITORS SEE THEIR READERS

Because readers—not advertisers—are the major preoccupation of every good magazine editor, it is important for a writer to understand just how an editor views those readers, what subjects he or she considers of greatest interest to them, and what techniques the editor considers most effective in gaining and holding readers' attention.

To achieve that understanding of the magazines you wish to write for, I suggest that you obtain copies of three recent issues (not necessarily three issues in sequence) and answer these six questions about the publication:

1. **Who reads this magazine?** Teenage girls? Stamp collectors? Sports fans? Bowlers? Young career women? Businessmen? Investors? Doctors? Single men with high incomes? Middle-aged couples whose chief interest is in their homes and gardens? People who travel on a budget? A wide general audience, difficult to classify? Scientists? Retired couples?
2. **What subjects interest these readers?** Money? Sex? Health? Politics? Fashion? Food? Sports? Entertainment? World problems? Ecology? Careers? Marriage problems? Films?
3. **What is the average length of the articles in the magazine?**
4. **What types of leads do the editors seem to favor?** Anecdotal? Narrative? Question leads? Opinion leads? Descriptive leads? Expository leads? Startling quotes? Scene-setting leads? "You" leads?
5. **What is the general tone of the writing?** Casual? Conversational? Staccato? Sardonic? Crisp? Straight exposition? Somewhat formal? Very formal?
6. **How are most of the articles in the magazine developed? What techniques do the writers seem to use most frequently?** Straight expository presentation? A string of anecdotes? A mixture of anecdotes, direct quotes, and exposition? Scene-by-scene construction? Heavy use of direct quotes? Dramatic narrative? Writer's opinion freely expressed?

Examples

Seventeen. Magazine market reports will offer you some basic information that you will find useful in studying *Seventeen:*

Monthly. Circ: 1,900,000.

Buys one time rights for nonfiction. [This means that the writer can have all other rights returned after the magazine has published an article. While this may have little value in most cases, in some others it can be important. If your article were republished in a book, for example, that could mean extra income. If it could be dramatized for television, all the income from the dramatization would belong to you, rather than being divided between you and the magazine.]

Articles and features of general interest to young women who are concerned with the development of their own lives and the problems of the world around them; strong emphasis on topicality and helpfulness. Send brief outline and query, including a typical lead paragraph, summing up basic idea of article. Also like to receive articles and features on speculation. Length 1,200–2,000 words. Pays $50–$500 for articles written by teenagers but more to established adult freelancers. Articles are commissioned after outlines are submitted and approved. Fees for commissioned articles generally range from $650–$1,500.

"Writers have to ask themselves whether or not they can find the right tone for a *Seventeen* article—a tone which is empathetic yet never patronizing; lively yet not superficial," an editor of *Seventeen* suggests. "Not all writers feel comfortable with, understand or like teenagers. If you don't like them, *Seventeen* is the wrong market for you. The best way for beginning writers to crack the *Seventeen* lineup is for them to contribute suggestions and short pieces to the New Voices and Views section, a literary format which lends itself to just about every kind of writing: profiles, essays, exposés, reportage, and book reviews."

This is very helpful background information, but by reading three issues of *Seventeen* closely, and by doing some research, you could come up with a more detailed report along these lines:

1. Who reads this magazine? Obviously, teenagers—and mostly women. Ages: 13 through 20 or so. This is indicated both by the articles featured in the magazine and by the ads. A former editor said that *Seventeen* serves as a "surrogate parent for many of the teens, who find that they can get reliable answers from us that they oftentimes cannot pry loose from their parents, their peers, or their friends."

2. What subjects interest these readers? The coverlines on recent issues gave a good indication of readers' special interests:

Coolness: Why Some Have It and Some Don't
Meet the Best Boyfriend in America
The New Sex Appeal—Nice Guys
Boy Crazed! When Boy Meets Girl
Why He Loves Your Long Hair
Hot Bikinis
Endless Summer!
Beach Bodies: How to Get a Perfect Tan
Gorgeous Lifeguards
Sex and the Prom: What Really Happens on the Big Night
Cool Clothes Under $25

The fashion and beauty section covered a wide range: "The Summer's Hottest Swimsuits," "Real-Looking Fake Tans," "Beauty Hints for Girls with Far Eastern Looks," "The Cut That Saved a Model's Hair," "What You and He Can Share and Wear Alike."

The section "Hot Talk, Cool Talk, and Earth Talk" consisted of brief treatments of a variety of subjects: a drink that caused many teenage deaths (Cisco); high schools that kicked military recruiters off campus; condominiums being built on Walden Pond; healthy snacks; and pollution caused by batteries that contain mercury and other toxic metals.

3. What is the average length of the articles in the magazine? The short items are often very short—75 to 150 words. Longer pieces range from around 900 to 2,500 words.

4. What types of leads do the editors seem to favor? Here are some typical leads:

Quote Lead

> My best friend and I were both virgins (most of my friends were) but then my boyfriend and I had sex. We really care about each other, so I felt it was okay. I didn't tell anyone, just my best friend. After that it was like she had to also. She ended up losing her virginity to some guy on a one-night stand. Your first time should be so special and shared with someone you really care about. I can't help but think she has made a big mistake. It's really made us grow apart.

> From "Friends and Sex: What Their Attitudes Mean to You,"
> by Debra Kent

Scene-Setting Lead

> A hip little coffee shop in downtown Manhattan seems like the perfect place to meet Matt Dillon for a chat and a bite to eat. Right? Wrong. The twenty-seven-year-old actor walks into the congested restaurant, takes one look around, grabs my arm, and says, "Let's get out of here."
> As we leave the fifty or so gawking faces behind us, he explains that crowded places make him nervous during interviews.
> "I don't feel I can speak . . ."
> "Intimately?" I offer.
> "Yeah. You know."

> From "In Person: Matt Dillon," by Claire Connors

Brief Summary Lead

> In the past three years, Jeffrey Abrams has sold six screenplays to major studios, including *Taking Care of Business,* starring Jim Belushi, and *The Rest of Daniel,* to star Mel Gibson. Not bad for a guy who just turned twenty-five.

> From a short piece in "Fresh Faces," by Stacey Colino

You Lead

> I'd like to see a show of hands here: How many of you have had a daydream about accepting an Oscar? Come on, admit it. You've thought about what you'd wear, who you'd thank, how humble you'd look while someone like Katharine Hepburn told a billion viewers that in all her years in the business she'd never witnessed a talent as amazing as yours. And how your ex-boyfriend, that snake, would see you on TV and exclaim to his dull-as-dishwater wife, *"That's* (your name here)! I used

to go out with her!" And then his wife would roll her eyes and think, "Yeah, right, like anyone that fabulous and gorgeous would almost talk to you."

From "Daydream Believer," by Beth Levine

5. What is the general tone of the writing? Almost all of the articles are written in a casual, relaxed, conversational tone. The editors urge writers not to "write down" to readers of the magazine, and not to preach to them or to exhort them.

6. How are most of the articles in the magazine developed? What techniques do the writers use most frequently? The editors seem to favor first-person, scene-setting, or direct quote leads for the major articles in these issues. A few pieces begin with general observations (for example, "Sensuous curves are back . . . but this time they're sleek and sinewy, not soft and smushy . . .").

In developing the articles, writers make heavy use of direct quotes, bring in an anecdote or two, and often address the readers directly. They rarely use straight expository presentation, except in a few very short items.

Ghost Town Quarterly. Recently, Sherril Steele-Carlin, a student at the University of Nevada, Reno, discovered a very small, special-interest magazine—*Ghost Town Quarterly,* published in Philipsburg, Montana. Here are excerpts from her analysis:

1. Who reads this magazine? The general readership seems to be older, retired people. Judging by the letters to the editor, many people discover the magazine while traveling through Montana. They are all interested in history and "ghost towning." I would say that most readers are probably middle income.

2. What subjects interest those readers? I believe they enjoy the outdoors, camping, fishing, and traveling (especially in motor homes). They are probably collectors of memorabilia or art of some sort. History of the West is definitely an interest.

3. What is the average length of articles in the magazine? Some were about 250 words, while several were about 1,000 words. The longest one in the issues I studied was 1,200 words. Almost every article included some type of illustration—photograph, map, or drawing.

4. What types of leads do the editors seem to favor? Almost all the leads were descriptive or scene-setting. For example,

The lush mountainside was slashed with burnt gold, russet, and charcoal of ancient buildings. There was a hush over the little town. A light haze of smoke drifted low, signalling the coming of cold weather. Even at late morning, the edges of the rain puddles were thinly crusted with ice.

Here the gold miners lived in the 1800's, when Warren, Idaho, was a rambunctious, rich new town. It was called Warren Meadows then. During the first 20 years or so, a handful of rough, determined men and women wrestled more than fourteen million dollars worth of gold out of the streams and the mountains.

5. What is the general tone of the writing? The whole feel of the magazine is casual, chatty, and folksy. Not unprofessional, just kind of "down-home." The articles are almost all conversational, without talking down or being too "cute."

6. How are most of the articles in the magazine developed? What techniques do the writers seem to use most frequently? The writers tend to use a string of anecdotes, tied together with description of another time and place. Many of the towns they are describing don't exist anymore, so the only way they have to share what life was like is to paint a word picture. Most of them do it very well. There were few direct quotes in any of the articles. Most were straight narration and exposition. In some of them the writers did express their opinions, including their comments on what should be done to preserve old historic sites.

Just typing up this analysis has given me an idea for *Ghost Town Quarterly.*

Backpacker. Charles Plueddeman, a student at the University of Wisconsin, Oshkosh, offered this analysis of *Backpacker:*

1. Who reads this magazine? Most readers of *Backpacker* are back-to-the-earth types. They are probably college educated or in the process of becoming college educated. They would probably support campaigns to save the whale and to prevent the slaughter of baby seals. They would also be in favor of protecting the redwoods, would fight nuclear power, and would want to close the national parks to motor vehicles. Their interests would include hiking, backpacking, canoeing, cross-country skiing, mountain climbing, and photography. They would not be interested in guns, hunting, or four-wheel-drive trucks. They would not read *Field and Stream,* but might read *National Geographic.* They might enjoy *Mother Earth News.*

2. What subjects interest these readers? A major portion of each issue is devoted to testing new hiking, camping, and skiing equipment, and the magazine's ratings carry a lot of clout in these markets. The contributed material (from free-lancers) includes first-person accounts of trips taken by the author in the United States or Canada. The magazine has also carried stories on such subjects as yoga, overcrowding the national parks, land management, outdoor or wildlife photography, and a piece about ways to avoid an encounter with grizzly bears.

3. What is the average length of the articles in the magazine? The shortest piece was about 800 words, and the longest about 4,300 words. The average length in the issues I studied was about 2,500 words. Each of the issues contained two long pieces (more than 3,000 words) and three or four short pieces ranging from 800 to 2,000 words.

4. What types of leads do the editors seem to favor? There are many first-person leads, and in other articles the author is a close observer or participant. For example,

> Gusts of wind swirled the densely falling snow. Three or four inches covered what had been dry ground the day before. It was a poor day to travel, but the thought of remaining inside my damp, gloomy tent did not appeal to me, so I prepared breakfast, packed my gear, and began the day's climb.
>
> Twenty-three days before, I had set out on skis to traverse the John Muir Trail. . . .

That is the lead to "High Sierra Ski Solo."

In an article about "How to Get Your Children to Hike with You," the author begins with a general observation but quickly focuses on her son:

Actual one-step-in-front-of-the-other hiking does not appeal to most children. But it appeals to many parents who want their children's cooperative, if not enthusiastic, company.

In our family, since my own level of willing participation falls far short of my husband Paul's hiking desires, he now relies on our 14-year-old son Jeremy for companionship in the mountains. By the time Jeremy was 10, he had climbed all 47 of the 4,000-foot mountains in New Hampshire. And he had started on the Adirondack 4,000-footers.

These two leads and others in the issues I analyzed indicate the editors' interest in establishing early the writer's personal knowledge and experience.

5. What is the general tone of the writing? The first-person stories are casually written in an easy, conversational tone. Some of the informational articles resemble good informational features in newspapers, filled with specific details and advice.

6. How are most of the articles in the magazine developed? What techniques do the writers seem to use most frequently? Often stories start with a picturesque scene or a description of a cold, frosty morning—perhaps the third or fourth day of the writer's journey. The author then takes the reader back to the beginning of the trip, or perhaps to the earlier point where he (or she) settled on the destination. The writer then proceeds with a step-by-step description of the journey, often building toward a climax—maybe a crisis, some sudden danger, or an achievement. The pieces often end with a comment about the experience. Stories are usually accompanied by maps indicating the route.

EXPERIMENT IN ANALYZING A MAGAZINE

In "Advice from Eight Editors," beginning on page 146, you will find suggestions to freelancers from the editors of a wide range of magazines: *People, Reader's Digest, Mother Jones, Cosmopolitan, McCall's, Modern Maturity, Seventeen,* and *Backpacker.* You might find it valuable to analyze two or three of these magazines after reading the editors' advice.

Your answers to the six questions discussed in this chapter will remind you of the topics that appeal to the readers of the magazines you study. In answering these questions, you will note the kinds of leads the editors prefer and the techniques used by other writers in their work for these magazines.

After you complete your analysis, you will be far better prepared than most freelancers to submit ideas and memos that will appeal to the editors of the magazines you study.

5

How to Offer Ideas to Magazines

What is the most effective way of presenting an article idea to a magazine editor? Here you will find copies of article memos and query letters that led to firm magazine assignments. You will also find a checklist to use in examining your own article memos.

When you write to a magazine to offer an article idea, the editor will usually be searching for the answers to these five questions as he or she reads your words:

Exactly what is the article idea?
Is it suited to my magazine?
Does the writer have special knowledge about this subject?
If the writer possesses no special knowledge, does he or she suggest some impressive sources who will be quoted in the article?
If given the assignment, will this writer be able to write an accurate, skillful, publishable article?

Because the editor's desk will be piled high with other papers—manuscripts, proofs, article proposals, memos, notes about telephone calls to be returned—the editor will expect you to answer those five questions as briefly as possible.

Professional writers use two different forms in presenting their ideas to magazine editors:

The article memo
The query letter

When written with care and skill, either of these two forms can give the editor the needed information in a few paragraphs—usually in no more than a single page. This makes it possible for the editor to reach an intelligent decision—and to reach it quickly.

Here we will look at both of these forms and examine some article memos and some query letters that have led to magazine assignments.

THE ARTICLE MEMO

This is the form I prefer. It seems to me to have several advantages over the query letter:

It *looks* more interesting than a letter.
It requires the writer to come up with a title for the proposed piece.
It forces the writer to bring the article idea into sharp focus.
It reminds the writer to cite sources.
It reminds the writer to mention his or her background, including any special qualifications to write this specific article.
It gives the editor a small sample of the writer's skill.

Literary agent Nannine Joseph taught all of her clients to use this form, and she advocated it strongly to magazine students at the Columbia Graduate School of Journalism.

The form itself is quite simple. See Box 5–1.

Box 5–1   *The Article Memo*

Your Name
Your Address
Your Telephone Number

THE TITLE OF THE ARTICLE
(Article Memo)
By _____ _____

Lead—Ideally, this should be the lead you plan to use in your completed article. In any case, it should be the same *kind* of lead—an opening anecdote if you mean to use one to begin your article, or a surprising statement lead if that is the kind you have in mind.

Capsule Statement—After gaining attention with your lead, you should tell the editor here, quickly, exactly what your article is about.

* * *

Sources—Here you should give specific details about your principal sources.

Your Qualifications—Are you a reporter? Have you written for other magazines? Do you have some special knowledge of this subject? Briefly indicate any special qualifications you have.

Additional Details—Do you have access to very good illustrations? When could you deliver the article?

A Typical Memo

As an example of the article memo form, I have unearthed one that I sent to a Sunday supplement (a magazine distributed with Sunday newspapers) when I was first beginning to offer ideas to magazines.

It is reproduced in Box 5–2 in the format commonly used by most free-lancers.

Box 5–2   *A Typical Article Memo*

Myrick Land
Address
Telephone Number

ARE YOU HELPING THE COUNTERFEITERS?
(Article Memo)
By Myrick Land

A few years ago, a man who hated to send conventional Christmas cards took a $5 bill, pasted his own picture over Lincoln's, and photographed the result. He made several prints on soft paper and mailed them to some friends.

One of the friends headed for the corner bar. "Somebody sent me $5 for Christmas," he told the bartender, "but it's funny, there wasn't any name on the envelope."

The bartender accepted the de-Lincolnized bill and it remained in circulation for three weeks, going from one unobservant citizen to another.

This casual acceptance of anything that looks like money helps account for a nationwide rise in counterfeiting, according to the U.S. Secret Service. Even professional counterfeiters have grown careless: One of them successfully circulated $1 bills on which Washington was misspelled "Wasihgton" and another omitted a crucial letter in a four-line legend on Federal Reserve notes so it read: "This note is legal tender for all debts, public and private, and is redeemable in *awful* money at the United States Treasury. . . ."

*   *   *

The U.S. Secret Service will be my major source for this article, and I have been promised the cooperation of the Chief, U. E. Baughman. The piece will describe other crude counterfeits and will tell readers how they can recognize counterfeit bills and what to do if they receive one.

I am a former reporter and feature writer on the Providence (R.I.) *Journal*. My articles have appeared in *The New York Times Magazine* and *Cosmopolitan*.

I can see ways to improve that memo now, but it passed the crucial test: I received the assignment. Incidentally, when the time came to write the article, I was able to use the same opening anecdote I had used in the memo. The piece was also published under the same title.

Incidentally, the subject of counterfeiting has been of strong interest to magazine editors for many decades. The *Reader's Guide to Periodical Literature* lists articles about counterfeiters and counterfeiting in almost every volume, from the beginning of the century through the early 1990s. Because of that continuing interest in the subject, you may wish to experiment with writing your own article about counterfeiting. You will find the necessary information and some suggestions about constructing such an article in "Experiments in Magazine Writing," beginning on page 162.

* * *

From your previous journalism courses, you undoubtedly understand the importance of the lead to any article intended for publication. But some beginning students in magazine writing are at first puzzled by the best method to handle two other elements in the article memo form—the capsule statement and the section describing your qualifications. A few examples may be helpful.

The Capsule Statement

This is a brief, precise statement of the central point of your article. It often appears in the second or third paragraph of an article memo, but some writers use it as the lead:

> If you've let an insurance salesperson sell you the most popular type of life insurance, you may be paying $100 to $500 a year more in premiums than you need to, three experts say. You could save that money by asking five simple questions before you make your next payment.

After reading those 50 words, the editor knows exactly what you are offering the magazine. Your next paragraph should describe your experts, and this should be followed by an indication of your own knowledge of the subject and your previous writing experience.

If you were proposing a personality article, your capsule statement would tell the editor why you feel the subject deserves space in this specific magazine:

> Although David Watkins has never before directed a film that cost more than $1,000,000, MGM is now ready to risk at least $50,000,000 on his next picture—a remake of "San Francisco."

Or

> Timberlake is a recluse, and even his closest neighbors know little about him. But an invention he has been "puttering around" with for the past five years could lead to the development of the first electric automobile capable of going 2,000 miles before it has to be recharged.

The capsule statement in a how-to article is often simple and direct:

This backyard storage shed could be built in 14 hours by anyone who knows how to use a saw and a hammer, and the cost for all the materials should be under $400.

A service article also often contains a brief, straightforward capsule statement:

Five famous cooks tell how they take the monotony out of the most standardized meal in most American homes—breakfast.

Focusing on Your Strong Points

If you haven't previously published articles in magazines, how can you convince an editor that you are capable of writing a successful piece?

You might consider these possibilities:

1. Emphasize your *other* writing experience. If you have published feature articles, for example, mention them and indicate the newspaper in which they appeared.
2. Focus on the experts you plan to quote in your article. This is particularly important if your own achievements as a published writer are limited.
3. Describe anything in your university studies that qualifies you to carry out the research required for the article.
4. Emphasize any special experiences you have had that give you a special knowledge and understanding of the subject you will be writing about.

Here are a few samples based on article memos prepared by students who had never had a magazine article published:

Emphasizing Other Writing Experience

I have been feature editor of the student newspaper at the University of Wisconsin–Oshkosh for the past two semesters, and three of my feature articles have been published in the Milwaukee *Sentinel.*

Focusing on the Experts

Dr. Adrian Scott, who has concentrated on the study of teenage acne for three years, will be one of my major sources. I have also set up interviews with Dr. Edith Wallace, a Milwaukee psychologist who has examined hundreds of troubled teenagers, and James Q. McPherson, chief counselor to students at the largest high school in Los Angeles.

Focusing on the Writer's Studies

As a history major, I have carried out some special research on the development of casinos in Nevada. I also have access to a series of oral histories in which casino owners describe some of the more imaginative schemes to cheat casinos over the past 35 years.

Emphasizing Personal Knowledge

I have spent at least four weeks in very remote camping areas every winter for the past four years. During my first years I made some dangerous mistakes and in one case I could have frozen to death if a fellow winter-camper had not appeared just after my tent was blown down during a blizzard. I will be able to describe the possible consequences of the most common errors made by winter-campers and to offer specific advice on how to reduce the dangers.

You will almost always be able to come up with a special qualification for writing the article you are proposing. Focusing on the experts is particularly easy since there are experts on almost any topic you decide to write about.

One reminder: Never emphasize a negative point when offering an article suggestion. Do not say,

This may not sound like a very interesting subject.

If you can't make it sound interesting, then you shouldn't offer it. And don't confess:

Although I have never written for magazines. . . .

Editors know that every writer has to start somewhere, and if your article memo is written with skill and is perfectly typed, that offers two indications that your approach to magazine writing is professional. If you also suggest a strong idea well suited to the magazine, and if the editor believes you know a great deal about the subject or have chosen impressive experts to quote, you will often be encouraged to write the piece on speculation.

I would recommend that any beginning free-lancer experiment with the article memo form. At the same time, I realize that many successful free-lance writers never use it. They prefer a different form, which we shall now examine.

THE QUERY LETTER

Many writers feel that the query letter is simpler, easier to write, and less formal than the article memo.

Margaret Davidson, a Wisconsin free-lancer, used a query letter in suggesting an article to the editor of *Private Practice,* a magazine for doctors. See Box 5–3.

Box 5–3 *A Typical Query Letter*

Mr. Llewellyn H. Rockwell, Jr.
Editor
Private Practice
3035 Northwest 63rd, Suite 299
Oklahoma City, Oklahoma 73116

Dear Mr. Rockwell:

Might you be interested in an article on "Older Doctors in Wisconsin May be Required to Take Written Tests"?

A proposal being studied by the Medical Examining Board here would require physicians over 60 to take written and oral tests to show they have kept current in their field. Physicians are already required to show that they have 30 credits of continuing education when their licenses are up for renewal every two years.

As might be expected, the proposal is meeting with opposition from area doctors. The 1,500-word article I have in mind would describe the controversy here.

In those three tightly packed paragraphs, Davidson focused on the central point of her article proposal. To underline the significance of the development, she then wrote,

I think this would be of special interest to your readers because Wisconsin may soon become the first state in the country to impose such a requirement. But it may well not be the last. Surely other states will be watching closely what is happening here.

In the closing paragraphs of her letter, she indicated her special interest in the subject and summarized her qualifications:

I am especially interested in the issue because my father is a 67-year-old physician. I am only too well aware of the time he spends reading medical journals and keeping abreast of what is happening in his field. But I wonder how successful he might be in taking examinations after all these years.

I teach journalism at the University of Wisconsin–Oshkosh and cover news of this part of the state for the *Milwaukee Journal*.

Thank you for your consideration of this idea. I look forward to hearing from you.

The editor was attracted by the article idea and impressed by Davidson's special knowledge and qualifications. He gave her the assignment.

One Idea Presented Two Different Ways

When free-lancer Celia Scully happened to spend a little time at an exhibition of "collectibles" one afternoon, she met a talkative postcard dealer from Los Angeles who spoke enthusiastically about collecting postcards as a hobby.

"I left with his business card and one antique postcard," Ms. Scully recalls. She also realized that she had accidentally run across an idea for a magazine feature.

She first wrote a simple query letter to an editor she knew. It is shown in Box 5–4.

Box 5–4

Jerry Reedy, Editorial Director
Odyssey
300 South Wacker Drive
Chicago, IL 60606

Dear Jerry:

Would you be interested in a 1,500-word article on getting started in the postcard-collecting hobby—which some antique dealers claim is the third largest hobby in the United States?

The article would include tips on what to look for in typical tourist shop postcards, something of the hundred-year history of postcards, descriptions of highly valued art and advertising cards as well as information on one of America's most unusual shrines two miles north of Orrin, N.D., featuring a pictorial record of the continent in postcards. . . .

My interest in postcard collecting started with a childlike fascination with turn-of-the-century "see-through" cards from the World's Fairs in Paris and St. Louis. Various antique dealers, whom I've interviewed, see deltiology (also known as cardology) as "the cheapest form of art you can buy," "a good investment," and "a fascinating way to record a whole social history." Since most travelers and tourists inevitably spend a few minutes and often a dollar or two at the postcard stand, your readers might enjoy knowing how to combine the collecting business with pleasure.

Best wishes for the New Year.

Reedy found the suggestion "intriguing," but reported that matters were unsettled at the magazine at that time and that it might be better for Scully to try the idea somewhere else.

"His encouraging letter led me to try a better-paying market, *Travel and Leisure*, which was new to me," Scully says. "I decided to write a better query letter, giving the new editor an idea of my writing style before getting into the 'meat and potatoes' of the piece. However, I've never been one to sit down and dash off the perfect lead. I always need something to trigger my thinking. In this case a lengthy wait in a supermarket checkout line was a stroke of luck. Glancing through a copy of *Reader's Digest*, I ran across a quotation from *Farmer's Almanac*. There was my opening line: 'A real friend is someone who takes a winter vacation on a sun-drenched beach and doesn't send a card.' With that, the rest came easily."

Her revised opening is shown in Box 5–5.

Box 5–5 *Revised Opening*

Pamela Fiori, Editor
Travel and Leisure
1350 Avenue of the Americas
New York, NY 10019

Dear Miss Fiori:

A real friend, according to *Farmer's Almanac,* is someone who takes a winter vacation on a sun-drenched beach and doesn't send a card. Chances are that that friend is buying postcards all right; he just isn't mailing them. Like hundreds of other Americans, he may be a deltiologist—a serious collector, an image junkie, a social historian, or simply a postcard nut.

"Postcard Fever" tells readers in 1,500 words about deltiology, which some antique dealers rank as the third most popular hobby in the United States today. The article would include tips on starting a collection, what to look for in typical tourist shop postcards, descriptions of highly valued art and advertising cards, and tidbits of the 100-year history of the ubiquitous postal. There's even a shrine to postcards located at the exact geographical center of the North American continent near Orrin, N.D.

Ms. Scully then mentioned her own early interest in collecting postcards and quoted the remarks of various antique dealers about the reasons for collecting them.

In this presentation she also listed three of her sources (one of whom had been in the collectibles business for 52 years), and added,

My credits include articles in *Travel, Holiday, Odyssey, Grit, Antique Monthly, American Collector, Antique Trader Weekly, National Antiques Review, Writer's Digest, Lady's Circle, Ladycom,* and *The Travel Agent,* to which I am contributing editor.

Travel and Leisure responded favorably, but asked Scully to write the piece at half the length she had suggested—to cut it from 1,500 words to 750.

"This started out to be a low-paying, first-time assignment at $200 plus expenses," Ms. Scully recalls. "But as it turned out, they liked the piece so much that they ran it in several regional editions and paid extra, so that for 750 words (plus a sidebar they later requested), I was paid more than $700—or just about a dollar a word. And the door was opened for more assignments at much better pay."

Because she had taken the trouble to work out the first paragraph of her query letter carefully, she was able to use it as the lead for the published article.

An Idea for the *Post*

Richard D. Rothschild, a Connecticut free-lancer, needed just four tight paragraphs to convince *The Saturday Evening Post* that he had an idea for an article that would appeal to the magazine's readers.

See the full letter on page 44.

Richard D. Rothschild
133 Byram Shore Road
Greenwich, Connecticut 06830
203-531-0333

October 9, 1990

Mr. Ted Kreiter, Executive Editor
The Saturday Evening Post
100 Waterway Boulevard
Indianapolis, Indiana 46202

Dear Mr. Kreiter:

Moments after lowering your bikes from the car, you glide along the banks of the lazy Connecticut River under a piney scented canopy. Next, you are pedaling slowly past The Elms, Marble House, and Beachwood, Newport's palatial "cottages," on your way to sapphire waters, salty air, and the sandy crescent of Goosberry Beach.

"By Car and Cycle Along New England's Spectacular Coast," the suggested article, takes readers on six short, fascinating rides to savor scenery and history and break up an otherwise tiring car trip.

A nonchallenging way to introduce the family to the joys of bicycle touring, the invigorating rides also explore quaint, Victorian Block Island, white-sailed Marblehead, historic Salem, and unspoiled Gloster, Rockport, and Annasquam.

Three weeks after I receive your OK, I can deliver 2,000 words on the pleasures of travel by car and bicycle, illustrated by six outstanding rides. 35 mm color is available (samples enclosed). And, if you wish, sidebars can be included with detailed route descriptions, small route maps, or information on how to plan other car/bike trips.

Are you interested?

Please let me hear from you, and thanks,

Richard D. Rothschild

encl: Clips, Slides, SASE   file:W/SATEVEP.QRY.

This one-page query letter brought Rothschild his first assignment from the *Post*. The five-page article, retitled "Yankee Pedaler," was featured in the July/August, 1991 issue.

The opening paragraph of the published article was based closely on the first two sentences of the query letter, with some additional details:

> Within moments of lowering your bike from the car, you are riding along the banks of the lazy Connecticut River under a pine-scented canopy. The route is a loop— a 23-mile circle of sorts—and takes two and a half hours to complete. Back at the car you catch your breath en route to the next stop, this time to pedal past Marble House, the Breakers, and Newport's other palatial "cottages."

An Article Suggestion for *American Collector*

Many editors ask that article memos or query letters be kept to a single page. Some say they would prefer even shorter queries: three brief paragraphs, or two, or even one.

I agree that ideally an article suggestion should run no more than one page. Editors have an enormous amount of reading to do, and a long, rambling letter or memo may leave a completely negative impression. If you are long-winded in describing your idea, will you be equally unselective in writing your article?

Randy Ormsby of *American Collector* chose a query letter from Bob Oliver as a model for writers who might wish to write for his magazine. Note Oliver's success in arousing Ormsby's interest with the opening sentence:

> When Neil Levy pulled out that one strategic book, the wall swung forward revealing a secret compartment.
>
> "I couldn't see myself building a whole mystery room without a secret compartment," Levy said.
>
> The tall, bearded Law School Dean added the library to house his collection of 2,000 paperback mysteries when they overflowed all available shelf space in the rest of his house. And he built for a capacity of 3,500 books, so he's not through yet.
>
> "This all started because my wife Jane is a garage sale nut," Neil said. "I had to have something to do at sales, so I started collecting mysteries, particularly the older ones." Levy's oldest paperback is a 1942 *The Thin Man* by Dashiell Hammett that he picked up for 10 cents. His collection includes sets with old-fashioned elaborate art-work on the cover, and sets written by big literary names under pseudonyms.
>
> Would you be interested in seeing a piece of about 750 words on Dean Levy's collection—on speculation? If so, would you prefer color or black-and-white photos?

Oliver's intriguing lead and his use of natural dialogue undoubtedly helped persuade Ormsby that he could write a lively article. It was also a good idea to offer to write the piece on speculation. After a free-lancer has written successfully for a magazine, an editor is often ready to offer a guarantee on pieces that do not work out. There is a certain amount of risk-taking whenever a writer approaches a new magazine, and it is helpful to the editor if the writer recognizes that.

A FEW COMMON ERRORS

Vagueness is always a flaw in a query letter or article memo. It may be worthwhile to look at some of the other common faults:

Slow Beginning

It is not unusual for an editor to receive a letter which seems to begin in slow motion:

> I am a free-lance writer who has lived in Wisconsin for the past 15 years, but spent much of my earlier life in New York City. Since coming to the midwest I have worked in a shoe factory, helped paint a bridge, spent two years as a waiter, then switched over and became a taxi-driver. I started taking evening courses at the University of Wisconsin about three years ago, first in engineering, but then switching over to the liberal arts. I'm now concentrating on English, and my special interest is in the writing courses.

This may seem exaggerated, but it is not. Editors sometimes have to read two or three pages before they can discover exactly what it is that led the writer to write to them in the first place. Many will give up after reading the first page or so.

Complimentary Opening

Queries often begin with overly flattering compliments:

> I've been reading *Redbook* for years, and I think it's the best magazine in the world.

Or

> I know most magazines would be too cowardly to present the article I want to write, but I think your magazine has the guts to print anything and not to worry about losing a few pages of automobile advertising.

Such statements may be sincere, but in a query letter these are just waste paragraphs. Your loyalty to the magazine or your admiration for its courage cannot be factors that influence the editor's decision about your proposal.

Frank Criticism

Sometimes free-lancers try the opposite approach:

> To be honest with you, your recent issues have been pretty bad. I don't know why you decided to waste eight pages on that trivial story about how Presidents spend their vacations. If you want to hold on to your subscribers, you're going to have to do better than that. Before it's too late, I'm going to give you a chance to publish something that's worth publishing. It's a story that may upset a few of your old-lady readers, but it'll help you get back some of the respect you've lost over the past few months with all the fluff you've been featuring.

Some editors would shrug off this belligerent opening, but others would toss the letter aside.

Offering a Bargain

Some writers assume that editors may be attracted by the chance to save a few dollars:

> I know that your regular rate for a 2,500-word article is $1,000, but I would be ready to accept $500 for this piece.

Or

> I am eager to have this article published, and that's more important to me than the money. You won't have to pay me anything for it.

These generous offers could actually have a negative effect. The writer seems to be implying that an editor might accept an inferior piece of work just to save a little money. Editorial budgets are often limited, but they are not *that* limited. If a magazine ordinarily pays $1,000 to beginning free-lancers for publishable 2,500-word articles, that is exactly what you should expect to be paid. If the magazine is going through a difficult period and is trimming payments, the editor will bring up that subject of a lower payment and you can then decide whether to accept or reject the magazine's offer.

WHY EDITORS SAY NO

These minor flaws are found most often in the work of amateurs. But there are other deficiencies or problems that lead to the rejection of many thousands of article suggestions year after year.

I asked editors to list the most common reasons for rejection of article ideas, and these were the ones most of them cited.

The writer hasn't bothered to analyze the magazine he or she is trying to write for.

This led almost every list. Attempting to sell an article to a magazine you have not studied closely and analytically is "the greatest single waste of a writer's time," said a *Reader's Digest* editor.

Each year the *Digest* receives many hundreds of article proposals (and completed articles) that do not contain a single anecdote. Because the use of anecdotes has long been recognized as one explanation for the *Digest*'s extraordinary popularity all over the world, the failure to include an anecdote or two in an article memo "indicates that the writer has not read the *Digest* closely," according to the editors who make decisions about acceptance or rejection of free-lance work.

Sometimes the writer's lack of understanding of a publication can be indicated rather subtly. "We are specifically directed to the 18- to 34-year-old woman," a *Redbook* editor said. "When you talk about children in *Redbook,* they are always under eight. The

Redbook reader is not likely to have teenagers. If a writer sends us an article proposal that focuses on teenage problems, we know she hasn't read the magazine closely and analytically."

Casual reading of a magazine is not enough, editors agreed. They often receive contributions from writers who say they have read their magazines for years and are astonished to discover how far these writers are off target. A thoughtful study of several issues is essential.

The article proposal is either too general or too vague. It lacks focus.

This ranked second among the reasons for rejection at most magazines. Beginning magazine writers (and some who have been trying to write for magazines for years) often leave a great deal to the editor's imagination. Editors mentioned such vague or general suggestions as these:

I would like to do an article about divorce.

We are planning to spend about ten days in San Francisco in June, and I would like to write a piece describing some of the most popular tourist attractions there.

I know there's been a lot of research about cancer, and I would like to talk to some of the researchers and find out if they're closer to finding a cure.

All of these writers were waiting for a favorable signal before doing the work that would be required to interest an editor in any of these subjects. Editors need more details than this before they can say yes.

"I'm not interested in vague proposals," one editor said. "'I'd like to do a story on nursing,' for example. Why *should* we do a story on nursing? What's the news peg? If a writer has done some research, she might tell us, 'In 1984 300,000 nurses left the profession. . . . Here's why they left, and here's how the problems that discouraged them could be overcome.' That gives me the kind of detail I need to reach a decision."

The writer fails to persuade the editor that the subject is significant.

"Writers should not oversell," an *Esquire* editor said, but then added that some make the opposite mistake. They fail to convince the editor that the idea they are offering is important. Any article idea presented routinely, without excitement, is likely to be rejected routinely.

Jim Ferri of *Travel/Holiday* also emphasized the need for writers to transmit some of the excitement they should feel when they undertake any magazine article. Ferri uses a single word to describe most of the unsuccessful query letters he receives: "boring."

Careless errors raise doubts about the writer's competence.

A few very demanding editors will reject an article suggestion (or even a completed manuscript) because they notice a single misspelled name or one obvious factual error. Yet year after year many thousands of free-lancers are careless enough to misspell the name of the editors from whom they hope to receive assignments.

Silvia Koner, former articles editor of *Redbook,* kept a folder filled with misspellings of her name. Writers who were submitting article proposals spelled her first name as follows:

Sylivia	Sylira	Sylvania	Cynthia
Silvie	Sivvia	Sally	Phyllis

They spelled *Koner* like this:

Kower	Konner	Kohner	Kroner
Koenig	Conet	Connor	Conar
Comer	Roner		

"Any editor has to feel that a writer who cannot copy down her name and title correctly is going to have trouble in writing 3,000 words," said Roberta Ashley of *Cosmopolitan.*

Other common flaws listed by many editors were these:

The writer does not convince the editor that the article will be authoritative.
The writer is proposing an article on a subject the magazine has already covered.
The writing is pedestrian and unimpressive.

CHECKLIST FOR AN ARTICLE PROPOSAL

With the comments of these editors in mind, it might be useful to test your article memo by using this checklist:

1. Is this a strong, fresh idea?
2. Am I certain that I am sending it to the right magazine?
3. Have I checked to make sure the magazine has not published a similar article in the past three or four years?
4. Will the title arouse the editor's interest?
5. Have I chosen the best possible lead?
6. Have I included an effective capsule statement that clearly indicates just what this article is all about?
7. Is the article idea tightly focused?
8. Have I given the editor enough information so he or she can make an intelligent decision?
9. Have I indicated specifically what authorities I plan to interview?
10. Have I told the editor enough about my own qualifications and background?
11. Is the article memo free of errors?
12. Even in this brief space, have I given some idea of my writing ability?
13. Have I checked a current issue of the magazine to make certain that I have spelled the editor's name correctly and have given the editor the right title?

This may seem an excessive amount of attention to pay to a page or page-and-a-half memo. But a great deal depends on the impression this brief document makes on an editor—or several editors, in many cases. A carefully crafted memo (or query letter) offering a promising article idea will be considered in even the busiest magazine offices.

AND NOW—THE NEXT IDEA

With the article memo or query letter in the mail, the next thing to do is to begin thinking about the next article idea.

You will naturally hope that the editor will respond both quickly and affirmatively, but you should accept two facts:

1. Editorial decisions can be slow. In rare instances you may receive a yes answer within two weeks, but often you may have to wait as long as two or three months before you know whether or not your article idea has been accepted.
2. Even if your idea is a very good one and the article proposal is very effectively written, the answer may still be no.

Professionals accept both those facts. Over the years many experienced magazine writers have learned to expect a negative answer to three out of every four article suggestions they submit. Because of that, they concentrate on keeping many article proposals in circulation.

Amateurs often fail to do that. Instead, many of them prepare a single article memo, mail it, and then wait. They build up their expectations based on a single article idea and then are deeply disappointed if the proposal is rejected.

To a professional, rejection is a normal risk. To the amateur, it is often a devastating blow.

Successful full-time free-lance writers often have at least a dozen ideas circulating at the same time. If they get three acceptances out of twelve, they are able to accept the negative reactions philosophically.

Because editors can be slow in responding, beginning magazine writers often raise the following question, which we shall examine in detail.

WHAT ABOUT MULTIPLE SUBMISSIONS?

Should a writer submit an article idea to only one magazine at a time?

Many editors would say yes. Their argument is this: Often several editors must read, consider, and discuss an idea before a decision is reached. If the writer is offering the same proposal to half a dozen different magazines, and two or three of them are interested in it, much editorial time is being wasted at the magazines that like the idea but do not end up publishing it. Those magazines that lose out may be less receptive to future submissions from that writer.

Some writers disagree. Editorial decisions take too much time, they say. Why should the writer wait four or five weeks to hear from one magazine, then perhaps have to start over if the answer is no? (With some article ideas, the passage of time could reduce the appeal of the idea, or even make it unpublishable.) Besides, they say, most editorial decisions are negative—therefore, the chance of two magazines accepting the same article proposal is quite small.

Having been on both sides, I can understand both arguments.

My suggestion is this: If you do decide to make multiple submissions, inform editors that you are doing that. You should be completely honest in your dealings with editors, just as you expect them to be honest in their dealings with you.

Usually you should take a chance by submitting your ideas to one magazine at a time, in my opinion. But you do not have to wait months for a response. If you have not heard from an editor in four or five weeks, you are justified in writing to request a decision.

Your letter should be short, calm, factual, and unemotional:

Dear Mr. Iverson:

On November 3, I mailed you an article suggestion, "How to Save Money by Taking Your Vacation in the Fall."

As you can understand, this article should appear in April or May, since readers will then have time to alter their vacation plans if they find my article persuasive.

I would prefer to write this article for your magazine, but if it does not seem right for you I would like to try the idea on some other editors.

Would you let me have a decision as soon as possible? I am enclosing another copy of my article memo with this note.

If that does not bring a reply within ten days, you would then be justified in submitting the proposal to another magazine. You might want to send a brief note to the first editor, informing him or her about the second submission.

A FINAL REMINDER

Always enclose a self-addressed, stamped envelope (SASE) when submitting a query letter or an article memo, or when writing a follow-up letter to an editor.

Finding
the Facts
You Need

Magazine editors reject many articles because the research is too skimpy. Here you will find some specific suggestions that could help you discover the details you need to know about your subject.

Assume that you have just heard about two developments that might offer promising subjects for magazine articles:

Edward Albee has completed a new play, and someone in the drama department tells you that he plans to stage a trial run at a theater within easy reach of your campus.

Dr. Milton Davis, a medical researcher who has spent ten years studying the causes of headaches, has been appointed to a visiting professorship at your university.

You take a look at *Writer's Market* and see immediately that an article about Albee and his new play might interest such specialized magazines as *Dramatics Magazine* or *Playbill.* You also realize that if you can obtain a fresh, revealing, wide-ranging interview with the playwright you might be able to place the piece in one of the major periodicals, such as *The New York Times Magazine,* that seem receptive to articles about widely known theater personalities. All this is apparent from a quick survey.

If Dr. Davis has something new to say about the causes and cures of headaches, you would have a much wider range of magazines from which to choose. Most magazines of general circulation occasionally feature articles on health, and many of them carry such pieces in almost every issue. You would also discover several publications with a special interest in the details of medical research.

After confirming the possibility of finding magazines that might be ready to respond favorably to these two ideas, you are now ready to undertake preliminary research. What is the best way to begin?

Some writers believe in just going to the nearest library and plunging in. They would start looking through *Readers' Guide to Periodical Literature* and the card catalogue (or library computer listings), searching for everything they could find under the three obvious headings: "Albee, Edward," "Davis, Milton," and "Headaches."

That approach has been used many thousands of times and is often effective. If you have the time for a leisurely search, you may find this a satisfactory way to begin. But since few students (and few professional writers) have much time to spare, you might want to experiment with a more systematic method of gathering the material you need.

You could start by getting basic information, and then move on from there, going into greater and greater depth until you are convinced that you have as much background information as you need—first for your article memo, and then for the complete article.

Let's begin with Edward Albee.

THE SEARCH FOR FACTS ABOUT ALBEE

Unless you happen to know a great deal about Albee, his life, and his work, you might want to start with the most basic of all the biographical information sources: *Who's Who in America.* This entry offers only the barest details, such as the titles of his previous plays. But you will almost always find the current mailing address at the end of each biography, and that will be useful to you later when you reach the point to set up an interview with Albee.

To supplement the few lines in *Who's Who,* you could then look for the reference shelves where most libraries keep a number of standard works easily available. Here you would probably find several volumes devoted to twentieth-century writers, and some of those would offer additional information about Albee. In *Contemporary Authors* (published by Gale), you would discover a much longer and more useful sketch of the playwright's career, and you would also find some direct quotes that might suggest topics that you will wish to touch on when you get around to your interview with Albee.

Checking on Recent Developments in Albee's Life or Career

Some of the biographical entries may be two or three years old, and you will want to discover whether there have been later developments that will influence your article. To check on this, you should look up Albee in the available newspaper indices, such as *The New York Times Index* and the index issued by *The Washington Post.*

Discovering What Other Magazine Writers Have Published about Albee during the Past Few Years

You do not wish to duplicate what other magazine writers have written about Albee. To prevent that, you will want to check on any major piece about him.

Your basic guide to the most important recent pieces is *Readers' Guide to Periodical Literature,* which lists articles appearing in about 160 general magazines.

Looking for Material in Specialized Reference Books

In addition to biographical material about Albee, you will want to discover what has been written about him in reference books that cover twentieth-century theater.

In *Modern World Theater* (Ungar), you will find brief descriptions of six of his plays. You will find reviews of some of his work in *On Stage, Selected Theater Reviews from The New York Times, 1920–1970* (Arno).

Long quotations from other major reviews and lengthy articles analyzing Albee's work appear in *Contemporary Literary Criticism* (Gale).

You may not use much of this material, but it will give you necessary background for your article.

Looking for Chapters or Complete Books about Albee

In most recent books about the American theater or the theater in the twentieth century, you would find at least passing references to Albee, and in many you would find chapters about him and his work.

In many libraries you would also discover books about Albee and his plays. In the largest research libraries you could find as many as seven or eight of these, including one entitled *Who's Afraid of Edward Albee?* If your library does not have the books that sound most useful to you, a reference librarian could probably help you obtain copies through an interlibrary loan.

Requesting an Interview

After this extensive preliminary research, you might want to write to Albee (using the address given in the current *Who's Who in America*) to tell him that you plan to write an article about him and his new play. You could describe the extent of your preliminary research, list the specific publications you have in mind for the article, and then request a brief interview by telephone.

In your note, you should indicate precisely when you plan to telephone. It might be a good idea to say that you will make a second call—again at a clearly specified time—if you fail to reach him the first time.

Once you have done this much work, you should be ready to write a memo to the magazine that interests you most strongly. If necessary, you could then go on to your second choice and your third.

When you have received a favorable response, you could then approach a reference librarian to request expert assistance in discovering other significant material about Albee you have not turned up in your own exploration. A librarian can guide you to unpublished Ph.D. dissertations and to manuscript collections in special libraries. Some of these materials may seem far too specialized to be of any value to you, but it is always useful to know what is available.

Although this library research will prepare you for the final stage, the article should never be based entirely (or even principally) on what has previously appeared in print. Your research merely gives you a base for the interviews with Albee (and with some of his friends, some of his critics, and others involved in the production of the new play). Your article should add to the store of material that will then be available to those who will be writing about Albee in the future.

THE SEARCH FOR FACTS ABOUT HEADACHES

In the early stages of your research for an article on headaches, you would consult the same three basic reference sources.

Who's Who in America would give you a brief biography of Dr. Milton Davis if he has achieved wide recognition as a medical researcher. If you don't find his name there, you could check the regional volumes (such as *Who's Who in the East*) or see whether he is listed in one of the many specialized biographical reference books now being published.

The New York Times Index would lead you to stories about any recent major developments in headache research and could include a news story or two about Dr. Davis if his work has gained national attention.

In *Readers' Guide to Periodical Literature* you would find a list of articles about headaches published in major magazines in recent years. You might be surprised—and encouraged—by the number of magazines that have shown an interest in this subject. For example, in a single year all these articles were published:

"About Those Headaches"—*Redbook*
"Pain Is All in Your Head"—*Vogue*
"Help for Tension Headaches"—*Science News*
"Got a Splitting Headache? Dr. Seymour Diamond Spells Relief B-i-o-f-e-e-d-b-a-c-k"—*People*
"Complete Help for Headaches Guide"—*Mademoiselle*
"Migraine Comes Out of the Closet"—*McLean's*
"New Ways to Ease Your Headache Pain"—*Ebony*

And during the same year, *Science* offered an article under this title:

"Perivascular meningeal projections from cat trimegial ganglia: Possible pathway for vascular headaches in man."

Research in Depth

After reading the articles in general magazines, you will want to discover what is being published currently in more specialized publications. In the Government Documents section of your library you will find *Index Medicus,* published by the U.S. Department of Health and Human Resources. This is a monthly listing of articles in the medical field published anywhere in the world, and the size of the volumes may seem intimidating at first. But the index will lead you to the most valuable recent articles about headaches, and a reference librarian can help you obtain copies of those that sound most useful.

Choosing the Books That Will Be Useful

You might want to begin by looking up brief articles about headaches in such volumes as *The Book of Health: A Medical Encyclopedia for Everybody* (Van Nostrand Reinhold), which you will find on the reference shelves.

You will also need to settle upon a few book-length treatments of the subject, and you may be surprised again by the number available. One large library lists 28 of them in its catalog.

One suggestion: Check the publication date before selecting a book about headaches. Although an earlier book may be worth reading because of the writer's skill in presenting basic background information, it could have one serious flaw. It may fail to reflect recent discoveries and current theories.

Should you try to read all 28 books if you find that many in the library you are using? I don't think so. At some point you have to make some arbitrary decisions about the amount of background research required. You might read a chapter or two in several books, looking for the two or three or four volumes that are current, authoritative, detailed, and clearly written.

And Now—The Interview

As in your work on the Albee article, you should always recognize that the library research is only the beginning of your preparation for writing a magazine article. But by following the steps outlined here, you have prepared yourself to use your interview (or interviews) with Dr. Davis to focus on what is new and significant in the results of his 10-year study.

DISCOVERING SPECIALIZED REFERENCE BOOKS

As the brief descriptions of the search for information about Albee, Dr. Davis, and headaches indicate, libraries contain thousands of specialized reference books that can be of enormous value to magazine writers. And these books are often overlooked.

Here are a few examples of biographical volumes focusing on prominent people in various fields:

Politicians:	*Who's Who in American Politics* (Bowker)
Architects:	*American Architects Directory* (Bowker)
Scholars:	*Directory of American Scholars* (Bowker)
Scientists:	*American Men and Women of Science* (Bowker)
Psychiatrists:	*Biographical Directory of the American Psychiatric Association* (Bowker)
Artists:	*Who's Who in American Art* (Bowker)

A reference librarian can help you find other books that will give you basic biographical information about who's who in such fields as advertising, insurance, engineering, music, education, and business.

In addition to hundreds of biographical volumes, large libraries offer specialized reference books in an extraordinary range of subjects. If you were researching black history, you might find as many as 17 major reference works, including *Blacks in America, 1492–1970: A Chronology and Fact Book* (Oceana). If you wanted to make a comparison between U.S. and U.S.S.R. military aircraft, you would find the basic information you needed in *Jane's All the World's Aircraft* (McGraw-Hill). *American Popular Songs from the Revolutionary War to the Present* (Random House) would give you details about 3,600 popular songs.

You will discover about 2,000 reference books listed and described in *How to Do Library Research,* by Robert B. Downs and Clara D. Keller (University of Illinois Press). Some of the subject fields that these volumes cover are

Baseball records
The women's rights movement
Film history
Supreme Court opinions
Slang terms
Folk music
Automobile production statistics
Poisonous plants
Trailer parks
Foundation grants
Emergency medical aid
Indian tribal history
Patent applications
Major events in world history

This is a very brief selection from the wide range of reference volumes listed by Downs and Keller. You might want to spend an afternoon at your university library to discover how many of these books are easily accessible to you. When you have spent some time as a free-lance writer, you may find that thumbing through any of the reference books that arouse your special interest can suggest magazine article possibilities.

USING DATABASES

In recent years, many writers have turned to the computer for help in their research. The formal name for this is *database research,* and you have probably used a simple form of it in searching for specific books in your library.

At least 2,000 databases are now available, and new ones are being developed every month. Here are three examples:

Full-text Database. NEXIS stores away in the computer the full texts of articles published in more than 125 newspapers, magazines, and newsletters. It also makes available the texts of stories distributed by the wire services (such as Associated Press) and those carried by the network news.

Abstract Database. Food Science and Technology Abstracts makes available brief summaries of articles in more than 1,200 journals on food science, chemistry, biochemistry, and related fields. Abstracts in many other fields are being introduced each year.

Statistical Database. CENDATA provides current data about the population, housing, and businesses gathered and analyzed by the Bureau of the Census.

A Few Words of Caution

Experts on database research caution those who have not used this method of gathering information to first see how much material they can obtain through traditional means of research (such as those discussed earlier in this chapter). One consideration is the sometimes surprisingly high cost of some database research. A search can cost you from $35 to more than $200 an hour, the authors of *Search Strategies in Mass Communication* report. They add this note:

> If there is time, it makes more sense . . . to do a search by hand rather than pay for a computer search. A data-base search may be called for if [you] are looking for information about an event or a topic that is so recent that it may not have made its way into the printed indexes and library sources.

If you do decide to experiment with database research, the authors of *Communications Research: Strategies and Sources* (R. B. Rubin, A. M. Rubin, and L. J. Piele) offer these suggestions:

1. First see how much you can find about your subject through a traditional, manual search. "The more you know about your topic, the more effective your search will be."
2. At the same time, "Don't entertain the illusion that you can exhaust all possible sources related to your topic. It is, of course, important to be as thorough as possible. . . . But you will never find all possible sources."
3. Narrow your focus before you begin the database research. Exactly what do you need to know that you have not discovered through your traditional research? "The first step is to develop a concise, one-sentence statement of your research question."
4. Look for some expert help at the beginning. "It is good to start by making an appointment with the librarian who coordinates the on-line search services at your university library to discuss the available data bases. . . ."
5. Obtain an estimate of the cost in advance, perhaps from the librarian. "Since costs vary widely, you should investigate these carefully before you begin the actual search."

AN EXPERIMENT WITH RESEARCH

Because inadequate research is often cited by magazine editors as a reason for rejection of manuscripts, it would be useful to carry out an experiment in researching a subject that appeals to you.

You could begin by choosing any one of these broad subjects, or by selecting another topic that is of special interest to you:

Backaches
Baldness
Camping
Bowling
Photography

Stamp collecting
Jogging
Dating
Women's rights
Abortion
ERA
Censorship
Cheating
Controlling tension
Home furnishing
Money
Searching for a job
Marriage problems
Learning disabilities
An entertainment personality
A sports personality
A major political figure

After settling on one of these 22 broad subjects—or selecting a different one of greater appeal to you—you should then bring the general topic into tight focus, looking for an aspect of the subject that could be developed into a magazine article.

For example, rather than writing a general piece about backaches, you might decide to explore the most common causes for backaches among people in their fifties and sixties and test that idea on *Modern Maturity.* For an article on bowling, you might be able to discover the seven errors commonly made by beginning bowlers. For indoor gardening, you could advise readers about half a dozen plants that *anyone* can grow successfully.

You will find other examples of the methods experienced writers use in bringing subjects into tight focus in Chapter 3, "Finding Article Ideas."

While narrowing your subject, you should also make a list of the magazines most likely to be receptive to your article. Visit the periodicals room of a large library or a major newsstand if you have not already become familiar with the publications that might be interested.

After these preliminary steps, follow the procedure outlined earlier in this chapter for researching the subject you have chosen.

Some interviewing will be essential for almost all magazine articles. One editor complained that many writers who approach him seem more comfortable with library research than with interviewing, and therefore offer him articles that consist simply of a regurgitation of available material. Before conducting your interviews, you may find it useful to examine Chapter 7, "Developing Your Skill as an Interviewer."

Once you have completed your library research and your interviewing, prepare an article memo or a query letter for the magazine (or magazines) you have chosen. Ask your professor and your fellow students to take a close, critical look at the article proposal. Consider all their suggestions, make any necessary changes or corrections, and then test the idea on an editor.

When you reach the point of submitting a well-planned, carefully researched, skillfully revised article memo or query letter to an editor, you are on your way to becoming a magazine writer.

7

Developing Your Skill as an Interviewer

Have you ever emerged from an interview with major questions left unasked, and with sketchy notes of the answers you did receive? Here successful interviewers offer detailed suggestions about the steps they take in preparing for and conducting an interview.

The skills you need for effective interviewing can be developed only through practice and experimentation.

Adaptability is the chief requirement. You will learn early that an approach which works well with a relaxed, self-assured interviewee may not work at all with someone who is afraid of being misquoted and who concentrates from the beginning on finding some polite way to get you out of his or her office.

Because interviewing is the most important source for many of the magazine articles you will write, it is useful to review the factors that determine whether or not a session will be productive.

Among the major questions to consider before, during, and after an interview are these:

Have you chosen the right person to interview?
Do you know enough about the person to interview him or her successfully?
Do you have a series of questions prepared in advance?
Are you certain you will come away with accurate notes of the interviewee's responses?

If your source asks you to treat answers to your questions as "off the record," have you decided how to respond?

If you feel that one of your questions may irritate your interviewee, when will you ask it? How will you phrase it?

If the interviewee asks you to submit your completed article for approval, how will you respond?

Let's examine these and some other important questions in some detail.

1. CHOOSING THE RIGHT PERSON TO INTERVIEW

Sometimes beginners are too casual in selecting interviewees. You are looking for the best possible source when you write for magazines, and it is a mistake to settle for people simply because they are easy to reach and eager to cooperate. By going to some additional trouble early, you can often quote an authority who will impress both your editor and your readers.

When I was teaching a magazine writing course in Australia, one of my students was writing an article about financial aid available to university students. He needed to know whether the government was about to reduce the grants that made it possible for many thousands of students to continue their education. He tried to get this information from officers in the university administration, but the responses were not very helpful.

"I don't think they know any more about what's going to happen in the next year or two than I do," he told me.

"Don't limit yourself to the campus," I suggested. "If you could go anywhere in Australia to get an answer, who would you interview?"

"Somebody in the Prime Minister's office," he said.

"Well, then, why don't you give his office a call?"

He laughed. "Why would they want to talk to me?" he asked.

"They may not, but the only way to find out is to try."

When I offered to pay for the long-distance call, he finally agreed. I could tell from his expression that he was still convinced that it would be impossible for an unknown student a thousand miles from Australia's capital to obtain a statement from such a lofty source.

The Prime Minister of Australia, the Honorable Gough Whitlam, happened to pick up the phone. Whitlam listened patiently to the hesitant voice from far-off Queensland, joked about his costly method of doing research for a journalism course, and then gave a quotable answer to the student's question: "As long as I am Prime Minister," he said, "the government will never reduce the funds available for student grants."

Occasionally you will fail in your effort to reach the specific person you would like to interview and quote. Then you may settle for a substitute: the senator's administrative assistant rather than the senator, for example. But I would not settle for the lesser figure too quickly. Especially in writing for a mass-circulation magazine, you are expected to use energy, skill, and imagination in your approach to someone who can speak with authority.

2. DISCOVERING SOMETHING ABOUT THE BACKGROUND OF YOUR INTERVIEWEE

If you know little more than the name and the title of someone you are interviewing, the thinness of your knowledge will soon become apparent, and you are not likely to have a very productive session.

Often (not always) you will be interviewing people who have gained a certain prominence in their fields. You may find that their careers are summarized in either the national *Who's Who in America* or in one of the regional editions—*Who's Who in the East, Who's Who in the West,* and so forth. In most libraries you will also find shelves filled with other biographical reference works that offer information about writers, scientists, academics, political figures, major industrialists, and others who have had outstanding careers in many areas.

You obviously know *something* about the person you have chosen to interview. Otherwise there would be no point in setting up the appointment. But you should supplement your general knowledge with as much specific background information as you can obtain in advance. Often a secretary will be able to give you copies of previously published interviews and other material that is otherwise difficult to locate.

3. PREPARING YOUR QUESTIONS

Some experienced writers do not bother to prepare questions in advance when they set up an interview. They have full confidence in their ability to improvise and have been doing this for decades with apparent success.

Other writers type out 25 or 30 questions before *any* interview. Some of these follow that list faithfully. Others rarely glance at it once the session is underway, but obviously find it comforting to know that it is available to refer to if their minds suddenly go blank.

I think dependence on improvisation is dangerous for beginning magazine writers. You are likely to find that your lack of preparation raises doubts in the mind of the interviewee about your competence to write the article you have proposed. And you may fail to ask some important questions.

I also have some reservations about 25 carefully composed questions. Once you have gone to all that trouble, you may be tempted to ask them, one by one, and your precise planning may make the interview too rigid. Often an interviewee makes an unexpected, intriguing comment that you should follow up immediately, without regard to the list you have written out in advance.

The method I use—which may or may not be the right one for you—is to sketch out the most important questions I want to ask. I do not write them out in full sentences. If I were interviewing someone who had discovered a new drug to reduce the pain of migraine headaches, I might write these notes on a card or a slip of paper:

How discovered?
Any side effects?
Works for all cases?

How tested?
When available?

Incidentally, in any interview it is important to ask your questions in some logical order. If you skip from point to point, your random questions can lead to scattered, fragmentary answers.

You should also avoid asking questions that can be answered with a monosyllable: yes, no, right, sure. A question that begins with the words *why* or *how* is most likely to lead to the kind of answer you will find quotable.

Keep in mind that you're looking for much more than just *facts* when you conduct an interview. You will need anecdotes, revealing details, and striking quotes to bring your article to life.

If the person you are interviewing makes a *general* statement that sounds promising, follow up immediately by asking for *specific* details that support that general observation. For example,

Interviewee: The Senator isn't really very good at dealing with the people who work in his office.
Interviewer: You've seen some problems in his method of dealing with them?
Interviewee: Yes, I have. For one thing he's pretty distant with them. Pretty remote . . .
Interviewer: For example?
Interviewee: Well, he didn't even know that his secretary's mother had been in the hospital for five weeks and wasn't expected to live. And he has trouble remembering the names of half the people who work for him.

By asking a series of follow-up questions, the interviewer will probably end up with a usable anecdote that will help round out his portrait of the senator.

Incidentally, it's important to show genuine interest in what the people you are interviewing say. If you do, they will often respond by volunteering the kinds of details that make your article more readable. Many of the people you interview are eager to have an audience, and they know that through your article they may reach hundreds of thousands or millions of readers.

4. ARRANGING THE INTERVIEW

When you have very limited time, you will probably have to use the telephone to set up an interview. It is important to identify yourself quickly, describe the article you are researching, and give a brief indication of the purpose of the interview.

If you have time, I suggest that you consider writing a letter instead. It should also be brief and specific and should prepare the way for a follow-up telephone call at a clearly specified time.

For example,

Dear Professor Gates:
I am writing an article about procrastination that I plan to submit to *Reader's Digest,* and I would appreciate a chance to discuss the subject with you.

I know that you have carried out extensive research on the causes of procrastination and have also counseled students who find it difficult to complete major projects.

Since procrastination is a common problem, I think your advice would also be valuable to the millions of readers of the *Digest*.

I will telephone you Friday morning, March 6, at 10 to work out a convenient time for an interview. If I do not reach you then, I will try again on Monday morning, March 9, at 11.

Thank you for considering my request.

If you have previously published a magazine article or two, you could include a paragraph stating, "My work has appeared in. . . ." Or if you have special knowledge or experience that qualifies you to write about the specific subject, you should also indicate that: "I am a psychology major. . . ." Or "I have done some research in the field. . . ."

5. OBSERVING YOUR INTERVIEWEE

Sensitivity to the person you are interviewing is of major importance. If you are dealing with someone who is not accustomed to being interviewed, you should take a few minutes to put the interviewee at ease. If the person you are interviewing is obviously very busy, you should indicate that you recognize this and offer to limit the time for the interview or to come back at a more convenient time.

Celia Scully, a free-lancer who has written for more than 30 magazines, told me of a session she had arranged with a psychologist who had gained a great deal of attention because of his theories about the best way to control obesity.

"He was in Reno to conduct a series of workshops, and all the media wanted to talk to him," Scully said. "As a beginning free-lancer at that time, I knew that I would be low on his list. I had been given an appointment at 4:35, and he had a television interview coming up at 5.

"When he came in, he looked beat. I thought he was probably wondering how he could get out of the session altogether, so I said, 'I know you've had a tough day. Would you like to take a break before we start?'

"I knew I was taking a chance, because he could have responded by suggesting that we cancel the interview entirely. But instead his face brightened up immediately and he said: 'Yes, if you could just give me time to send out for a milkshake that is thick and gooey and full of calories, that'll give me the energy I need to talk to you for ten or fifteen minutes before the TV interview.'

"I agreed—and ended up with a really valuable one-hour interview, while the TV crew had to wait."

6. SETTING THE TONE

The first two or three questions often determine whether an interview is going to be productive. At the same time you are studying the interviewee, he or she is also observing you and soon decides whether you have taken the trouble to learn something about his or her background, whether you are sympathetic or hostile, and how competent you are.

"If you try to imitate Mike Wallace or Dan Rather, you are likely to come across as a phony," warns free-lancer Celia Scully. "The successful interviewer has to use a method that is consistent with his [or her] personality."

Some inexperienced interviewers are too formal and businesslike, probably because they are concentrating entirely on their own objective of gathering as much information as they can as quickly as possible. Often writers who have done a lot of interviewing spend three or four minutes helping the interviewee relax, and then almost imperceptibly slip in the first of their questions.

It is also a mistake to spend too *much* time on casual conversation before starting the interview. As soon as your interviewee seems at ease with you, you should introduce your first question.

7. MAKING NOTES

I've known a few writers who felt they could record the results of an interview accurately without making notes. Most of us recognize that our memories are not that dependable. And some of the people you interview will begin to have doubts about your accuracy when they notice that you are taking only occasional notes or none at all.

Many reporters and magazine writers develop a primitive form of shorthand over the years. They get into the habit of using one-letter, two-letter, or three-letter abbreviations for some common words:

w	with
w/o	without
b	but
u	you
s	said
wh	when
whr	where
ap	approximately
est	estimated
M	Monday
F	Friday

As a beginning magazine writer, you might want to consider the advantage of studying shorthand or speedwriting, since there are obvious limitations to this kind of "reporter's shorthand." It is essential to record precisely any words you plan to quote, and it can be awkward if you have to ask an interviewee to speak more slowly so that you can make sure you are quoting accurately.

Of course, there is another possibility:

8. USING A TAPE RECORDER

I was surprised to learn that many of the experienced free-lancers I interviewed while working on this book use tape recorders rarely. Some do not use them at all. Those with the strongest reservations listed these reasons for staying away from recorders:

The sight of a tape recorder inhibits some interviewees. They become more guarded in their choice of words and may refuse to answer some questions at all, not wanting to have their words permanently recorded.

The battery may go dead during a crucial interview.

Interference from some unseen electrical device may make it impossible to understand the words on the tape.

Transcribing a one-hour tape can take several hours—and you may end up with only a few sentences of any real value. Tape-recorded interviews tend to go on and on, because the session itself seems so effortless. The real work for the writer is merely postponed.

Still, the tape recorder can be a very useful tool, and I believe solutions exist to most of the drawbacks those free-lancers mentioned:

Begin by asking if the interviewee has any objection to being taped. I think you will rarely run into an objection.

If you feel a tape-recorder is making an interviewee uncomfortable (even after the agreement to your use of the machine), turn it off. Make sure the interviewee sees that you have put it to one side, and switch over to making written notes.

Check the recorder carefully before any interview. If you have any questions in your mind about the strength of the batteries, replace them. And if the recorder itself is not dependable, get a new one.

For any important interview, make written notes even though you are also taping the answers.

Do not tape too much. If you just turn the tape recorder on and let it run for two or three hours, you will find yourself facing hours of tedious and unnecessary listening. Your "pause" button will make it possible for you to edit as you go, recording only those exchanges that are likely to be useful.

Transcribe selectively. There's no point in carefully typing out page after page of material that you will end up discarding.

One other suggestion: If you haven't had much experience with a recorder, stage a few test runs. Don't wait until you have a crucial interview before practicing enough to feel confident about your mastery of the machine.

9. KEEPING AN INTERVIEWEE TO THE POINT

Although it is a mistake to hold rigidly to the questions you have written out in advance because an interviewee might unexpectedly volunteer something of strong interest that you will want to pursue, it is also a mistake to allow your source to wander aimlessly. If an interviewee begins telling long, pointless anecdotes or offering information of no possible use in your article, you should be ready to draw the discussion back to the subject diplomatically.

One free-lancer said, "I listen patiently for a minute or two in such cases, but I cut in as soon as the person I am interviewing pauses to draw a breath. I'll say something like, 'That is very interesting,' or 'I'd like to hear more about that some time.' But then I add quickly: 'That was a very good point you were making a moment ago. I want to be sure I have it right. You were saying. . . .'"

10. ASKING THE DIFFICULT QUESTION

It is usually best to wait until late in the interview to ask a question the interviewee might resent. If you ask it too early, the person you are questioning might become defensive and uncooperative.

Most experienced free-lancers lead into such questions with remarks such as these:

"I've heard conflicting reports about why you resigned from your last job. Exactly what were the circumstances?"

Or

"As you know, you have been criticized for your opposition to the E.R.A. I'd like to give you a chance to respond to those comments. . . ."

Even though you must choose the best time to ask a question your interviewee might be reluctant to answer, you should not avoid asking it. You are the reader's representative when you are conducting an interview, and you should try to get answers to every question that might be in your readers' minds.

11. IF AN INTERVIEWEE REFUSES TO ANSWER . . .

"If an interviewee avoids responding when you ask a crucial question, you should re-phrase it and try again," said Charles Stokes, who has conducted interviews for maga-zines, newspapers, radio, and television. "If he keeps dodging, you should then quote your questions and his evasive replies. They should be quoted verbatim, and the reader will recognize what has happened. 'There must be some reason why he refuses to respond frankly,' most readers will decide."

12. CHECKING DIRECT QUOTES

If you use a tape recorder, you do not have to worry about the possibility of misquoting a source. If you don't use one, and have any uncertainty in your mind about the accuracy of your notes, I would urge you to telephone the interviewee to double-check all direct quotes.

Some magazines now use researchers who will telephone sources to check the quotes. It is far more troublesome to resolve problems when an article is about to go into print than it is to work them out earlier.

13. IF AN INTERVIEWEE SAYS, "THIS IS OFF THE RECORD . . ."

Some free-lancers say they end a session immediately if a source insists that his or her remarks are "off the record." Why talk to someone if what you are told cannot be published? they ask.

I think this is the right decision most of the time—but not always. Sometimes an "off the record" revelation will lead you to other sources that can be named. And frequently the source will agree that *some* of the information can be published, even if the source cannot be identified.

You gain nothing by cutting off an interview abruptly before you are sure that you are wasting your time.

14. A TRAP TO AVOID

Occasionally someone you interview may request that you let him or her see the completed manuscript. In my opinion, your answer should be a firm no.

Frequently, people who ask to read a piece "just to make sure that you have all the facts right" will then attempt to impose a subtle censorship. Some will try to turn an objective article into a publicity story for themselves.

You can double-check facts and direct quotations with your source without submitting the manuscript for approval. Many experienced writers do this checking by telephone, reading off only the specific material obtained from that source.

There is one exception to this general rule: If you write a first-person "as told to" article, the one whose byline appears on the article along with your credit line should approve the manuscript line by line.

A FINAL WORD

The techniques of conducting an interview can be described, but the art must be discovered. Experience in interviewing many different people for many different purposes is essential for anyone who hopes to do work of any significance.

At first you may be preoccupied with the mechanics of arranging the appointment, writing out the questions, making notes during the interview, or keeping an eye on the tape recorder.

Once you have passed that early stage, you should begin to focus on the central purpose of these sessions. You should ask questions that probe more deeply, concentrate on observing your interviewee, adapt quickly if some promising point begins to emerge unexpectedly, and pursue every promising lead, determined to get the full story.

Over the years you will learn to record in your mind far more than the questions and answers. You will be able to reveal the character of your interviewee and to recapture vividly the scene as well as the words.

THE Q&A ARTICLE

At some point you might wish to experiment with an article based on in-depth interviews with a single person. These Q&A (question and answer) pieces appear occasionally in many magazines, but three publications have featured them prominently over the years: *The Paris Review, Playboy,* and *Rolling Stone.*

The Paris Review interviews have been collected in two volumes under the title *Writers at Work,* and the *Playboy* interviews in the book *The Playboy Interview.* If this form interests you, you might want to study these volumes carefully, because planning, conducting, and editing such an interview (or series of interviews) is not as simple as it may seem.

At *Playboy,* for example, an interviewer may spend a month or more researching the subject's life and interviewing friends and enemies before actually questioning the subject. In some cases the writer submits *several hundred* questions to a *Playboy* editor, according to G. Barry Golson, editor of *The Playboy Interview.* The editor discusses those questions with the writer before the interview begins, suggests some others, and may join in editing and arranging those finally selected. Writers are instructed to "spend as much time as the subject [will] give them—and then ask for more." Writers rarely come back with less than five or six hours of tape, Golson says in his introduction to *The Playboy Interview,* "and, in recent years, twenty hours of recorded conversation have not been uncommon."

The editors recognize that publishing the complete, unedited tape would not be satisfactory. They work with the writer "to sift and refine the raw verbiage or a tape transcript into a linear, continuous conversation," Golson says, with the emphasis "on what the eye could read rather than on what the ear could comprehend. This meant there was always a process of distillation and condensation, of reshuffling and rearranging, but with sufficient faithfulness to the original that the material had the verisimilitude of natural, spoken conversation. It was never a matter of 'improving' a person's language, but of squeezing out the repetitions and meanderings, the pauses and false starts. . . ."

Interviewees have a chance to check for *factual* accuracy before the interviews are published, but the magazine resists "attempts to sanitize the conversation."

A Suggested Experiment

At one university a professor arranges for students to interview each other, with the interviews being videotaped and then analyzed. This is a very useful exercise because beginning interviewers are often so preoccupied with the mechanics of asking questions and making notes that they do not have a very clear idea of how they appear to interviewees.

If videotaping is not possible, you should tape-record one of your early interviews and then ask yourself a series of questions:

Did I take enough time to make the interviewee feel relaxed?

Did I avoid wasting too much time on preliminary conversation before moving into my first question?

Did I tell the interviewee clearly the purpose of the interview?

Were my questions clearly phrased?

Did they flow in a logical sequence?

Did I ask follow-up questions when the interviewee said something provocative or significant?

If I had a potentially difficult or embarrassing question to ask, did I choose the right time to ask it? Did I phrase it skillfully?

If the interviewee went off on a tangent, did I bring the person back to the central points without wasting too much time?

Did I come away with as much usable material as I expected—or more?

That final question is the real test for a successful interview.

8

Organizing Your Material and Writing a First Draft

There is no single method for organizing your material and writing your first draft. But an examination of the methods followed by some experienced free-lancers will suggest some procedures you might find worth trying.

If you had a chance to observe the working habits of a dozen successful magazine writers, you would notice the wide variations in the methods they follow in organizing their research material and in writing a first draft.

You might see two or three who were extraordinarily efficient. These writers return from their research trips with their notes carefully arranged, the leads to their articles already chosen, and the general shape of the pieces clear in their minds. They settle down to a typewriter without hesitation, with all the material they are likely to need arranged in neat stacks. They begin typing immediately, pause occasionally to check a fact or to locate a missing detail, stop now and then to revise a page, and will sometimes emerge after a long, unbroken session with a publishable full-length article. After the editors have read and approved it, the copy editor often finds that he or she has nothing more to do than to put in the paragraph marks and double-check the capitalization and punctuation to make sure it conforms to the magazine's style.

At the opposite end of the spectrum are the writers who sometimes sit immobile for hours—or even days—after completing the research on a complex article. Surrounded by stacks of notebooks, untranscribed tapes, unread documents and pamphlets and articles from professional journals, they often seem paralyzed, unable to make a start.

If you are one of the writers who is capable of organizing an article in your mind and writing it in near-finished form without hesitation, obviously you need no advice or help regarding this stage of magazine writing. But if you are a member of the far larger group—those who sometimes feel overwhelmed by the mass of material they have collected—it may be helpful to examine some of the steps various professionals take to turn an accumulation of research notes into a first draft.

SEPARATING THE MOST USEFUL MATERIAL FROM THE REST

Although some editors insist that "You can't do too much research," you may sometimes begin to question that statement. On a long, complex article you may find that you have gathered great stacks of documents, pamphlets, speech texts, articles, books, and notes about your subject, and the mere quantity of this material can become a problem. Surrounded by this clutter, you may find it difficult to make a start.

I suggest that you take some time to examine this accumulation. As you look at each item, you should have these questions in mind:

Is this something central to my article that I will want to have handy as I work on my first draft?

Is this something I won't need immediately, but will want to read closely before I do my revisions?

Is this something I am unlikely to need at all for this article?

You may be surprised to discover that a great deal of the material you have gathered can be set aside at this stage. I wouldn't discard anything yet, but I would remove as much as possible from my desk so I could concentrate on the essential notes and documents.

You will discover that people you interview often hand you copies of their speeches or their dissertations or their articles for professional journals even though these are entirely irrelevant to your article. I think you should always accept such material, and before you complete work on your piece you will want to examine it just on the chance that it might offer a usable detail or two. But at the moment you are concentrating on reducing the bulk of the material early, and I would separate the essential research from anything that seems of only marginal value or interest.

You will have a general idea of what you have collected but for the first time you can begin to see how it will all fit together. You may also discover at this point that you will need a few details that you overlooked. If these are minor, it may be best to go ahead on your first draft without them, knowing that you can leave a few blanks to be filled in later. Obviously if one or two of the missing facts are of major importance, you should try to track them down before you go any further.

Recognizing that an article is more than a collection of facts, I would also at this stage ask myself whether I had gathered the *variety* of material I needed for an effective piece: anecdotes, direct quotes, descriptions of places and people, dramatic illustrations.

MAKING YOUR MATERIAL MANAGEABLE

Most writers' notebooks I have seen contain a jumble of material in no particular order. You may actually save time by pausing early to work out some simple method of locating and retrieving the various items in your notebooks.

There are four possible methods of doing this:

1. You can simply go through the pages and use numbers or lines or symbols to call your attention to the most useful material. You might write the number "1" beside an anecdote you are planning to use as your lead, and "2" next to your notes for a capsule statement. Your sequence of numbers would give at least a rough indication of the order in which you are planning to use your material.

2. If you are not certain about the order, but wish to locate the most valuable notes quickly, you might use either lines or symbols to mark the various types of material. A single line down the side of one page could mark the strongest quotes, for example; double lines could be used to call your attention to very good anecdotes; triple lines could indicate something else—essential facts, statistics, or other details. Or you could underline the best quotes and use a series of symbols to call your attention to the other important material you have gathered. Some writers decorate their pages with a series of symbols: X ! + *

3. The third method—which I would recommend—is to use a copying machine to make duplicates of each page of your notes that you consider useful. Once you have this second copy, you can shuffle your notes back and forth until you decide the most effective order for the use of your material. This single step makes your notes more accessible and more easily manageable.

4. The fourth method is to go through all your notes, typing up each element on a separate card or sheet of paper. Very systematic writers sometimes do this, and I understand the advantages of this approach. I myself would find this a rather deadening step, and I would be afraid that it would use up some of the energy I need when I settle down to work on a first draft.

ARRANGING YOUR MATERIAL IN ROUGH ORDER

Sooner or later you will probably want to place your research material in a series of stacks.

In the first stack I suggest that you place anything that is likely to supply the lead to your article. If you are still trying to decide whether to use a specific anecdote or a particularly startling statistic, I would place both in this stack for the moment. If there are three or four potential leads, you could put them all here until you make your decision.

In the second stack you could put the notes you will need when you write your capsule statement.

In the third you could put the notes covering the next element you plan to use just after your capsule statement. If you lead off with an anecdote, you might wish to use a strong direct quote here, or a revealing statistic, or an expository paragraph.

You should continue with a fourth stack, a fifth, a sixth . . . as far as you can go in arranging your material in the order of likely use. You can always change the order later, but this stage has the specific value of helping you see a possible sequence for your presentation.

You will probably be uncertain about just where you will fit in some of your material. I suggest that you *group* this remaining collection. In one stack you could place the anecdotes you have not yet found a spot for, in another all the remaining useful quotes, in another the statistics and general background information. This will make it easier for you to locate what you are looking for when you are writing your first draft and your subsequent drafts.

Some writers feel that this rough arrangement of material in stacks is the last step necessary before they start work on a first draft. Others add one more preliminary step:

WRITING AN INFORMAL OUTLINE

Most professional magazine writers who use outlines do not write the kind of outline you may have been taught to prepare for some of your high school English classes. Whenever I think of these outlines, I always remember the stately progression of Roman numerals, capital letters, Arabic numerals, and small letters:

I. Early history of the state
  A. Arrival of the Spanish explorers
    1. Discovery of the Pacific
    2. Relationship with the Indians
      a. First meetings
      b. Early conflicts
  B. Beginning of agriculture
    1. Cultivation of maize
    2. First grape harvest

Rather than following this form, many free-lancers jot down a series of casual, informal notes. For example, if a writer had gathered material for an article focusing on the perils of the first year of marriage, the outline might be as simple and informal as this:

1. Lead anecdote: Brad & Linda
2. Capsule statement: First 12 months reveal problems most likely to lead to divorce
3. Anecdotes illustrating most common problems: Sex—Harry & Louise, Money—Tom & Anne, Lack of communication—Brad & Linda, Different values—Charles & Marie
4. UCLA survey about major problems
5. Advice from experts—Dr. Winslow, UCLA, Dr. Everstone, marriage counselor
6. How to get help (and where)
7. Closing anecdote (How Brad & Linda solved their problems)

These notes wouldn't mean much to anyone except the writer, but for some free-lancers these would serve a useful purpose. The notes concentrate the writer's attention on the need for a logical structure and make it less likely that he or she will include extraneous material or leave out anything that is essential for the development of the article.

In this case, the writer might be reminded of one possible problem when looking over the outline. Is most of the anecdotal material being used too early? There is the lead anecdote quickly followed by four others illustrating the most common problems facing couples during the first 12 months of marriage. Would it be better to introduce the UCLA survey just after the capsule statement, and then scatter the illustrative anecdotes more evenly through the piece? The writer might decide that would be a good change, or might decide that it would weaken the effect. The outline at least indicates a possible problem, and this suggests that it would be a good idea to experiment with the two different presentations.

THE MOST DIFFICULT STEP

Everything up to now has been preparation. It is tempting to some writers to dawdle over these early stages for days, postponing as long as possible the instant when they must settle down to writing.

Ideally, with the material now arranged in stacks and perhaps also outlined on paper, the writer should be ready to tap out a strong lead, follow with a brief, clear capsule statement, and then go on with quotes and anecdotes and statistics and expository sections until reaching an effective closing segment.

Actually, many writers—including a few experienced professionals—often bog down when it comes to writing the lead. A writer will begin with a very revealing anecdote, and then decide that it requires too much space. He or she will try a direct quote and then realize that it does not focus on a major aspect of the article. The writer will test a third possibility, then a fourth, then a fifth—discarding one because it is too confusing, another because it is too vague, another because it is undramatic.

Because they recognize how much time can be wasted in an unproductive search for the ideal lead, some writers have developed a way of getting past this barrier.

They begin by writing a later section of the article—perhaps the segment that will come immediately after the lead. "Begin with the third paragraph or the fourth paragraph," a *Look* editor used to advise writers who were stymied in their work on a piece. "You can always come back to the lead later."

When they do that, these writers often find that what they thought might be the third or fourth paragraph of their articles turns out to be a very effective lead. Their problem had been *excessive* anxiety about the opening section. Once the inhibition produced by that anxiety had been overcome, the most significant and intriguing point had emerged almost unconsciously.

Successful free-lancers offer two other suggestions you may wish to consider if you find that it is difficult for you to get started on a first draft:

Convince yourself that this is just a test run—that every sentence and every paragraph you are now typing can be discarded if it is unsatisfactory. If the lead is weak, it can be dropped from the second draft. If the capsule statement is too vague, it can be completely reworded. If an anecdote takes up too much space, it can be cut to half its present length.

All this is true, of course, but some writers must remind themselves of these facts. Even a bad beginning is better than no beginning at all, but some writers find it difficult to accept that. They become unnecessarily defensive about rough drafts.

"Anyone who looked at one of my first drafts would wonder how I've managed to support myself as a writer for more than thirty years," said a free-lancer who has published about 200 magazine articles and 15 books—including some best sellers. "I throw in everything, type as fast as I can, and never look back until I've finished a draft. Words are misspelled, the grammar is often shaky, and if I can't find a particular fact I need after a quick search of my notes I either leave a blank space or put in something I know I'll have to correct later. The one thing I've learned not to do is slow down. I race along until I reach the last paragraph."

That writer never lets anyone see his first drafts. They're not written for other people—they're written for himself. They bring his material together in the roughest possible form, but they give him a clear idea of what he has and what he still needs. He then sets about refining this into a publishable manuscript.

Some writers cannot work that way. They are too conscious of the flaws in their writing to ignore them even temporarily. They cannot go on to paragraph two until they have perfected paragraph one.

For those who find (after experimenting) that they cannot rush through a first draft, a different kind of first step may be possible:

Begin by writing and polishing the separate elements in an article, without regard to where they will be used in the completed piece. For example, choose a particularly good anecdote you know you will want to include somewhere in the article. Write it, edit it, revise it, and then set it aside (or save it on your computer disk). Choose another and another and follow the same procedure. Then select the best quotes from your notes, type them out exactly as you plan to use them, so they can be placed at the proper point later when you are assembling your first draft. Do the same with expository paragraphs, case histories, statistical material, and each of the other elements you think you will find useful.

Once you have written each of these separate parts, arrange them in order and *then* begin putting together a draft that will be much closer to final form than those produced by writers who prefer to do quick, rough drafts.

In the next three chapters you will find specific advice about improving your lead ("The First Hundred Words"), varying the techniques you use in presenting material ("How to Hold a Reader's Interest"), and focusing on writing skill ("Developing Your Own Style").

You might find it helpful to read those chapters before you begin working on your second, third, and fourth drafts of your first major article. But for the moment the essential step is to *begin*—to organize your material in the order that now seems most logical and effective to you, and to start writing.

You should be quite critical of your work before you submit it, but don't be too critical too early. That can paralyze you.

9

The First Hundred Words

Many readers decide whether or not to continue reading your article after glancing at the opening paragraphs. Here you will find examples of 13 types of leads developed by some experienced magazine writers.

"If the first hundred words of a magazine article aren't right, the ones that follow won't matter. No one will bother to read them."

That was the advice offered by one experienced magazine editor when he gave an assignment to a beginning free-lancer.

To illustrate the extraordinary importance of the first words a reader sees on a magazine page, the editor would sometimes reach over and pick up two issues of his magazine. He would flip through them and indicate a specific article in each issue.

"Read the first hundred words or so of each of those pieces," he would suggest. "Then tell me which of the articles has caught your interest so strongly that you find it difficult to stop reading it."

When the writer told him which of the pieces he was most eager to keep reading, the editor would nod. A readership survey indicated that that article had been read by almost 90 percent of the magazine's enormous circulation, while fewer than 30 readers out of a hundred had read all of the second article.

Readers are impatient. Editors know this, and that is why some of them feel justified in reaching an affirmative or negative decision about an article after reading the first hundred words or so of a manuscript.

This may seem unfair, but free-lancers who ignore this fact handicap themselves severely. It is impossible to exaggerate the importance of the lead to a magazine article.

Some editors show a strong preference for two or three kinds of leads. Others are receptive to any type of lead that will attract and hold the attention of the readers.

As a beginning free-lancer, you may wish to examine a variety of techniques professional writers have used over the years to lead readers into the body of their articles. Obviously, you should not merely copy what others have done in the past. Magazine writing is not that mechanical or limited. But you should recognize why these opening paragraphs have been used, and then develop leads that will pass the same tests.

THE ANECDOTE LEAD

Many experienced free-lancers begin most of their articles with an anecdote—a brief story that makes a point.

"The 'Problem' Child" in *Family Health* magazine begins quietly:

> At age 12, the boy was removed from school by his doctor because of a "nervous breakdown." As a young child he had spoken late. He was never a good student, and his teachers regarded him as a problem. He had no friends. Both his parents were sadly resigned to his being "different." How else could they explain his odd mannerisms, the religion he had made up and the hymns he constantly chanted to himself?
>
> Everyone who knew the child was convinced he was headed for a life of failure and suffering. But he surprised them all: His was a life of triumph and achievement. His name?
>
> Albert Einstein.

After gaining the reader's attention with this brief story, the authors quickly indicate that the evolution from a maladjusted early childhood to a very productive adulthood is not at all uncommon, and they offer suggestions on "six ways to bring out the best in any youngster."

* * *

In *Discover,* Jared Diamond used another opening anecdote with a surprise ending for an article about some unusual artists:

> Siri's drawings brought her acclaim as soon as other artists saw them.
>
> "They had a kind of flair and decisiveness and originality"—that was the first reaction of artist Elaine de Kooning; her husband, famed painter Willem de Kooning, agreed.
>
> Jerome Witkin, an authority on abstract expressionism who teaches art at Syracuse University, was even more effusive: "These drawings are very lyrical, very, very, beautiful. The energy is so compact and controlled, it's just incredible. . . . This drawing indicates a grasp of the essential mark that makes the emotion."
>
> Having seen the drawings but knowing nothing about who made them, Witkin guessed correctly that the artist was female and interested in Asian calligraphy. But

he didn't guess that Siri was over eight feet tall and weighed four tons. She was an Asian elephant who drew by holding a pencil in her trunk. . . .

When told of Siri's identity, Willem de Kooning responded, "That's a damned talented elephant."

Diamond adds some surprising details:

Actually, Siri was not extraordinary by elephant standards. Wild elephants often use their trunks to make drawing motions in the dust, and captive elephants often spontaneously scratch marks on the ground with a stick or stone.

He then goes on to raise a question about whether human beings are the only animals who are capable of creating art. We are not surprised that birds sing and wild animals do courtship dances, he observes, and should not reject out of hand the idea of elephants demonstrating an ability to draw what they see—or imagine.

THE NARRATIVE LEAD

Many magazine leads now make use of a technique that was borrowed from writers of fiction: the narrative (or story). You could easily believe that the following example was the opening of a short story:

The hardest part was dyeing his sun-streaked hair Clairol midnight black. He splattered globs of hair color all over the bathroom, and as he squeezed a thin white strip of glue onto the fake moustache, he noticed with irritation that the purplish-black dye had stained his fingernails. When he pressed the moustache to his upper lip, he inhaled a whiff of glue. It made him feel high, confident; it put him in the mood. He looked into the medicine-cabinet mirror and was struck by the face staring back. Gone were the tanned, blond good looks that had prompted a sports-writer to dub him the "golden boy golfer." The dark moustache and hair dye transformed Rick Meissner into somebody else: a bank robber.

Actually, that is the opening paragraph of "Out of the Rough and Into the Slammer," an *Esquire* article by Kathleen Maxa. In the second paragraph, Maxa offers a straightforward factual statement:

In June, 1977, Rick Meissner became the first card-carrying member of the Professional Golfers Association (PGA) to turn bank robber, a part-time career that brought him a measure of fame he never achieved on the tour.

Obviously, she could have given the reader those facts first, but she apparently felt that the scene-setting paragraph was a more effective opening. Much of the rest of her article is also offered in a dramatic narrative, focusing tightly on the central figure.

THE SERIES-OF-EXAMPLES LEAD

"Milking Medicare" in *Common Cause* opens with brief reports on three surprising episodes:

When Betty Morris got a call from someone saying she was updating her Medicare records—and asking if she was suffering from arthritis, bursitis or any heart problems—she allowed that she did have a little arthritis in one finger.

Soon, a big box loaded with expensive medical equipment showed up at her door. When Morris called the company that had sent her the equipment, she was told not to worry about paying for it—Medicare would. . . .

John McCarthy told a similar caller that he had Parkinson's disease. Soon he received two orders of costly medical equipment designed for people stricken with severe arthritis and confined to their beds. McCarthy plays golf and jogs.

Jean Ellison says she never spoke to anyone before a wheelchair showed up at her door. Ellison, who mows her own lawn and bowls regularly, says the wheelchair came with a letter saying it was issued by Medicare.

After offering these three examples, Vicki Kemper and Peter Montgomery assert that "fraud, abuse and overpayments . . . consume up to 10 percent of Medicare's overall costs." They could have opened the article with that general statement, but these startling examples leave a stronger impression than a summarizing assertion about abuses.

THE FIRST-PERSON LEAD

Now used in many magazines, the first-person lead often focuses on a common problem many readers of a magazine will recognize immediately. In "Are You a Black-Cloud Lady?" Catherine Black begins with this self-analysis:

Somewhere along the way, I became a genius at fearing the worst.

When lying on a hot, sparkling beach in Tahiti, I will close my eyes and picture thieves forcing open the window of my New York apartment, or my boss in a blind rage, preparing a resignation letter I will be forced to sign on my return.

A worst-case scenario is never far from my mind: Headaches are potential brain tumors, coughs are lung cancer, foggy-headedness is the first sign of Alzheimer's. I've rushed home in the middle of the day, convinced that I left the oven on or the door unlocked. (I'm always wrong.) And when I fly, which is often, I board the plane filled with a dire premonition that I'm about to plunge to my death.

She then observes:

At their most harmless, these abstract fears can make us tense and uncomfortable. But they aren't always harmless. Ironically enough, fearing the worst can sometimes make it happen.

She then offers advice from several experts on ways to control these fears.

* * *

In the *Philadelphia Inquirer Magazine,* Dick Pothier began his article, "My Heart Was Killing Me," with this vivid first-person account:

I would not call an ambulance. Despite my gasping as I struggled to button my shirt, despite the terror that my disabled heart might finally be spent, I couldn't believe I was dying. A noisy ambulance would be too embarrassing. No, I would be cool and take a cab.

But as I stepped out into the street that chilly Thursday, January 19, 1989, I knew I was in trouble. I needed to walk two blocks, but I couldn't go more than 30 feet without stopping. My lungs were filling with fluid, slowly drowning me. Panting, I leaned against a car. A few more steps. A telephone pole. A mailbox. Still, I couldn't bring myself to cry out: "Please! Somebody help me!"

After those two opening paragraphs, Pothier retraces the story of his heart attack, and then tells of his long wait for a heart transplant.

THE STRAIGHTFORWARD STATEMENT LEAD

Many magazine articles begin with a simple, direct statement of the main point. In "Ten Truths You're Never Told About the Job Interview," Lisa Collier Cool chooses this approach:

The job you've always wanted could be just one interview away. Before that crucial meeting with a prospective boss, wouldn't you love the opportunity to look inside her mind and discover exactly what she's *really* looking for? We asked several powerful decision makers to reveal their secret interview strategies and to share the surprising reasons they hire the candidates they do. Here's the inside information on how you can edge out the competition, score a magnificent impression, and *win* a job offer.

After that straightforward lead, which includes the capsule statement, Cool offers some surprising suggestions to readers of *Cosmopolitan* who are about to face the tension of a job interview. Among her revelations:

Most interviewers decide whether or not to hire you during the first five minutes.
Interviewers may test you if they suspect you're lying on your resume.
The stranger the question, the more important it is.
Several interviewers admit that they try to tempt applicants to make the wrong move.

This article depends heavily on direct quotes from a wide range of sources to back up these and other points. Cool recognized the need to use clearly identified sources—people who often make decisions on whether or not to hire someone—for the ten suggestions rather than simply stating her own conclusions based on extensive research.

THE SURPRISING STATEMENT LEAD

Dr. Lewis Thomas, president of New York's Memorial Sloan-Kettering Cancer Center, is a distinguished physician and biologist. Therefore he is able to make a statement that might be dismissed as nonsense if offered by a free-lance writer with no professional experience as a biologist:

> Warts . . . can appear overnight on any part of the skin, like mushrooms on a damp lawn, full grown and splendid in the complexity of their architecture. The strangest thing about warts, which have such a look of toughness and permanence, is that they can be made to go away by something that can only be called thinking. That is one of the great mystifications of science: warts can be ordered off the skin by hypnotic suggestion.

In his article, "Warts, Brains, and Other Astonishments," Dr. Thomas recognizes that some readers—perhaps many of them—will doubt this opening assertion:

> Not everyone believes this, but generations of internists and dermatologists have been convinced of the phenomenon. And there have now been several meticulous studies by good clinical investigators, with proper controls. In one of these, 14 patients with seemingly intractable warts . . . were hypnotized, and the suggestion was made that all the warts on one side of the body would go away. Within several weeks the results were indisputably positive; in nine patients, all or nearly all of the warts on the suggested side had vanished, while the control side had as many warts as ever.

If you plan to write a surprising statement lead, you should anticipate a skeptical response from editors and readers, and you should be ready to establish the accuracy of your statement almost immediately.

THE SURPRISING QUOTE LEAD

Once widely used, the surprising quote appears less frequently now. Two examples follow:

> Baseball is the favorite American sport because it's so slow. Any idiot can follow it. And just about any idiot can play it.

> Left-handedness is a stigma of degeneracy.

The comment about baseball was first quoted by Gore Vidal, and Art Hill uses it to introduce an enthusiastic article about the sport in *Esquire*. After attracting the reader with the surprising quote, Hill spends the rest of the article refuting it.

The statement about left-handedness was made, quite seriously, by a famous nineteenth-century criminologist, Cesare Lombroso. In *Is It Sinister to Be Left Handed?* Jack Fincher asserts that there is still a lingering trace of the absurd idea that left-handers "are somehow both wicked and inferior."

THE QUESTION LEAD

Dr. Daniel N. Stern begins "Diary of a Baby" with three questions:

> What goes on in a baby's mind when he's gazing at your face? How does a baby feel when he's hungry? How does a mother's mood affect him?

After arousing the reader's interest with those questions, Dr. Stern quickly establishes his qualifications for answering them:

I have been pondering such questions for more than 20 years—as a father, psychiatrist and researcher.

In the past, he says, both parents and scientists could only guess what babies were thinking. "But now," he writes, "because of advances in scientific observation, we know more about the early years than ever."

Some magazine editors have a strong prejudice against the question lead. But this *Reader's Digest* feature demonstrates the usefulness of such a lead for some articles.

THE YOU LEAD

Jenni Gaspard introduces "Binge Shopping: Are You a Victim?" by addressing the readers of *Beauty* directly—as *you*:

The price tag doesn't matter. It says, "Buy me" like all the others. The saleswoman, a siren, shows you an orange shirt. You hate orange—you'll take it. You move on to the next department, where Ralph and Calvin beckon to you like long-lost friends. Like a shark that has to keep moving or die, you can't stop shopping. Except this is not shopping—that implies selectivity. Your problem is you can't stop *buying*.

Ordinarily this kind of lead is effective only when many of the readers of a magazine see themselves as fitting into the situation the author describes.

THE QUOTE LEAD

In *M inc,* Peter Becker introduces the central character in "The Man Who Broke the Banks" with this lively direct quote from someone who knew him well:

"Everybody on the hill knew Joe. Nicest guy you could ever want to meet. Got some money, you take it to Joe. Joe'll take care of it. He's a banker. Then one day, *da boom!* No Joe. Joe's gone with $13 million. Vanished into thin air. Suddenly everybody wants to know: Where's Joe Mollicone?"

After offering that description of Mollicone, the author then gives a quick summary of the facts about the missing banker:

Joe was last seen on November 8, when his son, Joe III drove him to Boston and dropped him off at the Logan Airport Hilton. Four days later, when people heard that Joe had embezzled $13 million from Heritage, customers flooded the bank to make withdrawals. The run on Heritage bankrupted the Rhode Island Share and Deposit Indemnity Corporation . . . and spun the entire state into an economic crisis. . . . Suddenly 35 percent of the state's population couldn't get its money.

A direct quote should be used as a lead only when it arouses the reader's interest immediately. It also must focus attention on a central point in the article, as it does here.

THE SINGLE EXAMPLE LEAD

Chris, a political-science student at California State University–Northridge, in Los Angeles, used all the time-honored tricks to pass his courses without cracking a book: He peeked at fellow students' computer-scanned test-answer sheets, wrote notes on his hands, legs and shoes, paid a friend to take an exam for him and surreptitiously changed more than one grade from a D to a B in a teacher's record book. In fact, in the five years it took Chris, 24, to graduate he recalls only one or two courses he passed *without* cheating.

"It's not that I cheated more than other people," says Chris, who is self-employed and who requested that his last name not be published. "I was just more creative."

After that lead in *People,* the authors (Eileen Garred, Doris Bacon, Nancy Matsumoto, and Sarah Skolnik) observe,

Chris may be exaggerating his own inventiveness, but he is, sadly, not far off the mark in his estimation of his fellow students. . . . A study released this week by Rutgers University concludes that an alarming 67 percent of today's college students cheat at some point in their undergraduate years.

THE OPINION LEAD

The No. 1 problem today is not ignorant students, but ignorant professors. . . .

That is the opinion of Professor Camille Paglia, who teaches at Philadelphia College of the Performing Arts.

She goes on to say in her second paragraph:

American professors have been institutionally impelled, by graduate education and then by the universities that employ them, to become narrower and narrower.

Professor Paglia's article appeared in *Image,* the Sunday magazine distributed with the San Francisco *Examiner.* The coverline prepared readers for her bold statements: "Rough Trade: Camille Paglia Slaps Academia Around."

Relatively few magazines are receptive to strongly stated opinion leads. Editors who feature them must be convinced that the author's opinions will be of real interest to most of their readers.

THE DESCRIPTIVE LEAD

For an article about jellyfish in *Smithsonian,* Jack and Anne Rudloe first paint the scene:

As we approached the pass between the barrier islands of Apalachicola, Florida, we began seeing the cannonballs, a white one here and a purple freckled one there, each pulsating, all moving in the same direction. Soon the soccer-ball-size jellyfish were so thick they turned the ocean into a vast polka-dotted sea. There were millions of them, moving crosswise to the currents, pulsing along in formation, filling the water from surface to bottom.

After attracting your attention with that vivid description, the Rudloes set out to persuade you that a jellyfish is not a "stinging blob of slime" but a biological marvel—and a "creature of fragile beauty."

CHOOSING YOUR LEAD

Although thousands of magazine leads would fit into the 13 categories illustrated here, thousands of others would not. And even though many magazine editors have shown a marked preference over the years for some of these traditional forms, others encourage their writers to experiment.

In any case, your lead should emerge naturally from the research on your article. An effective lead can be written only if you have shown imagination in selecting a subject, have focused sharply on one aspect of that topic, have been thorough in gathering background information, and have conducted enough well-planned interviews.

Once you have done that, you should examine your notes thoughtfully, without any rigid advance determination to write an anecdote lead or a narrative lead or a surprising statement lead. Your lead should grow out of your material, and if you do *not* see at least two or three very strong possibilities as you reread your notes, that could be a warning that you are not yet ready to write your article.

Once you are certain that you do have all the material you need, you may want to submit a potential lead to these six tests:

1. Is this lead certain to arouse the interest of readers of the magazine I have in mind?
2. Is it brief?
3. Is it clear?
4. Does it focus on an important point?
5. Does it set the right tone for the article?
6. Even if it is acceptable, is it the *best possible* lead? Do I have other material or could I obtain other material that would give me a still stronger lead?

Any lead that passes all those tests (in your own opinion and in the opinion of your fellow students and your journalism professor) should also satisfy a demanding magazine editor.

You have now solved the first major problem in writing your article. In the following chapter, "How to Hold a Reader's Interest," you will find some suggestions about how to retain a reader's attention through the remaining 900 or 2,400 or 3,400 words of your article.

10

How to Hold a Reader's Interest

Even though the lead attracts a reader, he or she will sometimes give up on an article after reading a few hundred words. What causes that loss of interest? And how can you—as a writer—hold the reader's attention?

Every magazine editor is confronted periodically by manuscripts that get off to a very promising start but then grow less and less interesting, page by page.

During my days as an editor, I often tried to analyze such articles. Often the writer had accomplished a great deal. He or she had

Chosen an intriguing subject
Conducted extensive research
Organized the material logically
Eliminated obvious faults or errors

But even so there was one problem the writer had *not* solved—and it was overwhelming. The writer had not succeeded in holding my full attention after the first few paragraphs of the article. The lead was effective, but after a page or two my interest began to flag, and by the time I reached page four or five I would pause to flip through the manuscript to discover just how many more pages I would have to plow through.

The verdict any editor has to give on such a manuscript is obvious. Unless the difficulty can be spotted and overcome, the submission must be rejected. Editors know how quickly readers will stop reading and turn the page if an article begins to bore them. A magazine that publishes too many articles that trigger such a reaction among readers will soon be in deep trouble.

If a reader (including that crucial first reader—the editor) is interested enough to *begin* reading an article with considerable anticipation, what causes the attention to begin to drift?

Seven faults in magazine writing can cause a reader to grow restless. These range from the failure to give an early statement of what the article is about to the overuse of facts in the opening section. Those flaws can be overcome by close attention to the following suggestions.

LET THE READER KNOW PRECISELY WHAT THE ARTICLE IS ABOUT WITHIN THE FIRST THREE OR FOUR PARAGRAPHS

Editors sometimes toss a manuscript aside after reading the first two pages, irritated because the writer has not yet given them a clear indication of the subject. Not all articles require a brief, summarizing capsule statement, but many of those written for general magazines do, and when one is needed, it should be introduced early.

If you decide that an article you are working on would benefit from this kind of quick summary, you should consider using it just after your lead. Occasionally a writer will use it as the lead.

The capsule statement for a brief article on self-esteem published in *American Health* appears in the opening sentence:

A major study reveals that the egos of kids—especially girls—are likely to take a sharp nose dive when the youngsters enter their teen years.

The article, by Judy Folkenberg, reveals that 60 percent of the 2,350 girls studied were satisfied with themselves in elementary school, but only 29 percent remained self-confident and satisfied by the time they reached high school.

* * *

The closing words of the *first* paragraph in an article by Jennifer Warsen make clear what the piece is about:

It wasn't until my hair began falling out that I got really frightened. My normally shiny, strawberry-blond mop was brittle, dull and coming out in handfuls. My skin was dry and yellow, my fingernails were scaling away, and I hadn't menstruated in nearly six months. I was dying. I was a 19-year-old college sophomore, and from the age of 15 I had alternated between periods of *anorexic starvation, bulemic purging,* and *attempts at stopping* that invariably ended in failure.

After that closing sentence, a reader will have no doubt at all about the focus of this first-person account.

* * *

In *Marriage,* Celia Scully presents her capsule statement for "The ABC's of Returning to School Successfully" in the form of a series of questions she assumed would be going through the minds of many mature women who were considering the possibility of completing their university studies:

> Can I do it? Am I too old? Will younger students accept me? Can I get back into the routine of studying, writing themes, taking—and passing—tests? What will it do to my family? And, finally, do I have the right to spend so much money on myself?

In these few lines Scully gives the reader a clear idea of the ground she plans to cover in her article.

Clearing up the uncertainty in the reader's mind about the central point of an article is not difficult. In many cases it is done less directly than this, and you may prefer a more subtle approach. If your opening anecdote is chosen carefully, for example, no direct statement from you may be necessary. Or a striking quotation from an authority could serve the purpose.

In any case, a writer should be aware of the annoyance some readers feel when they read paragraph after paragraph without discovering exactly what the article is about.

LEARN TO BE SELECTIVE

A second problem commonly found in the manuscripts that lose a reader's attention is lack of selectivity.

Inexperienced writers often try to tell readers more than they want to know about a subject. The writer becomes completely absorbed in all the information that turns up during the weeks of research and is convinced that these details will be of equal interest to his or her readers.

Most successful magazine articles have a limited purpose and are rather tightly focused. The writer is not trying to tell readers all about the subject. The writer recognizes that the reader has a *casual* interest in this (and many other) topics and should not be overwhelmed with details.

Experienced free-lancers routinely set aside *most* of the material they have collected. Although it seemed worth noting when they were doing their research, this discarded material no longer seems essential.

RECOGNIZE THE VALUE OF ANECDOTES

Undramatic presentation is characteristic of many unsuccessful articles.

Even though the writers of such pieces might recognize the value of an opening anecdote, they do not make effective use of such stories in the body of their articles.

Even in personality pieces, these writers often depend on flat declarations rather than illustrative anecdotes. Their manuscripts might include such observations as these:

He is sometimes short-tempered with his employees.
She has a reputation for extravagance.
He is often late for appointments.

Each of these general statements leaves a rather vague impression. In each case a skillfully written anecdote would have made two contributions to the article:

The basic point would have been made much more vividly.
The use of an anecdote would have varied the presentation of the article.

For an article entitled "Murder: The Amateur's Crime," I used several anecdotes to support the capsule statement: "Seven out of ten murders are committed by plain, ordinary citizens who wouldn't think of parking next to a fire hydrant or stealing a pair of socks off a counter."

I gave two examples of conscientious murderers:

Most murderers are sincerely shocked when they first realize that they have killed someone. A Boston woman shot her husband, then offered her blood for a transfusion.
    The law-abiding instinct is so strong in many of them that it is impossible for them to avoid capture. A man in Arizona had almost eluded the police after killing an in-law, but stopped for a red-light as he neared the state line. He was astonished later when asked why he had not rushed across to safety in the adjoining state, beyond the jurisdiction of the cops who were following him.
    "Why," he replied, "it's against the law to go through a red light."

Another brief anecdote in the same article offered an unusual motive for mayhem:

A bank executive killed a bartender who asked him, "What will you have, Shorty?" He was just over five feet tall and had always resented being called Shorty.

Of course, these would not have been used in a serious, analytical article on the same topic.

RECOGNIZE THE VALUE OF DIRECT QUOTES

Weak articles often make little or no use of direct quotes. The writers sometimes routinely summarize or paraphrase all of the comments made by those they interview.

This is usually a mistake. Quotes must be used selectively, and there is no point in including those that are dull, rambling, or confusing. But in general, writers should realize that they are losing a valuable element in an article if they fail to make some use of direct quotes.

In "Walking Tall With Michael J. Fox," in *Cosmopolitan*, Chris Chase allows Fox himself to tell much of the story:

"When I was twenty-one I could drink a hundred beers, go to bed at four, and feel great a few hours later. Last night, I had a couple of glasses of wine with dinner, went to bed at eleven-thirty, and thought I was gonna die in the morning."

Fox comments about his additional caution now that he is a husband and a father:

"I used to eat red meat. I used to eat *live* meat. But . . . We had a lot of heart disease in my family. My father passed away from heart disease, so if I get rid of the red meat and the smoking, then maybe I can get away with something like not exercising. I'm gonna hedge my bets, although there's always that one person that lives to be a hundred and eight, and goes, 'I drank a pint of whiskey every day and ate chicken fat off the floor.'"

About acting as a career:

"What I do is so silly anyway. It's not like I have a real job or anything."

About life with his two-year-old son Sam:

". . . you don't play with kids so much as you try to prevent them from killing themselves. They want to stick their tongues in the fan, they want to lick the electrical socket, they want to put the corkscrew in their ear."

These direct quotes seem to me far more revealing than any summary by the author would be.

An earlier magazine profile of a brilliant actor, Richard Burton, included two somber and memorable quotes.

About the high and low points of his career:

"Most actors of . . . ability, ah, go through cycles . . . which, ah, one time you're at the top, you can do nothing wrong. I've been at the top, where . . . for five or six years I was at the Old Vic, and all the films I did were big smashes . . . between the ages of 26 and 32. . . . And then I took a dive. . . . *Cleopatra* was part of the down period. . . . If you examine the careers of other actors, you'll find that they all take dives. . . ."

About the dark period in his professional and personal life:

"For six years, I sort of went out of business. It was as though a ghost figure was pretending to be me. . . ."

These are from a well-remembered *New York Times Magazine* personality piece by Barbara Gelb.

Gelb weaves in more than a dozen quotes, some thoughtful, some amusing. They are important elements in her profile, and they also contribute a useful variation to her presentation.

LEARN TO BE SPECIFIC

Writers sometimes weaken their work by using too many generalized statements. They may feel that on the basis of extensive research they are qualified to make such statements as these:

Many restaurants include hidden charges in their bills.

Mail service in England is far superior to the service available in the United States.

At least one-third of all the major operations being performed each year in the United States are unnecessary.

Those statements may be true or they may be false, but in any case a writer is unjustified in offering them to magazine readers unless it is possible to support them with convincing evidence and specific examples.

In documenting the first statement—about restaurants—James Villas began by calling on the reader's own recollection of a common experience:

> It happens every time you sit down in a fancy restaurant—as well as in a few not so fancy ones. As you study the menu and wine list, a little calculator in your brain starts clicking away automatically. What's this going to cost? In the past, despite your calculations, you've always been surprised when the final bill arrives, but this time you're determined to analyze every single charge that could conceivably be made. Appetizers, main courses, maybe a small salad and side vegetable for two, wine, tax, tip. You come up with a figure that can't possibly be off by more than a dollar or two. But when the bill is presented, you suddenly realize your nice, well-planned, $60 dinner for two has somehow soared to $75. You think about haggling with the captain, but instead you simply sit there, shell out, and admit once again to being taken.

In his capsule statement, Villas states that restaurant managers are among "the shrewdest breeds in creation when it comes to reaping an extra buck" and offers to reveal the tricks they use that lead to those bloated restaurant checks. "I've learned quite a bit that might help save you lots of money," he says.

In the body of the article, Villas avoids the possible monotony of a series of generalized statements about hidden charges or overcharges. He includes such specifics as this:

> At the Four Seasons in New York, many customers do not realize that a charge of $2.75 per person is added for "bread and butter."

> When a waiter at the Jockey Club in Washington asks casually, "And would you care for a nice Caesar salad?" you shouldn't say yes unless you're ready to increase your luncheon tab by $4.50.

> At many restaurants, when the captain or the waiter "simply recites the specials in glowing terms, never mentioning a price," you should recognize the reason for the oversight: "The charge can be astronomically more than for any dish on the menu."

Villas had obviously carried out extensive research over a long period of time, and his generalized warnings would have been useful to many readers. But, unlike some beginning writers, he realized that the reader's interest would be renewed by the use of these specific illustrations.

LEARN TO PACE OUT YOUR PRESENTATION OF FACTS

In many articles, the reader must be given a considerable amount of information. Inexperienced writers often yield to the temptation to present the essential facts in a lump, early. This is another common cause of loss of reader interest.

In writing an article about the Western Australian city of Perth for *National Geographic*, Thomas J. Abercrombie realized that many of his readers knew little about the city. In addition to offering a number of scenes of life in Perth, he wanted to include such facts as these:

Population: 925,000
Fastest growing major city in Australia
Capital of Western Australia
Most isolated capital in the world
Distance from England: 12,000 miles
Founded: 1829
Climate: Average of 10 hours sunshine daily in the summer. Mild winters. Cool
     ocean breezes.
Early settlers: Not prisoners, as in Sydney. Mostly landed gentry.
Western Australia deposits: uranium, diamonds, gold, bauxite, nickel, oil, gas,
     cobalt, chrome, molybdenum, tantalum, vanadium
Leading producer and marketer of solar-energy devices
Many millionaires
First Western Australia gold rush: 1885
Iron boom: 1950s
Nearest neighboring city: Adelaide, 1,700 miles east

As this brief sampling indicates, Abercrombie had a great deal of specific, factual information that he considered of interest to the readers of *National Geographic*. But rather than cramming all—or most—of these details into his opening page, he used just four of them there:

Capital of Western Australia
Population: 925,000
Nearest neighboring city: Adelaide, 1,700 miles east
Distance from England: 12,000 miles

The other details were scattered through his 13 pages of text. As a result, there was no feeling of clutter—of a number of facts that had to be absorbed too quickly.

Sometimes a writer has to supply fairly complex background information to make it possible for a reader to understand the article. That was the problem Lowell Ponte faced in his *Reader's Digest* piece, "How Artificial Light Affects Your Health." Here it becomes particularly important to avoid overwhelming the reader with unfamiliar material. Readers who begin to feel that it is going to be difficult to follow the writer's presentation are likely to give up and turn the page.

Recognizing that problem, Ponte first attracted the reader by focusing on a single victim of a certain kind of artificial light:

In the quiet town of Cheshire, Conn., Annette Mara was pleased to learn that her children's elementary school had installed new energy-saving lighting. But when fall classes began in 1978, her nine-year-old son Timmy returned home each day close to tears. "My eyes hurt, Mommy," he told her repeatedly.

Ponte then underlines the seriousness of the problem by reporting that 16 of the teachers in Timmy Mara's school also said they were suffering from "unusual headaches and eyestrain."

The first general details about the lighting are given in the third paragraph. Ponte describes the "new high-pressure, sodium-vapor lights" and observes that they "distorted colors in the classroom, causing students to confuse red books for orange."

After that easy-to-read introductory segment, Ponte then began to bring in further details, step by step:

Paragraph Five: Description of Edison's incandescent light.

Paragraph Seven: Description of the common fluorescent light developed during the 1930s.

Paragraph Eight: Description of the high-pressure sodium-vapor lights responsible for the eyestrain suffered by Timmy Mara.

If Ponte had led off with this more complex material before first convincing readers that a new kind of lighting could cause problems, many would have drifted away.

IMPROVING A MANUSCRIPT

This chapter has offered a brief survey of some of the flaws that may cause readers to lose interest in your work even though you have chosen a good subject and have researched it thoroughly. When confronted by that difficulty, you might want to reread your article, asking yourself these six questions:

1. Have I made it clear early just what this article is about?
2. Have I been selective? Have I discarded unessential material?
3. Have I made effective use of anecdotes in both the lead and the body of the article?
4. Have I made adequate use of direct quotes?
5. Have I used specific details rather than general statements?
6. Have I paced out my presentation of essential facts? If I have to include material a reader might find difficult to understand, have I led up to it carefully and presented it step by step?

This checklist is not all-inclusive, of course. But when examining your article for these possible flaws, you are likely to notice any other fault that might be present. Once you begin taking a cold, critical look at your work, you will no longer be blinded by the easy self-satisfaction of the amateur.

If you decide the introduction of two or three anecdotes or the use of a few direct quotes would improve a piece, you should not simply insert them mechanically. Whenever you make a basic change in a magazine article, you should be ready to revise it carefully.

When you recognize the importance of renewing your reader's interest periodically, and when you learn a variety of ways of accomplishing this, you have taken a major step toward professional writing.

Professionals realize that once the attention begins to wander, they are in danger of losing the reader forever.

11

Developing Your Own Style

Should a writer set out to develop a unique, immediately recognizable style? What style appeals most strongly to magazine editors? Both of these questions are examined here.

Some students are confused by the word *style*. They seem to feel that it is something *added* to writing to enhance its flavor, the way salt and pepper are sprinkled over a fried egg.

This is a misconception. The style is *in* the writing, not added to it.

Style is "the particular mixture of words, constructions, rhythms, and forms of expression characteristic of a writer," the noted writer Jacques Barzun has observed.

Your own writing style began developing when you wrote your first essay, poem, short story, or article. You have undoubtedly refined it since, and you may now wish to improve it by paying close attention to your choice of words, by concentrating on simple, direct expression of your thoughts, and by experimenting with the structure of your sentences and paragraphs.

Some students believe that a writer's style should be immediately noticeable—that it should call attention to itself. Although it is true that some famous writers have immediately recognizable styles, this is not a requirement for success as a writer. Many readers prefer authors who are more subtle and less showy. In magazine writing, a clear, direct, simple presentation is acceptable, and some editors do not favor special flourishes.

They feel the reader's attention should be focused on the substance of the article, not on the writer's style.

E. B. White has written one of the most useful analyses of style in the closing chapter of *The Elements of Style,* 3rd ed., by William Strunk, Jr., and E. B. White (Macmillan). You will probably wish to read the entire chapter, but a few brief excerpts will indicate the author's emphasis on simplicity, naturalness, and clarity in writing:

> Write in a way that comes easily and naturally to you, using words and phrases that come readily to hand. But do not assume that because you have acted naturally your product is without flaw.

> Revising is part of writing. Few writers are so expert that they can produce what they are after on the first try.

> Rich, ornate prose is hard to digest, generally unwholesome, and sometimes nauseating.

> Clarity, clarity, clarity. When you become hopelessly mired in a sentence, it is best to start fresh; do not try to fight your way through against the terrible odds of syntax. Usually what is wrong is that the construction has become too involved at some point; the sentence needs to be broken apart and replaced by two or more shorter sentences.

> Style *is* the writer, and therefore what a man is, rather than what he knows, will at last determine his style.

As White observes, both your virtues and your faults will be reflected in your work. If you are lazy, you will settle for clichés of thought and expression. If you are thorough and meticulous, each paragraph will be carefully crafted. If you do not read widely, your articles may seem thin. If you are a voracious reader, this can enrich your writing.

As you concentrate on perfecting your style, you should begin reading more analytically than ever before. Observe the methods followed by other writers in gaining and holding their readers' attention.

You will also want to eliminate any faults that may get between you and your readers and muffle the sound of your voice.

By studying weaknesses found in the work of many beginning writers, you will be able to focus your attention on some problems that could be present in your own early manuscripts.

USE OF UNFAMILIAR WORDS

Jacques Barzun offers this general suggestion about the choice of words:

> Prefer the short word to the long; the concrete to the abstract; and the familiar to the unfamiliar.

Even usually skillful writers occasionally display this fault. When the novelist Vladimir Nabokov (author of *Lolita*) translated *Eugene Onegin* into English, he used these words: *curvate, dit, shippon, rememorating, sapajous, millitude, dulcitude.*

The critic Edmund Wilson observed that the talented Russian novelist had one great fault as a translator: He had chosen English words that "most readers have never seen and will never again have occasion to use."

Some will argue that there is nothing wrong with occasionally sending a reader to a dictionary. If that were the actual result you achieve when you introduce an uncommon word in a magazine article, I would agree. But I believe most readers are irritated when a writer uses many unfamiliar words, and they respond by turning to another article.

You should also consider carefully before using some words that are easily understood but might make your work sound pretentious. *Residence* is a perfectly acceptable word and in some sentences would be the right choice. In other sentences it might be better to write *house* or *home.* No rigid rule can be given about word choices, but in the examples that follow I would at least consider using the simpler, shorter word:

position	job
endeavor	try
utilize	use
verification	proof
ascertain	find out

OVERUSE OF THE SIMPLE, DECLARATIVE SENTENCE

You have probably been cautioned many times to avoid writing sentences that are too long or too complex. This is good advice. But some beginning writers go too far in the other direction. Sometimes they write paragraphs consisting of a cluster of very simple, declarative sentences:

> Davison finished high school in 1939. He then went into the army. He spent five years there. He was discharged because of a leg wound. He then returned to Iowa. He was a farmer for three years. In 1947 he started his own business. He was very successful.

Each of those sentences is direct and clear, but a succession of them is monotonous.

Sometimes when I question such a passage, the writer mentions Hemingway. I realize that he or she can point to a paragraph such as this one in "The Killers":

> Outside it was getting dark. The street-light came on outside the window. The two men at the counter read the menu. From the other end of the counter Nick Adams watched them. He had been talking to George when they came in.

Or these lines from *A Farewell to Arms:*

> There were some aviators in the compartment who did not think much of me. They avoided looking at me and were very scornful of a civilian my age. I did not feel insulted. In the old days I would have insulted them and picked a fight. They got off at Gallarate and I was glad to be alone. I had the paper but I did not read it because I

did not want to read about the war. I was going to forget the war. I had made a separate peace.

Although there may be some superficial resemblances between the Davison paragraph and the two passages by Hemingway, some basic differences exist. The Davison paragraph consists of a series of flat, factual statements. The sentences do not vary in form. A subtle variation is present in the structure of Hemingway's sentences, although a casual reader may not notice this. Also, Hemingway has deliberately stripped away every unnecessary word for a specific purpose: to present a tightly compressed description of a dramatic scene.

In any case, you should not have to cite another writer's achievement in defending your own work. You should be able to prove that you have developed your own effective style.

PASSIVE CONSTRUCTIONS

"The active voice gives writing a sense of strength, energy, vitality, and motion," Jefferson D. Bates observes in *Writing with Precision*. "The passive voice slows things down."

While you should not eliminate the passive voice from your work, you should avoid using it habitually.

At times the passive voice serves the purpose of focusing the reader's attention on the most important element in a sentence. For example,

The President was shot at 1:07 P.M. today.

That seems to me stronger than

An unknown sniper shot the President at 1:07 P.M. today.

Writers who *overuse* the passive often tell you that something happened but do not tell you what caused it to happen. For example,

An order was given that the investigation be stopped.

Or

It was decided that in the future appointments would be made by the company president.

Who gave the order? Who made the decision? The writer should let the reader know unless those details are unimportant. If the writer doesn't have that information, he or she should continue the research until these facts are discovered.

Once that is accomplished, the writer can then shift to the active voice and offer specific details:

General Wilson stopped the investigation.

Or

The company president decided that he would make all future appointments.

Your sentences will often be shorter and clearer when written in the active voice.

EMPTY PHRASES

Manuscripts are often weakened by the use of phrases that contribute nothing. You should watch for unnecessary words such as these:

As has often been said . . .
It has been pointed out that . . .
It is expected that . . .
Due to the fact that . . .
There have been statements to the effect that . . .

Writers who use such phrases are usually backing into their statements. While you may be able to justify the use of such constructions once in a great while, usually you should eliminate such empty phrases.

VAGUENESS

You should not fill your article with too many facts and figures. But when you do use one, it should be stated precisely. Do not say,

Many millions of dollars have been wasted on the new tank.

Instead say,

Each of the new tanks cost $23 million more than the contractor originally estimated. The total cost overrun will be $690 million.

Your article gains force through the use of specific details. "A man in his forties" could be 41 or 49. You should know his exact age, and if it is important you should give it precisely: 43. "About a hundred miles north" is acceptable in some cases, but "Ninety-three miles north" would be better. "A few years later" is vague. "Four years later" leaves a sharper impression.

The reader may begin to wonder about the thoroughness of your research if you use too many vague statements and approximations.

WORDINESS

After writing a first draft, you should watch for expressions such as these: *at the present time, on a few occasions, in a number of instances*. You can substitute a single word for each of these: *now, occasionally, often*.

This is the first step in eliminating wordiness. You should go through sentence by sentence, looking for any unessential word. For example,

Wilson, *who is* 40 *years old, then expressed his strong feelings about the waste of time involved* in filing *a whole series of* "worthless reports nobody is ever going to take a look at."

Each of the italicized words can be cut without loss. The 34 words in the paragraph can then be reduced to 16:

Wilson, 40, objected to filing "worthless reports nobody is ever going to take a look at."

Once you've done such trimming, you might want to reread the shortened version to make certain you have not cut too heavily. You can always reinsert any detail that strengthens your manuscript.

CLICHÉS AND TRITE STATEMENTS

"I don't see anything wrong with using clichés in magazine articles," one of my students once said. "Everybody understands what you mean if you say that something is 'as old as the hills' or that somebody is 'as brave as a lion.'"

At first this argument may seem persuasive. Clichés become clichés because they are easy to understand and are memorable. The first person who said that something was "as old as the hills" obviously made a strong impression on those who heard the comparison. That's why the words were repeated.

But by now those words have been used so often that they make little impression on most readers. And the writer who uses them contributes nothing new—he or she is merely echoing someone else's thought in someone else's words.

You've probably learned by now that you should not write that a new television star was "the apple of her father's eye," but you may be less conscious of the need to eliminate trite or obvious statements from your manuscripts.

I have run across statements such as these in the work of some beginning writers:

Christmas has become too commercialized.

Millions of Americans are moving from the northeast to the warm sunbelt states.

The early years of childhood are very important.

All of those statements are accurate, but none of them introduce a fresh thought. You should not tell readers what they already know.

You *could* include a vivid illustration of just how commercialized Christmas has become, just how many people are moving from Massachusetts to the sunbelt states, or just how much a child learns before entering kindergarten.

The generalized statement would be trite and ineffective. A specific example would make the point in a way the reader would remember.

PERFECTING YOUR STYLE

Eliminating these common faults will clear away some barriers between you and your readers. To achieve an impressive style, you will also need to concentrate on several positive objectives. You can test your manuscripts by asking a series of questions:

Is my writing clear?
Is it dramatic?
Have I chosen the exact word?
Is there some variety in sentence structure and sentence length?
Is there an easy flow from beginning to end?
Have I discovered the right form for my article?

By taking a close and critical look at your writing, you can develop a style that will appeal to most readers—including that important first reader, the editor who can determine whether or not your work is published.

12

Discovering the Right Structure for Your Article

Finding the most effective form for your article may require experimentation. A close study of published articles will give you an idea of the wide variety of forms used by successful magazine writers.

In most well-written magazine articles, the skeleton is invisible to the casual reader. But it is there, artfully concealed beneath the smooth surface of anecdotes, direct quotes, summarizing paragraphs, statistics, and other elements—and it may be worthwhile to examine a few published articles to discover just how the professionals who wrote them structured their work.

You will find that there is no single form—or dozen forms, or 21 forms—for a magazine article. Fortunately, you do not have to attempt to duplicate what others have done. You have an almost unlimited choice in the way you structure an article, as long as your method works. But you should keep in mind that the *lack of any form at all* was mentioned by many editors as a major reason for rejection of articles, even when the writer had selected a promising subject, researched it thoroughly, and directed the work to a likely magazine.

Each year thousands of people who would like to write for *Sports Illustrated* or *Ski* or *Modern Maturity* or *The New Yorker* type up their notes haphazardly and rush them off to those magazines.

One editor speculated that many of those beginners are confused because many published magazine articles *appear* to be effortlessly written. The structure is completely hidden, and the language is relaxed and colloquial. In some cases, the editor observed, weeks—or even months—of experimentation was required to achieve that appearance of ease.

An editor at *Reader's Digest* emphasizes that learning to structure an article is almost as important as learning to write with skill.

Because the structure often is not immediately visible to even the attentive reader, it may be helpful to take apart a few magazine articles to see the underlying form.

We will begin with a brief, simple piece, then move on to some more complex articles, and conclude with an examination of one of the most famous magazine features ever written—Lillian Ross's famous profile of Ernest Hemingway.

A BRIEF ARTICLE

In *National Geographic Traveler,* Joseph Anthony found a very effective form for a simple article that focuses on a single central point. In a piece entitled "What Will You Do?" he accomplishes a great deal in just one-and-a-half magazine pages.

Using a first-person lead, Anthony begins by describing a situation that anyone who travels frequently might someday face:

> I'm not in the habit of checking into hotels without two francs to rub together, but in this case I had no choice: A thief had stolen virtually everything of value (cash, traveler's checks, credit cards, and passport) from me and my companion just a few hours earlier, and we hadn't been able to get anything replaced.
>
> We were vacationing in the south of France, and we were broke—and I mean *flat* broke. Relying on the kindness of strangers, I told the night manager we could settle the bill the next day, and she decided we looked honest enough to trust.
>
> With all the ads trumpeting credit card and traveler's check services—immediate replacement, instant emergency cash, and so on—we weren't too worried. . . .

Anthony then contrasts the picture given in those ads with the reality:

> *The Image.* MasterCard International boasts of its world-wide emergency card-replacement program, which allows customers to pick up new cards at more than 62,000 replacement centers, usually within 24 hours. . . .
> *The Real-Life Experience.* The only way MasterCard would replace my stolen credit card immediately was if I traveled from the south of France to a Paris office—a round-trip of more than a thousand miles.
> *The Image.* Bank of America's international network of locations allows its traveler's check customers to get emergency cash after local banks are closed.
> *The Real-Life Experience.* Bank of America's traveler's check department told us that we could get a $500 emergency advance at a hotel in central Cannes. We drove to the hotel—only to find it was closed for renovations. During a second, considerably testier call, Bank of America said it had no other emergency locations in the area. . . .

After reciting these experiences, Anthony then offers readers several specific tips on what to do to avoid the problems he and his companion ran into. (For example, you should have with you the central telephone number of your credit card issuer and of the bank that issued the card.)

Anthony then tells how his problem was solved the morning after the loss. He suddenly remembered that he had applied for an American Express card before leaving for Europe. He walked from the hotel to the local American Express office at 11 A.M., and by 2:10 P.M. walked out with a new card and $600 in cash and traveler's checks.

The piece closes on a light note:

> Probably the only person happier than I to see that new card with my name on it was the hotel manager.

AN UNUSUAL PERSONALITY ARTICLE

Frank Barnaba is a vice president of a small company in New Haven, Connecticut, and ordinarily he might not be considered a likely subject for a five-page article in *Reader's Digest*. Writer Mark Stuart Gill makes the reader want to know more about Barnaba with this lead:

> One icy winter night in 1980, Frank Barnaba sat in a New Haven, Conn., diner on his way home after a business trip. He heard someone weeping in the next booth. It was a girl about the same age as his 17-year-old daughter, Cheryl.
>
> Barnaba's instinct was to pay his bill and leave. As vice president of a water-treatment franchise, he was a busy man. But he remembered what his wife, Audrey, had once said: "Everyone is someone's child."
>
> When he asked if he could help, the girl blurted out a story that would haunt him forever. An honor student from nearby Seymour, Conn., Lisa had rebelled and run away. After living on the streets, she met a man who introduced her to cocaine. When she was addicted, he forced her to work as a prostitute.
>
> *This kid should be dreaming about her prom, not turning tricks,* thought Barnaba. *But what can I do?*

Gill then tells what Barnaba did. With the backing of his wife and daughter, he tracked down Lisa, talked to her for many hours at a New Haven diner, and encouraged her to take charge of her own life.

Nearly a year after they first met, Lisa called him to say she was going to leave the streets. Barnaba arranged to meet her at the diner.

"But Lisa didn't show," Gill reports. "Hours later, she was found in the city morgue, with enough cocaine in her veins to kill half a dozen men. Police couldn't decide whether it was suicide or murder."

After that striking opening story, Gill then retraces in detail what Barnaba personally has done to help many other teenagers and to bring information about the dangers of life on the streets to thousands of others.

The article focuses briefly on Barnaba himself, and then offers a series of vignettes of other teenage prostitutes Barnaba has advised and assisted. In aiding one of them, Barnaba was threatened by a pimp armed with a .45.

The cost was high, Gill says. The Barnabas twice mortgaged their house, and at one point they were $125,000 in debt because of Barnaba's obsession with helping the teen-agers.

With the passage of time, Gill reports, Barnaba's work brought him praise and help, including a $400,000 grant from the Justice Department's Office for Victims of Crime. The focus throughout the article is on people, and Gill ends by quoting Barnaba:

> "There's no secret to what I do. I don't have a fancy 12-step program to gain kids' confidence and reform them. I just have one step: Be there for children and help them take control of their own lives. Ultimately they have to save themselves."

* * *

This article, entitled "Savior in the Streets," moves swiftly, and at first you may not be conscious of the skill involved in weaving together the stories of Barnaba and four of the teenagers. Although the structure is not easy to detect, it is there, as you will see if you read it in the July, 1991, issue of *Reader's Digest:*

1. Opening anecdote about Lisa
2. The founding of an organization called "Paul & Lisa" to help teenagers
3. Barnaba's own troubled childhood
4. The story of Missy, one of the first teenage prostitutes Barnaba helped
5. The threat from a pimp
6. The change in the life of another teenager
7. Widening recognition of Barnaba's work
8. The cost to Barnaba and his family
9. The growth of "Paul & Lisa"
10. Barnaba's own view of what he does

Obviously, another writer could have chosen a different structure for this story. What is essential is that the article has a logical structure and is not presented merely as a collection of notes.

A MAJOR HEALTH ARTICLE

In "Those Mysterious, Maddening Allergies," Maxine Abrams first attracted the attention of *Cosmopolitan*'s readers by describing three reactions to allergies:

> Ann's eyes had been swollen for weeks. She'd changed her brand of eye makeup twice; then she wore none at all. Still, there was no improvement.

> Strange stomachaches had plagued Carole, but her doctor couldn't find anything wrong. "It must be stress," he concluded.

> Morgan's first ski trip was marred by a bad case of hives. The blotching and itching made her scratch until she almost bled, then kept her off the slopes.

The author then says,

These three women have *one* underlying problem—allergies.

Ann, a bank teller, has developed an allergy to money, especially to the coins she has to handle at work. "When she touches the coins, then rubs her eyes, she gets a rash."

Carole is allergic to preservatives found in many foods and wine.

Morgan is allergic to frigid weather.

After describing the problems confronting these three women, the author offers this capsule statement:

Hidden allergies can develop anywhere, anytime, in anyone, for any reason. They can drive us wild with their itching, spoil our looks with a rash, sap our energy with diarrhea and cramps, frighten us with fainting spells and breathing disorders. Severe reactions to food, insect bites, and drugs can be *deadly*. It's estimated that forty to forty-five million Americans suffer with allergies—and as many as eleven million more may have an allergy without knowing it.

She then focuses on several aspects of this problem:

1. The difficulties some doctors have in correctly diagnosing allergies
2. New testing techniques
3. Two conflicting theories about the cause of allergies
4. The wide range of substances that can cause an allergic response
5. The possibility of inheriting a tendency to suffer from an allergy
6. Eleven tips on "How to Outsmart a Hidden Allergy": for example, "Keep a two-week record of the foods you eat and any symptoms that follow," and "If your symptoms are new, take a hard look at any recent changes you have made in your diet, cosmetics, toiletries, medicine, or life-style."
7. Final advice: Find an allergist who won't give up.

Maxine Abrams covers many details in this three-page article. The reader comes away with a better understanding of the complexity of allergic reactions, a useful list of the most common causes, and a carefully presented series of steps to detect and control allergies.

A COMPLEX SCIENCE ARTICLE

If you are dealing with a very complex topic, you might want to read "A Fraud That Shook the World of Science," an article by Morton Hunt published in *The New York Times Magazine* on November 1, 1981.

This is the story of an investigation of two scientists at the Yale School of Medicine. The magazine's editors observe that the investigation (of charges of falsifying data) "shook the research community, overturned promising careers, and started an agonizing reevaluation of the scientific method."

Morton Hunt makes effective use of narrative throughout the article, beginning with the dramatic lead:

On a bright, cold morning in early February, 1980, Jeffrey Flier, a tall, mustachioed, young physician, boarded a train in Boston on his way to New Haven to carry out a distinctly disagreeable professional task. He was going to conduct an "audit" at the Yale University School of Medicine: He would spend some hours interrogating and examining the laboratory records of an associate professor there, one of whose published research papers on insulin metabolism had been called fraudulent by another researcher.

Dr. Flier—he pronounces it "flyer"—was well qualified for the assignment. He had trained in diabetes research at the National Institutes of Health (N.I.H.) in Bethesda, and now, though only 31, he was chief of the diabetes metabolism unit of Beth Israel Hospital in Boston and an assistant professor at the Harvard Medical School. He was intimately acquainted with the special technique of studying insulin metabolism used in the challenged paper and had been accepted by both sides as an impartial auditor.

Flier, recounting the events of that day not long ago, recalled feeling somewhat uneasy about the coming encounter. . . . [He] knew that, no matter how he acted, the meeting was bound to be stressful and humiliating for his interviewee, Dr. Vijay R. Soman. Still, Flier was not deeply anxious, since he felt confident he would find no evidence of overt fraud. . . .

After that quietly dramatic opening, the author retraces the story step by step, focusing on each participant in turn. The article should be read in full, but a few brief excerpts will indicate the effectiveness of this technique.

Dramatic Presentation

"I had expected graphs for each patient, showing the data plotted out and curves drawn through the points," [Flier recalled, in describing his first interview with the accused scientist, Dr. Vijay R. Soman], "but what he gave me was just a sheet of raw numbers.

"'Don't you have graphs?' I asked him. He seemed flustered, and said, 'Well, we threw away the individual graphs after a year because we had no storage space.'

"I started to feel uneasy. You don't throw away graphs with data that have just been published; it made no sense."

And later:

"I said, 'You do know how serious this is?' and he said, 'Yes,' and started to defend himself. He said he'd been under great pressure to publish as soon as possible so as to obtain priority for the finding. He said that the laboratory he worked in was oriented toward productivity and success.

"The situation had begun to seem strange and unreal to me. Vijay grew more and more disordered and irrational in his thinking and started to say peculiar philosophical things. I felt troubled and disoriented too."

Conclusion

In the aftermath segment of his article, Morton Hunt retraces the effects of the investigation on each of the people involved. About Vijay Soman, for example, he reports:

Soman disappeared from the Yale School of Medicine in April of last year, and by summer he and his family were back in Poona, India; nothing is known in American scientific circles of his life there today. All efforts to reach him have proved unavailing.

A FAMOUS PROFILE

Lillian Ross's profile of Ernest Hemingway is one of the most famous magazine articles ever published. It first appeared in *The New Yorker* and was later republished in two books: *Portrait of Hemingway* and *Reporting*.

To appreciate the full effect of the author's moment-by-moment, scene-by-scene construction, you should read the complete text. But the brief excerpts that follow will give you some impression of Ross's talent and her achievement.

Note her success in focusing your entire attention on Hemingway. Ross never intrudes and seems in fact to disappear completely from view during long stretches of the profile. Because there is nothing to impede your observation of Hemingway, you gain a vivid impression of what it would be like to spend several hours with him. His mood, his sometimes erratic behavior, even the rather querulous tone of his voice is communicated.

With her unblinking eye and her extraordinary attention to detail, Ross simply presents Hemingway to you and lets you reach your own conclusions about the kind of man he is.

The lead to this famous profile is simple and straightforward:

> Ernest Hemingway, who may well be the greatest American novelist and short-story writer of our day, rarely came to New York. For many years, he spent most of his time on a farm, the Finca Vigia, nine miles outside Havana, with his wife, a domestic staff of nine, fifty-two cats, sixteen dogs, a couple of hundred pigeons, and three cows. When he did come to New York, it was only because he had to pass through it on his way somewhere else. Late in 1949, on his way to Europe, he stopped in New York for a few days. I had written to him asking if I might see him when he came to town, and he had sent me a typewritten letter saying that would be fine and suggesting that I meet his plane at the airport. "I don't want to see anybody I don't like, nor have publicity, nor be tied up all the time," he went on. "Want to go to the Bronx Zoo, Metropolitan Museum, Museum of Modern Art, ditto of Natural History, and see a fight. . . . Don't want to go to Toots Shor's. Am going to try to get into town and out without having to shoot my mouth off. I want to give the joints a miss. . . ."

Scene-by-Scene Report

After that low-key introduction, Lillian Ross re-created Hemingway's visit to New York—a city he had never liked—moment by moment, episode by episode, drink by drink, beginning with bourbon in the airport cocktail lounge:

> Hemingway told the bartender to bring double bourbons. He waited for the drinks with impatience, holding on to the bar with both hands and humming an unrecognizable tune. Mrs. Hemingway said she hoped it wouldn't be dark by the time they got to New York. Hemingway said it wouldn't make any difference to him, because New York was a rough town, a phony town, a town that was the same in the dark as it was in the light, and he was not exactly overjoyed to be going there anyway.

Many writers might have noted Hemingway's quick trip to the bar and his order for double bourbons, since his drinking habits had often been commented on. Few would have observed so minutely his mixture of contempt and dread as he approached Manhattan:

> We were crossing the Queensboro Bridge, and we had a clear view of the Manhattan skyline. The lights were on in the tall office buildings. Hemingway did not seem to be impressed. "This ain't my town," he said. "It's a town you come to for a short time. It's murder."

At the hotel there is another scene that reveals his attitude toward New York, and it is offered without any comment by Ross.

Mrs. Hemingway goes over to examine a bookcase in their hotel room, and she discovers that it is filled with pasteboard backs of books—not real books.

> Hemingway put his briefcase down on a bright-red couch and advanced on the bookcase, then slowly, with expression, read the titles aloud—*Elementary Economics, Government of the United States, Sweden, the Land and the People*, and *Sleep in Peace*, by Phyllis Bentley.
> "I think we are an outfit headed for extinction," he said.

If Ross felt that Hemingway was overreacting to a hotel decorator's folly, she did not say so. She instead reported meticulously his preoccupation with the false book jackets:

> Hemingway went back to the bookcase and stood there stiffly, as though he could not decide what to do with himself. He looked at the pasteboard backs again and said, "Phony, just like the town."

Briefly Ross herself reappeared in the profile at this point. She asked Hemingway about his new novel, *Across the River and Into the Trees*. He had brought the unfinished manuscript with him.

> I wanted to know whether, in his opinion, the new book was different from his others, and he gave me another long, reproachful look. "What do you think?" he asked after a moment. "You don't expect me to write 'The Farewell to Arms Boys in Addis Abada,' do you? Or 'The Farewell to Arms Boys Take a Gunboat'?"

He commented about some critics of his work:

> "People think I'm an ignorant bastard who doesn't know the ten-dollar words. I know the ten-dollar words. There are older and better words which if you arrange them in the proper combination you make it stick. Remember, anybody who pulls his erudition or education on you hasn't any. . . ."

He makes a series of cryptic statements that Ross records without comment:

> He gave a short, rumbling laugh. "I am a strange old man," he said, "How do you like it now, gentlemen?"

He also suddenly begins boxing (without an opponent) or firing an imaginary weapon:

> [As we started across Fifth Avenue] a flock of pigeons flew by. He stopped, looked up, and aimed an imaginary rifle at them. He pulled the trigger, and then looked

disappointed. "Very difficult shot," he said. He turned quickly and pretended to shoot again. "Easy shot," he said. "Look!" He pointed to a spot on the pavement.

Mrs. Hemingway had suggested that her husband buy a new coat at Abercrombie and Fitch. Some writers might have decided that this would be a good time to close their notebooks and take a short break from reporting. Ross instead accompanied him to the store, watched every gesture, and noted his cryptic exchanges with the clerk:

> A tall, dapper clerk approached us, and Hemingway shoved his hands into his pants pockets and crouched forward. "I think I still have credit in this joint," he said to the clerk.
>
> The clerk cleared his throat. "Yes, sir," he said.
>
> "Want to see coat," Hemingway said menacingly.
>
> "Yes, sir," said the clerk. "What kind of coat did you wish to see, sir?"
>
> "That one." He pointed to a straight-hanging, beltless tan gabardine coat on the rack. The clerk helped him into it and gently drew him over to a full-length mirror. "Hangs like a shroud," Hemingway said, tearing the coat off. "I'm tall on top. Got any other coat?" he asked, as though he expected the answer to be no. He edged impatiently toward the elevators.

The Hemingway profile is widely recognized as a model in the use of the "I am a camera" approach to magazine writing. Some writers have falsely concluded that this kind of reporting is easy because little more *seems* to be involved than taking detailed notes and then arranging them in chronological order.

Actually, this is a particularly demanding magazine form. The writer must first exercise careful judgment in selecting a subject for such a piece. Then he or she must be constantly alert to the revealing but seemingly unimportant comments by the subject, and to encounters between the subject and other people, such as the one between Hemingway and the clerk at Abercrombie & Fitch. In the course of several hours (or even days), the writer will accumulate stacks of notes (in some cases, hundreds of pages). Selection again becomes a very important matter, and each significant episode must be presented crisply. It is absolutely essential to maintain pace.

This is a type of article that you might want to explore, but you should not try to do such a piece hurriedly or casually. It requires imagination, energy, patience, and skill.

CHOOSING THE STRUCTURE FOR YOUR ARTICLE

The examples cited here suggest the wide range of techniques used by professional magazine writers.

It would be a mistake to try to duplicate the form you find in someone else's work. You should analyze the material you have gathered, arrange it in the order that seems most natural, and then experiment until you are certain you have discovered the most effective way to present that specific material. Do not attempt to *impose* an arbitrarily selected structure.

You will want to make certain you have chosen the best possible lead and have used a capsule statement (unless you are sure that the reader will understand just what your article is about without such a statement).

Beyond that crucial early segment, the tests you should apply to the body of the article are simple:

Have you included everything that is essential?
Have you eliminated everything that is not essential?
Have you presented your material in a logical order?

For a more detailed look at your manuscript, you might want to use the "Checklist for a Magazine Article" in Appendix A. That will help you discover any weaknesses before you submit your article for an editor's judgment.

By taking a close, critical look at both the form and the content of your articles, you will gain the respectful attention of editors, who will recognize your professional approach even if they do not recognize your name.

FINDING THE RIGHT ENDING

Writers who pay close attention to the leads of their magazine articles are often rather casual in choosing the final paragraph or two.

This is a mistake. The last sentences of an article can leave a strong impression on your readers—including your first reader, the editor who is considering your manuscript.

Quotes are often used to emphasize a central point or to introduce a thought that the reader may carry away from the article. Some are used just because they are surprising or memorable.

The Ironic Quote Ending

Some writers prefer an ironic or amusing closing quote. For example, "A Cool Act of Murder" by Ken Gross tells the story of a widely respected doctor who is accused of killing his wife. She was found "tucked under a warm blanket with a pillow placed carefully under her head." A detective said after examining the scene of her death, "Whoever killed her, it was someone who loved her."

After recounting the story of the doctor's unsuccessful attempt to prove that he was too far away from home to be involved in his wife's death, the author quotes a detective who played a major role in the investigation.

"He's likable," says [Detective Bob] Anderson ungrudgingly. "In fact he was the nicest murder suspect I ever went after."

In *People,* Susan Schindehette and Sue Carswell closed their article about the break-up of the marriage of Donald and Ivana Trump with a quote about Ivana's future. After reflecting on Ivana's two failed marriages, a friend, Joan Schnitzer, forecasts that Ivana will undoubtedly marry again:

"She's the marryin' kind," she said. "But I think she'll kiss a lot of toads before she finds her handsome prince."

For "School for Scandal," an article about cheating on college campuses also published in *People*, the authors end with a quote from an acknowledged—but disappointed—cheater at California State University–Northridge:

> "It may be one way to pass," he says, "but if you really want to get good grades, you can't do it by cheating. I only got two A's the whole time."

The Reflective Quote

In *Reader's Digest*, "Cocaine: The Devil Within" tells the story of Kerri Miller, a college student who suffered a stroke and severe memory loss as a result of her prolonged addiction. The piece by Per Ola and Emily d'Aulaire ends with a quote from Miller:

> "Cocaine is a big lie. It promises paradise while it destroys everything around you. I know—I have seen the devil. He comes in a small glass vial."

A Look Ahead

In an article in *People* focusing on Prince Charles's deficiencies as a father the authors cite many episodes in which he seems not only distant from his sons William and Harry but totally indifferent to them. In conclusion the authors quote two observations by Dr. Henry Levant, author of *Between Father and Child:*

> "When [the sons of such fathers] grow up, they have trouble forming intimate relationships with their wives and children, and will repeat the experience with their own children, whether they like it or not," Levant says. He then adds: "All kids really need is one adult who's absolutely nuts about them."

The authors make their own final comment: "And that, in the person of their doting mother, William and Harry certainly have."

The "Encouraging Note" Ending

Writers sometimes offer the reader encouragement or advice in the closing paragraph. Concluding an article on "Those Mysterious, Maddening Allergies" in *Cosmopolitan*, Maxine Abrams addresses the reader directly:

> What should you do if your allergy is especially tough to detect? What you should *not* do is give up. If your problem persists and baffles one doctor, find another, more tenacious allergist who will persevere until the cause is found—and you're finally free of all those maddening symptoms.

Offering the Reader Other Sources

Service articles often end with a list of additional sources for readers who want more information.

Near the end of "Give Your Doctor a Checkup—It Could Save Your Life," Tamara Eberlein writes,

HELP—A PHONE CALL AWAY

Here, the numbers to dial and other ways to check on your doctor:

She follows with the names, addresses, and phone numbers of organizations readers can consult to get specific information about their doctors.

The Forecast Ending

It is fairly common for writers to feel that their intensive research qualifies them to offer a prediction about the topic they have covered in their article.

Martha Weinman Lear ends a thoughtful *Ladies' Home Journal* article, "Staying Together," with these words:

> There may again come times when the experts will start predicting the end of marriage, but marriage—in some form or another—will surely survive them once more.

> In another article about marriage—"The First Year: Marriage's Delicate Balancing Act"—the author ends with this comment:

> If the prospect of spending your newlywed years negotiating and struggling rather than kissing and snuggling leaves you cold, don't despair. Marriage isn't *all* work, and most first-year troubles do get resolved. Smoothing over the rough spots just takes time and commitment, but if you survive those first twelve months, you'll have the rest of your lives to share with each other. Now, what could be more romantic than that?

*   *   *

If you spend an afternoon in a library, you may be surprised to discover how many different types of article endings various writers have used. In planning the conclusions for your magazine pieces, you will have many choices—but the one thing you want to avoid is causing readers to turn the page, looking for more, because they don't realize that those final 50 words *were* the end of your article.

13

The Writer and the Law

As a magazine writer, you will need to understand the laws governing copyright, libel, privacy, and plagiarism. Here you will find an introduction to these laws and some examples of cases won—and lost—by other writers.

During your writing career you may face questions such as these:

Should you copyright your articles before you submit them to magazines, to make certain that no one steals your ideas?

If you want to quote about 100 words from a book, is it necessary first to obtain permission from the author?

If someone tells you that a person you are writing about was once arrested for shoplifting, should you quote that statement in your article?

How candid can you be in commenting on the ability of an actor or a singer or a writer?

In submitting photographs to illustrate an article, should you show only the people you have mentioned in the piece? Or is it all right to offer photographs showing other people in a situation similar to the one you have described?

Because questions such as these will arise during your career as a writer, it is important to know something about the laws governing copyright, libel, privacy, and plagiarism.

SHOULD YOU COPYRIGHT YOUR ARTICLES
BEFORE SUBMITTING THEM TO MAGAZINES?

This question is often asked by beginning writers. They worry about the possibility that editors will steal their article ideas and turn them over to staff writers or to favored free-lancers.

I have never known a professional writer who shared this fear. Those who have dealt with magazines for years realize that editors would no more consider stealing a writer's ideas than they would think of stealing the writer's tie or watch.

I believe the worry among beginners over this "danger" arises from a misunderstanding. Relatively few new, *original* ideas are offered to magazines. Thousands of obvious, *general* ideas are submitted regularly—and no writer has any claim to *ownership* of such ideas.

For example, the editor of a travel magazine might receive suggestions from 20 or more writers during a single year for articles about the least expensive way to travel to Europe. No one *owns* that general idea. The editor could easily reject 19 of those 20 proposals and still feel free to accept the twentieth one because of the special skill this particular writer demonstrates in researching and shaping his or her article. In that case, the editor is not buying the general idea but the specific presentation.

If you wrote to that same editor and proposed a piece about holidays in Greece or Hawaii or Mexico, it would be a mistake for you to believe that you were the *only* writer offering those suggestions. You might be competing with 10, 15, or 50 writers who had settled on the same rather obvious *general* idea. You have no greater claim to ownership than any of those other writers.

When a new television star appears, free-lancers routinely deluge the offices of magazine editors with proposals for pieces about this new personality.

All of these ideas are in the air. They belong to no one. If an editor is unimpressed by the angle you suggest or has reservations about your ability to write an acceptable article, the magazine will naturally reject your proposal. That does not mean that the editor is not free to accept an alternate suggestion for a treatment of the same general subject.

Hal Wingo, an editor of *People,* said that writers who offer his magazine some vague proposal for "an article about Barbra Streisand" sometimes believe that they have established a legal claim to all future articles about Barbra by making that submission.

Although you cannot copyright your article *idea,* you *can* copyright the specific words you use to express that idea.

In fact, you now have an automatic copyright as soon as you complete an article. Under the new Copyright Act that became effective January 1, 1978, anything you write will be copyrighted automatically even if you do not register it with the copyright office.

However, if you would be more comfortable if you knew that your article was both copyrighted and registered before it was submitted to an editor, the procedure is fairly simple.

You can obtain the necessary copyright application form by writing to

Register of Copyrights
Copyright Office
Library of Congress
Washington, D.C. 20559

You must submit two copies of the final version of your work to the copyright office and pay a small fee. On the title page of your copyrighted work you should include this notice:

Copyright © 19.., by ——————— ———————

Usually you will not need to obtain copyrights on your work. Once you sell an article, this step will be taken by the magazine that publishes the piece. Almost all magazines routinely copyright the entire contents of each issue. Ordinarily an editor will arrange for the copyright to be reassigned to you (after the magazine appears) if you make that request.

Even with the automatic copyright provided under the new copyright act, registration with the copyright offices serves as a useful record of ownership, just as a registered deed serves as a record of ownership of a house.

The new act has also lengthened the period of copyright. Before 1978, copyright was effective for 28 years and could be renewed for another 28. Under the new law, copyright remains in effect for 50 years after the author's death. An article you publish while still in college could remain in copyright for more than a century, and it is conceivable that your grandchildren could receive income from future publishers of the article far into the twenty-first century.

MUST YOU OBTAIN PERMISSION TO QUOTE PUBLISHED MATERIAL?

Under a doctrine called "fair use," you can quote *briefly* from copyrighted material "for purposes such as criticism, comment, news reporting, teaching . . . , scholarship, or research."

The precise number of words you can quote from a book without specific permission has never been firmly settled by a court judgment. In practice, many editors assume that it is all right to quote up to 250 words from a full-length *book* without requesting permission. (You should be sure to credit the source.) If you quote more than 250 words, editors will probably suggest that you make a formal request. Permission will often be granted routinely, but for longer quotations you may be asked to pay a fee.

Your letter requesting permission should go to the copyright owner (clearly indicated in the opening pages of most books). You should send a copy of the material you wish to quote and should indicate the magazine (or magazines) to which you plan to submit your article. Always include a self-addressed, stamped envelope (SASE).

If you are quoting from a short article, you may need to ask permission even when quoting 100 words or so because you will be using a higher *proportion* of the copyrighted material.

Court decisions provide no clear rule about such quotations from very brief material. Some authorities suggest that you ask permission if you wish to quote as little as two or three lines from a short poem, or a few words from a song lyric. This is probably the safest step.

The editors who publish your articles will be aware of these special requirements.

If you are writing a book rather than a magazine article, you will need to include many more details in your letter requesting permission. The copyright owner will want to know the name of the publisher, the publication date, the estimated price, and whether the book will be published in hardcover or paperback. The publisher of your book can provide a model "permissions letter," and if you are quoting from a number of sources your request form can be photocopied to save your time.

The Controversy over "Work Made for Hire"

One provision of the new Copyright Act has been attacked by many writers.

If a writer is hired to do an article, screenplay, or book, the work may be copyrighted in the name of the writer's employer and the writer may relinquish all rights to it.

This is the controversial provision in the Copyright Act:

Works Made for Hire—In the case of a work made for hire, the employer or other person for whom the work was prepared is considered the author for purposes of this title, and, unless the parties have expressly agreed otherwise in a written instrument signed by them, owns all of the rights comprised in the copyright.

This is not a new idea. For decades, hired writers have usually surrendered ownership of their work to their employers. But some writers hoped that the new Copyright Act would provide a fairer division of ownership and control.

Those who criticize the "work made for hire" passage in the Copyright Act sometimes cite the differences between the rights gained by Broadway playwrights over the years and those surrendered by Hollywood screenwriters.

The contrast is very strong. Plays are not ordinarily written under "for hire" arrangements, and playwrights retain an extraordinary amount of control over their works. The standard play contract requires that a producer consult the playwright before changing a line of the script, and the producer may also be required to consult the author on casting and on many other important details of production.

On the other hand, Hollywood screenwriters who work for hire may see their scripts changed beyond recognition or discarded entirely when a film is made. Few of them are even informed about the way their work is presented to the world.

If you object to giving up all control of your work (even though you are being paid a salary while writing it, or receiving a fee for your work), the new Copyright Act does recognize that your articles may be copyrighted in your own name "if the parties have agreed . . . in a written instrument signed by them. . . ."

This is something you might wish to consider when undertaking work for hire.

Although the copyright of a routine newspaper feature story may have little future value, that is not the case with a copyright in a major magazine article or a book or a screenplay. If you can negotiate a written agreement to protect those rights, you might be providing a precedent that will be important to other writers.

In any case, you should always be aware of what you are surrendering when you sign a standard "work made for hire" agreement.

SHOULD YOU QUOTE A STATEMENT CHARGING THAT SOMEONE YOU ARE WRITING ABOUT WAS ONCE ARRESTED FOR A CRIME?

You should be extremely careful about writing anything that asserts (or even implies) someone has committed a crime.

You will be running a great risk if you publish such a charge without absolute proof of the accuracy of the statement.

If you "impugn the honesty, virtue, or reputation" of someone, or if you "expose him to public hatred, contempt, or ridicule," you could be guilty of libel. The often-quoted words are from a decision of the U.S. Supreme Court (*Dorr* v. *U.S.*).

In a New York State court decision, the danger of accusing someone of a crime is mentioned specifically:

A publication is libelous on its face when the words impute to the plaintiff the commission of a crime. . . .

It can also be libelous to publish anything that tends to "degrade the individual or lessen the person in the estimation of an appreciable portion of the community" or that affects (or may affect) "his business, profession, or calling."

Many huge libel judgments have been awarded against newspapers and magazines in recent years, and this emphasizes the danger that can arise if you publish derogatory statements that cannot be proved in court.

You would be free to include a statement about an arrest for shoplifting if the person you are writing about had been tried and found guilty. You would need to dig out the records of the trial and to quote the verdict fairly and accurately. You may report "judicial, legislative, or other official proceedings" even when these include statements that are defamatory.

If you quote accurately and fairly statements made in a courtroom during a trial or in the state legislature or in Congress while they are in session, this material is "privileged" and you are not required to prove that the statements you quote are true.

It is important to recognize the *limitations* on privileged material. Some writers assume that any statement made by a police officer can be quoted without danger. That is not true. Privilege covers "official proceedings"—not the casual comments of someone who is regularly involved in such proceedings.

For example, if you were having a casual conversation with a police officer and the officer said "I'm certain that the contractors who are building those new apartments over on Center Street have been bribing the building inspectors," you would be running a great risk in publishing that unsupported statement. If the officer had enough information to conduct an investigation that led to charges being filed and if the contractors were convicted of bribing the building inspectors, then the evidence produced in court could be freely published. (Even if the contractor were not convicted, you would still be able to quote any statement made in court. You would also need to make clear that the contractors had been found not guilty.)

In some states many quasi-judicial and quasi-legislative proceedings are now privileged, but writers should never *assume* that they are dealing with privileged material without careful checking.

HOW CANDID CAN YOU BE IN COMMENTING ON THE ABILITY OF AN ACTOR, SINGER, WRITER, OR PAINTER?

Courts have long protected the rights of writers to comment with great candor about the performances of actors and entertainers and about the creations of authors, playwrights, painters, sculptors, and composers.

One often-quoted example of a rather cruel use of this right first appeared in a small newspaper in Iowa. It was later reprinted in a larger paper, the *Des Moines Leader*.

A reporter had attended a performance by the Cherry Sisters and then wrote this review:

Effie is an old jade of 50 summers, Jessie a frisky-filly of 40, and Addie, the flower of the family, a capering monstrosity of 35. Their long skinny arms, equipped with talons at the extremities, swung mechanically, and anon waved frantically at the suffering audience. The mouths of their rancid features opened like caverns, and sounds like the wailing of damned souls issued therefrom. They pranced around the stage with a motion that suggested a cross between a *danse du ventre* and fox trot— strange creatures with painted faces and hideous mein. Effie is spavined, Addie is stringhalt, and Jessie, the only one who showed her stockings, has legs with calves as classic in their outlines as the curves of a broom handle.

When the Cherry Sisters sued for libel, the Iowa courts refused to penalize the writer. The Iowa Supreme Court said the reviewer's words were protected under the doctrine of "fair comment." In its decision the court observed,

One who goes upon the stage to exhibit himself to the public, or who gives any kind of performance to which the public is invited, may be freely criticized.

Critics have complete freedom of expression "provided they are not actuated by malice or evil purpose in what they write," the justices said.

Exercising the same freedom, a reviewer in *The New York Times Book Review* offered this estimate of the talent of the popular novelist Leon Uris when Uris's novel *Topaz* was published:

Mr. Uris is flagrantly unable to construct a plot, a character, a novel, or a sentence in the English language—and [in *Topaz*] he takes 130,000 words to display his incompetence.

In *Newsweek* a reviewer noted that *Chesapeake,* a novel by James A. Michener, was 865 pages long, and then offered readers these two suggestions:

My best advice is don't read it; my second best is don't drop it on your foot.

Such comments are protected by courts because of the belief that there should be no restraint on candid discussion of the *public* acts of public figures. In *Hoeppner* v. *Dunkirk Printing Co.,* the Supreme Court explained the reasoning behind this doctrine:

Everyone has a right to discuss the personal deportment, behavior, and qualifications of one who occupies the public eye much more freely than he has to talk about a private individual in whose affairs the public has little or no interest. Just and reasonable criticism of a public person is not libelous. It would indeed be a sorry day for the country if men in public life were beyond censure.

Later, in *New York Times Co.* v. *Sullivan,* the Supreme Court broadened the protection offered to writers reporting or commenting on public figures. Unless a public figure could prove that a statement concerning his or her official conduct was published with "actual malice," the individual could not recover damages, the Court said. The plaintiff is required to prove that the statement was published "with knowledge that it was false or with reckless disregard of whether it was false or not."

"The Court voted to protect *some* false statements in order to make public debate more robust and uninhibited," William E. Francois observes in *Law and the Writer,* "and to reduce the threat of large damage awards in libel actions that were having a chilling effect on First Amendment freedoms."

It is important to keep in mind that this ruling applies to the *public activities* or *official acts* of public figures. You are free to write that an author has written the worst book you have ever read, but you cannot casually charge the author with forging a check or assaulting his or her spouse.

A REMINDER ABOUT DEFENSES IN LIBEL SUITS

In general, writers or publishers will offer one (or more) of these basic defenses when confronted by a charge of libel:

1. They may contend that the story they have published is true. It is not enough to assert this; the writer or the publisher must be prepared to prove it.
2. They may contend that the story is privileged. In many cases this defense is adequate even if the published statements are both defamatory and false. But the writer must be certain that the material he or she is citing *is* privileged, and the report must be fair and accurate.
3. Writers or publishers may contend that they are offering fair comment on a public figure. If the court agrees that the person who was written about is a public figure, writers and publishers have wide latitude in their reports and criticisms.

Other defenses are occasionally offered, but those just cited are the major ones.

Incidentally, courts now examine closely the motives behind the publication of derogatory material. Lawyers can question your selection of quotes, your arrangement of facts, even the reason why you omitted certain material from your article. If your responses reveal prejudice or animosity, this can be used to establish "actual malice," which can lead to a damaging verdict. Any writer who sets out maliciously to injure someone or to harm the person's reputation can be held accountable, and the penalties can be heavy.

IN SUBMITTING PHOTOGRAPHS TO A MAGAZINE, SHOULD YOU SHOW ONLY THE PEOPLE YOU HAVE SPECIFICALLY MENTIONED IN YOUR ARTICLE?

The answer is yes—this is always the safest course. And most magazines will ask you to obtain a signed permissions form from anyone who can be clearly identified in your photographs. The forms vary in phrasing, and you should obtain copies of the one preferred by the magazine that plans to use your article.

The caution about the selection of illustrations grows out of some complex and costly lawsuits involving major magazines. Two of the most famous cases arose because of photographs used in *The Saturday Evening Post*.

A *Post* article entitled "Never Give a Passenger an Even Break" portrayed taxi drivers in the District of Columbia as brazen, ill-mannered, contemptuous, and often dishonest.

As an illustration for the piece, the magazine used a photograph of cab driver Muriel Peay. She had not granted the *Post* permission to publish her photograph, and she sued, charging that the illustration placed her in a false light, indicating that *she* was brazen, ill-mannered, contemptuous, and perhaps dishonest. The courts agreed and gave a substantial judgment against the publisher.

To illustrate an article entitled "Mafia: Shadow of Evil on an Island in the Sun," the *Post* selected a photograph of five people playing blackjack. The gamblers were not named, but the photograph was accompanied by this caption:

High-Rollers at Monte Carlo have dropped as much as $20,000 in a single night. The U.S. Department of Justice estimates that the Casino grosses $20 million a year, and that one-third is skimmed off for American Mafia "families."

One of the five people shown in the photograph was James Holmes, and he could be easily identified. He said the picture and the caption placed him in a false light, and he sued for libel and invasion of privacy. A U.S. District Court agreed:

Certainly the caption is reasonably capable of amounting to a defamation, for one identified as a high-stakes gambler and of having a connection with the Mafia would certainly be injured in his business, occupation and/or reputation.

Often such "false light" invasion of privacy cases arise because of the combination of words and photographs. That was true in a suit against the *Ladies' Home Journal*.

A photograph of Mr. and Mrs. John W. Gill was selected to illustrate an article entitled "Love." They were seated on two stools, and Mr. Gill had his arm around his wife.

The caption read,

Publicized as glamorous, desirable, "love at first sight" is a bad risk.

The accompanying article said that "love at first sight" was the "wrong" kind and was "100% sex attraction."

The court decided that the phrases in the article would seem to apply to the couple shown in the photograph, and that this implied that Mr. and Mrs. Gill were "persons whose only interest in each other is sex, a characterization that may be said to impinge seriously upon their sensibilities." The Gills won their suit.

Incidentally, the Gill case illustrates the danger that can arise when a photograph is taken for one purpose and then used for another. The photo of the Gills was not taken for use with the article entitled "Love" but for an entirely different purpose. The editors selected it casually because it was available and seemed appropriate. Frequently photographers will try to get five or six uses out of the same photo—and that can be dangerous.

These "false light" suits have become fairly common since 1903, when the state of New York adopted the first law to protect privacy.

Louis D. Brandeis and Samuel D. Warren were early advocates of such a law. In a famous article, they wrote,

> The press is overstepping in every direction the obvious bounds of propriety and decency. Gossip is no longer the resource of the idle and vicious, but has become a trade, which is pursued with industry as well as effrontery. To satisfy a prurient taste the details of sexual relations are spread broadcast in the columns of the daily newspapers. To occupy the indolent, column upon column is filled with idle gossip, which can only be procured by intrusion upon the domestic circle.

Brandeis and Warren called for recognition of the "Right to Privacy"—the right of individuals to go through life without having their personal behavior written about in the press.

Hayes B. Jacobs, an experienced free-lancer, summarizes the effect of the laws that have been passed since that article was published:

> [You] cannot write just anything you want to about your fellow man; he is entitled to quite a degree of privacy, to quite a few secrets about his personal life. He has a legal right to lead his own life in his own way, without waking up some morning and discovering the public knows *all* about it.

Although many suits have been brought over "intrusion" into the private lives of people who could not be considered public figures, relatively few judgments have been awarded on this ground. When writers base their reports on a public record and present it fairly and accurately, courts are usually ready to accept this as a defense.

For example, a newspaper in New Mexico published this report:

> Richard Hubbard, 16, son of Mrs. Ann Hubbard, 532 Ponderosa, NW, was charged with running away from home, also prior to date, several times endangered the physical and moral health of himself and others by sexually assaulting his younger sister. Court ordered a suspended sentence to the New Mexico Boys' Home on the condition that he serve 60 days in the Juvenile Detention Home.

In this case, the charge of "invasion of privacy" was brought by the younger sister of the 16-year-old boy. Her attorneys said that the story "caused her to be regarded as unchaste, and that her prospects of marriage have been adversely affected thereby."

The newspaper proved that the reporter had been careful to use the exact words used in the official court records, and the New Mexico Supreme Court ruled that the story was "accurate, newsworthy, and exercised in a reasonable manner for a proper purpose."

A reporter's carelessness led to a substantial judgment in another suit involving privacy.

When a bridge collapsed in West Virginia, 44 people were killed, including a man named Cantrell. Cleveland *Plain Dealer* reporter Joseph Eszterhas covered the story, and five months later went to the Cantrell home to do a follow-up feature about the effect of the disaster on the family of one of the victims.

Mrs. Cantrell was not at home, so the reporter interviewed the children while a photographer took pictures of the children and of the house.

The article emphasized the family's poverty and described the old, ill-fitting clothes worn by the children and the neglected condition of the house. Although Eszterhas did not interview Mrs. Cantrell, he included this paragraph in his feature story:

> Margaret Cantrell will talk neither about what happened nor about how they are doing. She wears the same mask of nonexpression she wore at the funeral. She is a proud woman. She says that after it happened, the people in town offered to help them out with money and they refused to take it.

That paragraph was cited specifically in a judgment against the *Plain Dealer* for publishing "knowing and reckless falsehoods against the Cantrells."

The justices said,

> There was no dispute during the trial that Eszterhas, who did not testify, must have known that a number of the statements in the feature story were untrue. In particular, his article plainly implied that Mrs. Cantrell had been present during his visit to her home and that Eszterhas had observed her "wear[ing] the same mask of nonexpression she wore [at her husband's] funeral." These were "calculated falsehoods" and the jury was plainly justified in finding that Eszterhas had portrayed the Cantrells in a false light through knowing and reckless untruth.

A $60,000 judgment was awarded Mrs. Cantrell.

Because the doctrine of the "Right to Privacy" is still being developed through a series of court decisions, it is important for writers to be conscious of the need for special care when writing about nonpublic figures.

THE DISTINCTION BETWEEN PARAPHRASING AND PLAGIARISM

As a writer, you should usually *absorb* essential background material and then present your articles in your own form and in your own words.

You will, of course, also quote or paraphrase some previously published material in some of your articles. When you do, you should always be careful to give credit if you are using material that was *originated* by another writers.

General information can be used without giving credit. For example, if you were writing about a current volcano and wished to make some comparisons between that volcano and Vesuvius, you could use the italicized *facts* in the following passage from the *Encyclopedia Britannica* without crediting the source:

> Vesuvius is *an active volcano* that rises above the Bay of Naples on the *Plain of Campania* in *southern Italy.*
>
> Although it is a *relatively young volcano,* Vesuvius had been *dormant for centuries* before the great *eruption of A.D. 79 that buried the cities of Pompeii and Stabiae under ashes . . . and the city of Herculaneum under a mud flow.* The writer *Pliny the Younger gave an* excellent *account* of the catastrophe *in two letters to* the historian *Tacitus. . . .*

At this point the *Encyclopedia* quotes from one of Pliny the Younger's letters. If you decided to use that direct quotation or to paraphrase the letter, you would naturally give credit to Pliny the Younger.

Let me emphasize this: You would not *copy* the passages from the *Encyclopedia Britannica,* but you could use it as one dependable source for basic information about Vesuvius and would not be expected to give specific credit, because the *Britannica* did not originate this material.

You would also routinely consult various reference volumes for such general information as this:

The population of Brazil
The height of the Eiffel tower
The age of John F. Kennedy when he became President
How oil is refined
Medical researchers who have won the Nobel Prize

This kind of basic information may be used without giving credit. But if you run across *unusual* information in a reference volume, you should cite the source. For example,

> Did you ever think how many male and female ancestors were required to bring you into the world? First, you had a father and a mother. That makes two human beings. Each of them had a father and mother. That makes four more. . . . Again, each grandparent had a father and mother, making eight more. . . . So, on we go back to the time of Jesus Christ, 56 generations. The calculation indicates 139,235,017,489,534,976 births must have taken place to bring you into this world. All this only since the birth of Christ—not since the beginning of time!

You might wish to paraphrase this to get to the point more quickly. But if you wished to make use of that figure, 139,235,017,489,534,976, I think you should cite the source—*Mammoth Book of Trivia,* by James Meyers. (And, incidentally, it would be good to ask a mathematician to double-check Meyers's calculation.)

The rule many writers follow is to give credit to published sources unless they are *certain* the information is generally available.

In any case, you should always keep in mind the crime committed by writers who "borrow" other writers' work: plagiarism.

Plagiarism is literary theft. If you use another writer's *language* without giving credit, you are guilty of plagiarism.

If the work that is stolen is currently protected by copyright, the thief may be charged with infringement of copyright, and the penalties can be severe. In one copyright infringement suit the defendant was ordered to pay a $5,000 fine and substantial court costs.

Some plagiarists copy entire magazine articles or books, word for word, and proof of plagiarism is fairly simple in those cases. But other plagiarists disguise the theft by paraphrasing the original work, and these cases present juries and judges with far more difficult decisions.

Unfortunately, writers who are entirely innocent have occasionally had to spend months defending themselves against charges of plagiarism that turn out to be entirely baseless. The writers of a very successful play that opened with a murder that was committed in the theater audience had to defend themselves from an unsuccessful playwright who had chanced to use that same kind of opening. In another case, two writers happened to write stories about a woman who was elected Vice President of the United States and then became President. Each was serialized in a popular magazine—one ten years later than the other.

The writer of the earlier serial sued for copyright infringement, and the judges agreed that there were some similarities in the two works. But they observed,

> Similarities can, of course, occur from copying, but they may also occur by reason of the subject matter and setting with which both stories deal. . . . [It] seems more reasonable that the many similarities that do occur are those which are almost compelled by political imperatives rather than to conclude . . . that they are the result of either reading or copying the story of the plaintiff.

As a matter of fairness—and to protect yourself against even a suspicion of plagiarism—you should give generous credit to your sources. If an editor decides that the information you have credited to a single source is in fact generally available, the editor may remove the citation.

The most important advice I can offer is this: Remember that you are a *writer,* not a *compiler* of previously published material. Although you will consult other writers frequently for facts and background information, the value of your articles will depend on your own contribution. You should make extensive use of interviews and search out original sources (such as letters, diaries, journals, and similar first-hand reports) and should not settle for simply stringing together material previously gathered by other writers.

OTHER BOOKS YOU WILL FIND USEFUL

This brief treatment of "The Writer and the Law" can serve only as an introduction to the laws governing copyright, libel, privacy, and plagiarism. When you have time, you should read and study a few of the books that cover these subjects in much greater detail.

I would recommend these volumes:

Rights and Writers, by Harriet F. Pilpel and Theodora S. Zavin (E. P. Dutton & Co., New York, 1960). This very readable book grew out of a series of columns by Harriet F. Pilpel published in *Publishers' Weekly.* Many specific cases involving writers are described and analyzed, and the authors also include a lucid discussion of the laws governing libel, privacy, copyright, contracts, taxes, and censorship.

Law and the Writer, edited by Kirk Polking and Leonard S. Meranus (Writer's Digest Books, Cincinnati, Ohio, 1978). Lawyers, literary agents, journalism professors, and experienced free-lance writers contributed chapters to this book, and brief chapters serve as a quick reference for many legal questions. You might want to pay special attention to the chapters focusing on libel, invasion of privacy, copyright law, book contracts, subsidiary rights, and legal problems facing photographers.

The Protection of Literary Property, by Philip Wittenberg (The Writer, Inc., Boston, 1978). A widely used reference book by an authority on copyright, plagiarism, libel, and privacy.

Law of Mass Communications, by Harold L. Nelson and Dwight L. Teeter, Jr. (The Foundation Press, Inc., Mineola, New York, 1978). A well-organized and skillfully presented treatment of most of the legal questions that writers are likely to face. The authors offer many specific cases as examples and review the general principles that led to favorable or unfavorable court decisions.

Free-Lancing: Occasionally, Part-Time, or Full-Time

Many beginning magazine writers dream of making their livings as full-time free-lancers. What are the chances for success? Here editors, agents, and experienced free-lancers answer that question and offer advice to writers who wish to experiment with this career.

A few hundred people in America make their livings as full-time free-lance writers for magazines.

Thousands of others experiment with free-lancing for a few months or maybe for two or three years, and then return to the security of a job as a reporter or a public relations writer.

If you are thinking of exploring the possibility of full-time free-lancing, you may want to consider the advice offered by editors and writers who are familiar with both the rewards and the problems associated with this career.

Fulton Oursler, Jr., former Executive Editor of *Reader's Digest,* has observed successful magazine free-lancers all of his working life. He offers this portrait of those who survive:

> The successful full-time free-lance writer is extraordinarily hard-working. He must be looking for new ideas constantly. He's thinking today of something he'll be writing next week, next month, next year.
>
> He's always enthusiastic. He's in love with his current story, but he's eager to get to work on the next one and the one beyond that.

However great his success, that enthusiasm never diminishes. I've seen James Michener work 12, 14, even 16 hours a day when a book is going well.

The free-lancer is curious. Many are curious about everything, while others focus their attention on one particular area.

He's resilient. Every free-lancer must endure the experience of having work rejected. For most there will be long periods when things are not going well. But the successful free-lancer shrugs his shoulders and keeps on working.

Other editors and experienced free-lancers endorse the points made by Oursler. They also offer the following detailed advice to anyone who is seriously considering entering the field.

BE PATIENT

"Many beginning free-lancers want the success to come immediately," said Albert Rosenfeld, former Science Editor of *Life,* who has also been a very successful free-lance science writer. "They should recognize that it is difficult to become a magazine free-lancer, just as it is difficult to gain a reputation for skill as a lawyer or a doctor. Be prepared to take some time to make a breakthrough."

BE READY TO MAKE A SMALL BEGINNING

"The most important step for anyone who wants to be a free-lancer is to get into print early," said John G. Stewart, who has been an editor of three magazines, including *The New York Times Magazine.* "It doesn't matter whether you get any money for your early work, or whether only a thousand or two thousand people see your article. It's a start—and once you've published two or three pieces in a little regional magazine, you are a magazine writer. Of course, you shouldn't stop there."

LOOK FOR MAGAZINES THAT INTEREST YOU

"I enjoy writing for some magazines that might not interest other writers at all," said Roger Rapoport, who has been free-lancing since his undergraduate days at college. "I'm writing now for a magazine called *Americana,* which is not widely known but publishes some excellent historical articles, and for one called *Running,* because I'm interested in that sport. Also, *American West.* One of the great advantages of free-lancing is that you can choose. I think a beginning free-lancer should spend some time looking around, deciding just where he [or she] will *enjoy* working."

DON'T OVERLOOK MAGAZINES OUTSIDE NEW YORK

"I've found that magazines published outside New York are more receptive to submissions from free-lancers than those published in New York," said Wisconsin free-lancer Margaret Davidson. "The highly visible magazines receive so many thousands of article ideas that your letter is often handled routinely. Editors of smaller magazines will often write to tell you why they're turning down an article proposal, and that can be very valuable to anyone who is just beginning."

DON'T PREJUDGE MAGAZINES

"Some writers sneer at magazines they've never bothered to read," said Linda Stewart, whose articles have appeared in magazines ranging from *Harper's Bazaar* to *Family Circle*. "For example, they dismiss all the women's magazines, and assume that they're still filled with articles about how to clean your kitchen or how to sew. You may discover that a magazine you have always regarded with contempt is actually both well written and well edited."

CONSIDER THE POSSIBILITY OF SPECIALIZING

"If I were beginning as a free-lancer today, I would develop a specialty," said Ray Robinson, former editor of *Seventeen*. "I might choose something like financial writing. Someone who could write clearly and effectively about economics would be valuable to many editors."

Other editors and free-lancers suggested several fields for specialization: medicine, science, law, travel, child care, marriage problems, sports, entertainment.

KEEP MANY IDEAS IN CIRCULATION

"I can remember a time when my father put 50 article suggestions in the mail in a single day," said Fulton Oursler, Jr. "He believed a free-lancer should always have many article ideas circulating in all directions."

OFFER TO WORK ON SPECULATION

"I say specifically in my letters to editors for whom I've not previously written that I will write the article on speculation if it interests them," said New York City free-lancer Linda Stewart. "I think that sometimes makes the difference. And I am reasonably confident that the editor will want the piece when I submit it."

BE PERSISTENT

"Persistence counts as much as talent," several free-lancers said. Linda Stewart added, "Many talented people try once or twice, then give up. I hear them say, 'I could have written that' when they see someone else's article in a magazine. But the difference is that the published writer did not fool around with magazine writing for a few weeks or a few months. He [or she] kept trying one idea after another, one magazine after another."

A *Redbook* editor agrees about the importance of trying again and again. "I always feel that many writers get discouraged too easily," she said. "If you receive a personal rejection—a thoughtful one—you should always follow up with other ideas. Many times I have said to a promising writer, 'Please keep in touch with me. Although this particular idea doesn't work for us, and we are a very hard market to break into, I'd be very interested in hearing from you about other ideas.' And then I'm surprised because I never hear from that writer again."

DON'T WASTE TIME ON WEAK IDEAS

"I think a free-lancer should be objective enough to recognize whether he is offering an editor something worth the magazine's serious consideration," an *Esquire* editor said. "He should not waste his own time or an editor's time on routine, uninspired ideas."

Many other editors echoed this point. "If I were a free-lancer," one *Reader's Digest* editor said, "I would concentrate on coming up with article ideas and article titles that would be worth featuring on the cover. These ideas are obviously more difficult to find, but they are also far more valuable to any magazine."

EXPERIMENT WITH SEVERAL TYPES OF ARTICLES

"Some writers seem to settle into writing just one kind of article early and keep writing similar articles for years," a very successful free-lancer said. "They might write *only* personality pieces or *only* travel articles or *only* articles for highly specialized trade magazines. It seems to me that they're missing out on one of the great attractions of free-lancing—the chance to experiment with a great variety of article types."

If the idea of experimenting appeals to you, you might want to take a close look at some articles in each of several broad classifications, and then try to come up with promising ideas in each of the areas that appeals to you. This sampling of types of articles will suggest some possibilities:

A how-to-do-it article
An as-told-to article
A question-and-answer article
A personality piece
A trend article
An information piece
A medical article
A travel piece
A first-person article
A light essay
An opinion piece

A science article
A historical article
A quiz
An expose

As this far-from-exhaustive list indicates, you have a wide range of choices as a free-lancer. Although you may decide later that you prefer to devote most of your time to medical articles or pieces about television personalities, during your early years it would be good to explore a variety of possibilities.

LEARN TO WORK WITH EDITORS

"Some writers tend to regard editors as adversaries, or even as 'the enemy,'" said Philip B. Osborne, Assistant Managing Editor of *Reader's Digest*. "What they don't realize is that an editor is out there to run interference for the writer. I try to make my writers look as good as they can. That's my job. As an editor, I'm only as good as the writers I work with. And that goes for a magazine too. It's writers that keep us in business. If they do well, our magazine does well."

WHEN TO DRAW THE LINE

John Frook is a former *Life* editor who has also contributed to many other magazines as a free-lancer and has written successfully for television and films. He understands the role of editors and agrees that a good editor can be extremely valuable to a writer. But he cautions that some editors go too far in trying to take over stories.

> One editor asked me to go back and talk again to an American nurse who had volunteered to go into Afghanistan to care for the women and children who were casualties in the war there, and to convince her to say something ugly about the Russians. What a bonus it would be if she would also say something red, white, and blue about how wonderful the Americans were.
>
> Now, that good woman never gave a thought to politics. She was a nurse who wanted to help suffering people, and it didn't matter to her what their language was, their nationality, or their political views.
>
> I've been at this work long enough so I know I could have manipulated her into the kind of quote the editor was looking for. But it would have been wrong—and that's where the writer should draw the line.

YOU DON'T HAVE TO START AT THE BOTTOM

"I know many people advise beginning free-lancers, 'Start small but think large,'" said Philip B. Osborne of *Reader's Digest*. "I don't agree with that 'start small' business. If a writer has enough talent, and comes up with a really excellent idea, he might be able to publish fairly early in *Family Circle* or the *Smithsonian* or *Reader's Digest*. I don't want to make it sound easy, because it isn't—but it's possible. Anything is possible when you have the courage to think it.

"I always tell writers who aim for the *Digest*—'The odds are lousy, but the chances are good.' That may seem contradictory, but it isn't. The competition for space here is staggering. We get thousands of ideas every week. But still, a terrific idea, presented with real skill, will get through. And if we're confident the writer can develop that idea, and will stay with it through the revisions that are almost always necessary, we will work with him (or her) as long as it takes."

CHOOSING THE RIGHT TIME

"For beginning writers, the odds on landing an assignment from *National Geographic* are about a thousand to one," Robert Laxalt tells students in his magazine writing classes, quoting an estimate from one of the magazine's editors.

Laxalt himself had written for many magazines, including *Saturday Evening Post, True, Redbook* and *Atlantic Monthly,* and had published his first two books with Harper & Row, before he received his first assignment from *National Geographic*. One of those books—*Sweet Promised Land*—led to the assignment, because it convinced the editors he could write about the Basques with knowledge and understanding.

Once you have established a reputation by publishing widely, you'll discover that an assignment from the *Geographic* can keep you heavily occupied for as long as six months, Laxalt observes.

"For a major piece, you should expect to spend about a month on research, followed by four to six weeks in the field," he says. "You'll probably be brought to Washington before leaving, to face intense questioning by the editorial staff.

"When you turn in your first draft, both the editorial and the research staff go to work. One editor told the *Washington Post*, 'Research is firmly convinced that all writers are liars.' Often a researcher will retrace the same path you followed, and will double check every quote with the source. Going back to 13th-century journals on some stories is not unusual.

"You should also expect to be asked to rewrite. On one of my articles, about New Mexico, I went through four revisions."

Laxalt, who has written about 20 articles and book chapters for the National Geographic Society over the past 25 years, including one that gave him a chance to spend six weeks with gauchos in Argentina, tells his students that the final results justify all the grueling work.

"For one thing," he says, "nobody ever throws away a copy of *National Geographic*. Your articles can become a permanent part of school and home libraries for millions of readers."

MAKING THE BEST OF REJECTION

Richard Matthews, who has written for a broad range of publications, including *Country Living, Harrowsmith, Historic Preservation, Early American Life,* and the *New York Times,* decided to take a chance on full-time free-lancing after 16 years as a teacher. He recommends that magazine writers maintain a file of rejection notes, not as a record of past failures but as a possible reminder of a publication for future submissions.

"Occasionally a rejection slip arrives with a hand-written note," Matthews says. "It may be nothing more than a brief reason for rejection scribbled at the bottom of a form, but sometimes it's an invitation to submit again. I prize whatever is personal and encouraging. When I have an idea and don't know where to send it, I sift through the file to find possibilities and send off proposals."

Matthews then writes to the editor who wrote the brief note, saying "Thank you for your encouragement last time," or "Thank you for your comments."

He adds:

"That file has been a gold mine. Seldom do I make it into a magazine on first try; sometimes it has taken up to three years before an idea sells, but fully half the publications I've finally 'cracked' came out of my Retrievable Rejections folder."

MONEY AND THE MAGAZINE FREE-LANCER

"In the 1960s, when I was on *Life,* we wouldn't hesitate to pay $5,000 for a major article, and we would go higher than that if it was necessary," Albert Rosenfeld recalls. "Today, when free-lancers find a magazine that pays $2,500, everybody says, 'That's great!' Many of the national magazines rarely pay more than $1,500 for a full-length article now, and some pay as little as $1,000 or even $750."

The failure of magazines to keep up with inflation in their payments to writers is often mentioned by both free-lancers and magazine editors. "I don't see how people can afford to write for magazines," two editors commented.

One of the most widely known current magazine free-lancers, Hunter S. Thompson, also focused on this point:

I could raise some ethical questions with regard to journalism professors who tell young people that they should write for magazines at all. I pay 55 cents for a Mounds candy bar these days, but most of the magazines I used to write for are still paying free-lance writers the same fees they were paying when Mounds cost a dime. Magazines are an advertising medium, a means to an end, and if you don't teach this you are cheating your students. I lecture on this now and then, and I feel a certain responsibility to the people I talk to—and to the best of my knowledge there is no way that even a *good* writer, doing consistently *good* articles for 'good' magazines can make a decent living or even pay the rent on a comfortable apartment in New York . . . and if you doubt this, check the next issue of *Esquire* or *Rolling Stone* or *Playboy* for bylines you might recognize. Except for book excerpts, you won't find any.

While the $750 to $1,500 payments most national magazines now offer make it difficult for even a very hard-working writer to do more than squeeze by if he or she depends entirely on income from articles for all his or her living expenses, the same payments can be entirely satisfactory to those who free-lance part-time while receiving an assured income from newspaper reporting or from public relations or advertising, or from teaching or practicing law or delivering mail or working as a secretary.

Of the many thousands of articles published in magazines year after year, a high proportion come from these part-time or occasional free-lancers. A university professor contributes a monthly column to a magazine for florists. A reporter submits ideas regularly to both *People* and *Sports Illustrated*. A stockbroker writes about investing, and a home economist writes articles about food, personal finances, and home furnishings.

One great advantage of either part-time or occasional free-lancing is that a rejection (or a series of rejections) seems less catastrophic. An obvious limitation is that you cannot travel as freely on assignments, and you may write less than you would if you were free-lancing full-time.

Even very successful free-lancers often *supplement* their magazine income with book royalties, screen-writing or television-writing payments, fees from lectures, or fees paid for part-time teaching or for serving as consultants in fields in which they have gained recognition as experts. Some carry out special writing assignments for companies, trade associations, or government bodies.

Even with this supplementary income, full-time free-lancing can be hazardous. Writers who have built up a strong dependence on a few magazines that seem particularly receptive to their work may learn suddenly that two of the editors they have worked with harmoniously have resigned (or been fired). The successors bring along their own favored free-lancers, and the previously successful writers suddenly begin receiving polite rejections from magazines in which their work has been featured prominently for years.

Still another magazine folds, and a fourth reports that it is heavily overstocked and will be buying no more pieces from anyone for several months, reducing the market for the work of those free-lancers.

Unpredictable developments such as these are common in the magazine world. And even for the most experienced writers, every new magazine article is a gamble. I once heard of a writer who had sold 100 articles to the *Saturday Evening Post* and then had his 101st and *all* his subsequent articles rejected brusquely by a new group of editors.

Because of many factors—including worry about the cost of orthodontia for the children, or concern about possible illness, or the sudden recognition that they have put aside nothing for retirement—many writers who have had some success as full-time free-lancers end up reluctantly settling for a 40-hour week on a magazine staff or in some related field.

Others realize all the hazards involved but stay with the life they have chosen. Why? Listen to Al Rosenfeld:

An editor I've known for years once said to me, "I don't know how you can stand this kind of life. I need to know there's a salary check waiting for me every two weeks, that the company is paying for my group life insurance, that my family's health insurance is also being paid, that there's a little money in the bank for the kids' college education, and that when I get too old to work there will be some retirement benefits. I need the security of a full-time job."

You know what's happened to him since he first said that? He's been on *four* magazines—and every one of them has folded under him. Yet whenever I run into him, he still asks me, "How can you face all the uncertainty of free-lancing?"

Then Rosenfeld offers his own answer:

I know that I'm working in a changing field, and at times that can be disturbing. But I have this conviction—which may not be entirely logical—that things are always going to work out. I believed that as a young free-lancer, and I still believe that now.

Maybe a free-lancer has to be a special type of person. I don't mind living with uncertainty.

KEEPING RECORDS

In any free-lancing you do—full-time or part-time—it is important to keep accurate records.

Some free-lancers maintain elaborate journals in which they record every detail about their work. For most a simple card file will be sufficient.

You might wish to prepare a separate card for each article you write. For example,

Title: "How to Help Your Child Study"
Memo Written: April 3–5, 1991

Memo Submitted to:	Date Submitted:	Response:
McCall's	4/6/91	Rejected 4/21/91
Redbook	4/25/91	Rejected 5/15/91
Ladies' Home Journal	5/23/91	Rejected 6/9/91
		(Handwritten note)
Memo Revised:	6/18/91	
Revised Memo		
Submitted to:		
Parents	6/19/91	Accepted—on spec.
		Suggested length:
		2,500 words

On the back of the same card or in a separate file, you should list all of the expenses you have incurred in writing that specific article. These would include paper, copying costs, purchase of magazines or books, travel expenses, entertainment expenses, telephone expenses, postage.

If the Internal Revenue Service (IRS) accepts your status as a free-lance writer, many of the direct costs involved in your writing will be deductible. After you have made some sales to magazines, you may also be allowed to deduct a reasonable amount for a room in your home if it is used exclusively for your writing.

The rules regarding acceptable deductions change periodically, so you should consult the latest publications from the IRS covering this subject.

WHAT ABOUT AGENTS?

Many beginning free-lancers are convinced that there is only one way to succeed in magazine writing: Find yourself an agent.

Many magazine editors disagree.

"We rarely deal with agents," said Hal Wingo, Assistant Managing Editor of *People*. "We prefer to deal directly with writers."

Roberta Ashley, Executive Editor of *Cosmopolitan*, said, "Agents are not interested in magazines. There's no money in it for them. I've never had an agent sit down with a writer and come up with satisfactory ideas for *Cosmo*."

A *Redbook* editor observed, "With the exception of about five really good agents, is it of value for a writer to have someone represent her in dealing with magazine editors? I would say no. Many agents just take your material and put it in a blue folder and send it around. In a few cases they might be able to get the writer a few more dollars for an article, but they don't even do that very often."

Not all writers agree with these editors. Roger Rapoport sold his first pieces to several major magazines on his own but has been represented by the same literary agent for years.

Rapoport had pieces published in *The New Republic, Look, McCall's, The Atlantic,* and *Harper's* while still an undergraduate—a remarkable record that would seem to indicate that he didn't need much help.

As a result of the publication of that series of articles, Rapoport suddenly began receiving offers, including one to write a newspaper column and another for a book. On the recommendation of one of the magazine editors he had written for, he wrote to the Sterling Lord Agency.

He became a client, "and in a very short time the agency made a lot of contacts for me," Rapoport said. "They worked out a book contract, and they found a lot of magazines for me to write for regularly. I am free to offer ideas directly to magazines, and do that often, but I know the agency is also watching out for possibilities. They handle the negotiations over money and all the business details."

During your early years as a free-lancer, you will *probably* have to handle your own negotiations with editors. Later you will find the services of an agent valuable when you begin writing books, plays, television scripts, or film scripts.

A WORD OF CAUTION

Some literary agents advertise in writers' magazines, and their promises can be tempting to writers who have been discouraged by a series of rejections:

> Publish Now!
> Sell Your Manuscript!
> Make Money Writing
> Former Editor and Pulitzer Prize juror will critique and change your rough copy into
>   publishable work . . .

Tucked away in the copy for such ads you may find mention of the fee ("$12 minimum" . . . "$5 first $1,000, then less" . . . "reading fee—$20.").

Years ago Paul R. Reynolds, a very successful and highly respected literary agent, denounced those who charge writers a "reading fee" or "handling fee" or "collaboration fee" as "predatory sharks."

Many of these "so-called agents" rarely sell an article or book, Reynolds observed, and instead make their living from the fees they charge unpublished writers. (An ethical agent shares in the income he or she helps the writer to make. Ordinarily the agent receives 10 percent of the payments made for the writer's work.)

Before signing with any agent who advertises his or her services, I would ask these questions:

Do you charge a fee to read manuscripts?
How many of your clients have had work published within the past two years?
Could you name several of your most successful clients and tell me where I could find their published articles?

Later you can think about agents. Today it would be better to concentrate on coming up with a striking article idea and presenting it so effectively that an editor cannot say no.

When you have gained some success on your own, you can obtain a list of established agents by writing to the Society of Author's Representatives, 39½ Washington Square South, New York, N.Y. 10012. The society will send you a copy of "The Literary Agent," which offers some useful general information and a list of recognized agents. (As always, you should include a self-addressed, stamped envelope.)

15

Joining a Magazine Staff

What is your chance of finding a magazine staff job shortly after graduation? What is the best approach to a career in this field? An examination of the backgrounds of some current editors offers answers to these questions.

Teresa Gibbs of Pamplico, South Carolina, had just completed her undergraduate work at the University of South Carolina when she applied for a staff job at *Reader's Digest*.

Gibbs knew none of the editors at the *Digest,* so she sent her letter of application directly to editor-in-chief Edward T. Thompson. She began with a simple, direct statement about her attitude toward the magazine itself:

Dear Mr. Thompson,
    I have read and enjoyed *Reader's Digest* since my early teenage years. In a sense, the *Digest* and I grew up together—it has always been around my home.

She then emphasized her focus on magazines during her years at the university:

I have recently graduated from the College of Journalism at the University of South Carolina. During my three years in the accelerated program, I concentrated on many areas of magazine production.
    I was fortunate in having William Emerson, a former editor-in-chief of *The Saturday Evening Post* and *Newsweek* bureau chief in Atlanta, as my magazine writing instructor. His class was truly a reality course—complete with deadline

pressure, lengthy writing assignments and editing projects. He is also my advisor and suggested that I contact you.

On the design side of the spectrum, I had a course in magazine art direction under Kay Howie Jackson, the most successful art director in the state. In this class, I learned about magazine graphics in general and various layout techniques.

In four more brief paragraphs, Gibbs gave additional details about her background, including her experience in covering the state house for a South Carolina newspaper during her university years.

Thompson was impressed by the letter and the accompanying resume, and passed them along to a *Digest* managing editor, who contacted Gibbs. Before she was interviewed, Gibbs was asked to complete a series of written tests that the editors had devised to help determine whether applicants have the particular abilities required at the *Digest*.

First she was asked to critique the *Digest's* editorial and graphic content. Then she was to read major articles in various magazines, comment on the subjects covered, and indicate whether or not the articles were suitable for condensation in the *Digest*. If they were, Gibbs was instructed to condense them. Finally, she was asked to edit and condense an article that was actually scheduled for future publication in the magazine.

Gibbs passed the tests and was invited to visit the *Digest* to be interviewed by its editors. She did and within a few months after her graduation from the University of South Carolina, she joined the editorial staff in New York.

This direct approach to the editor of a national magazine by someone without previous experience on a magazine staff might fail nine times out of ten. But because it does succeed occasionally, it is worth trying. Three graduates of one of my classes in magazine editing at the University of Nevada–Reno found staff jobs on small magazines by approaching the editors a week or two after being graduated and expressing strong interest in working on those particular publications. One was hired as an assistant editor, quickly demonstrated her ability as a writer, copy editor, and layout artist, and then succeeded to the editorship a few weeks later when the editor who had hired her decided to move on.

PATHS LEADING TO MAGAZINE JOBS

There is a recognized pattern in the careers of many newspaper editors. Many of them start early carrying copy or working as cub reporters, and then move slowly onward and upward because they have demonstrated both ability and interest in editing and administration. The path leading to editorial positions on magazines is less visible.

Once in a great while a magazine will announce an opening publicly, through want ads in newspapers or *Editor & Publisher*. This is usually a last resort, however. Unfortunately, when such an ad appears the number of applicants is likely to be very large, and your chances of even getting an interview are reduced because the respondents will ordinarily include some people with previous magazine experience.

Other ways to find your first job in magazines include the following:

Beginning as an intern
Beginning as a free-lance contributor
Beginning as a very junior editor
Starting your own magazine

The variety of approaches to magazine staff jobs may best be illustrated by citing a few brief case histories.

Starting as a Summer Intern

Patricia Flood had just completed her undergraduate work at Smith and planned to go on to another university for graduate work in history the following September. She heard about a summer internship at *American Heritage,* applied, and was accepted.

Because the magazine had a very small staff, she was soon assigned to picture research, and then began writing captions for the pictures she had located. Then she began sending along suggestions for articles to the magazine's editors.

The summer ended and Flood was invited to stay on. After a few years at *American Heritage,* she met an editor at *Esquire* who was impressed by her work. When *Esquire* needed a new editor, he suggested that she apply. She joined the staff there in 1979, and in 1981 she was named executive editor.

Starting as a Reporter

"Many of our roving editors started on newspapers," said John M. Allen, former vice president of *Reader's Digest.* "That's where they learned how to do the necessary research and the importance of clarity and simplicity in writing."

John G. Stewart worked briefly for United Press before he became an editor at *This Week,* then *The New York Times Magazine,* and then helped found a special-interest magazine, *Africa Update.*

The shift from newspaper reporting to magazine editing usually occurs fairly early in most careers. Many magazine editors have had a few months or a few years of reporting or copyediting for newspapers, but relatively few have had long periods on papers before moving over to magazines. Some basic differences exist between the newspaper story or feature and the magazine article, and those who are very skillful in writing or editing for a daily publication may not do as well on a weekly or monthly magazine. The reverse is also true: Some very good magazine writers and editors would find the pace of daily journalism too demanding.

Starting as a Free-Lancer

Some writers start as free-lancers and remain free-lancers all their lives because they wish to escape the restrictions they see in any office job.

Others find editorial jobs attractive and begin to concentrate early in their careers on the two or three or four magazines where they would like to work.

Often a magazine's entertainment editor (who covers movies and television and occasionally plays) begins his or her career as a free-lance contributor. This may also be true of the medical editor and the sports editor on some magazines.

Not all free-lancers who join magazine staffs are that specialized. Some range widely in their choice of subjects, but they impress editors by their clear understanding of the needs of the magazines they write for.

Leonard Gross free-lanced for several years before joining the staff of *Look*. He had previously worked on newspapers and on the staff of another magazine, but the editors were most impressed by his unusual skill as a writer, his imagination, his energy, and his understanding of the kind of article that would appeal to the readers of *Look*. He later covered Latin America and Europe for the magazine.

Since *Look* folded, Gross has concentrated on books and has attracted the same wide readership there as he did during the years devoted chiefly to magazine writing.

Starting Your Own Magazine

Four of the most successful magazines of the twentieth century were founded by young editors with limited experience and very little money, but with clear ideas of the kinds of publications they wished to establish.

The stories of the founders of *Reader's Digest, Time, The New Yorker*, and *Playboy* will be found in several books available in most university libraries. If the idea of starting your own magazine appeals to you, you might want to study the experiences of these young founders: DeWitt and Lila Wallace (*Reader's Digest*), Henry Luce and Briton Hadden (*Time*), Harold Ross (*The New Yorker*), and Hugh Hefner (*Playboy*). This will give you some idea of both the risks and the possible rewards.

One striking fact about these four magazines is the failure of experienced publishers to recognize the possibility that they would succeed. Without exception, established publishers attempted to discourage the founders, absolutely certain that they were wasting both their time and their money.

It is no longer possible to begin a new magazine with $5,000 (the amount required to launch *Reader's Digest* in 1922), and the risks in this field are very high. About 300 new magazines are started in the United States each year, and fewer than 30 survive into a second year.

There are six obvious requirements for success:

A fresh idea—a conception of a magazine that differs sharply from those already being published
A strong appeal to an identifiable group of readers
A strong appeal to a sufficiently large group of advertisers who wish to reach that group of readers
An editor with a clear grasp of who these readers are and what will interest them
A business manager who understands all the details of magazine production and distribution
Adequate capital

Although failures outnumber successes by about nine to one, there have been some other notable triumphs in this field since World War II: *New York, People, Working*

Woman, and many other magazines, including some small, special-interest publications that have attracted loyal audiences and a sufficient number of regular advertisers.

If you have an idea for a specialized magazine that would have very strong appeal to 75,000 or 100,000 readers, or a general magazine that would attract at least a million readers, you might take a close look at *The Magazine,* a book written by Leonard Mogel (Globe Pequot) publisher of *National Lampoon* and former publisher of *Signature* magazine. Mogel offers much useful advice to anyone who is thinking of starting a magazine.

In founding a new magazine, you would be taking a major gamble. But so were young DeWitt and Lila Wallace.

Getting from Here to There

Because magazine careers begin in so many different ways, students are sometimes puzzled about the best way to begin the search for staff jobs.

You might want to consider two possible approaches:

First Approach

Choose two or three specific magazines you would like to work for.

Study those magazines thoroughly, issue after issue.

Begin submitting ideas to the editors of those magazines on a regular basis—ideally at least one idea every three weeks. Address your article memos to the same editor, and submit only those ideas that seem exactly right for the magazine.

Once one of the magazines indicates that it is receptive to your ideas, concentrate on that magazine exclusively for a period of time.

After the magazine has accepted three or four of your submissions, mention your strong interest in joining the staff as either a contract writer, a staff writer, or a junior editor. (A contract writer submits articles to a magazine on a regular basis and may be offered an annual guaranteed income if his or her work is especially valuable to the publication.)

Request an interview with the editors and emphasize your strong interest in a full-time arrangement with the magazine.

Whether this approach works or not depends on many factors. There may be no staff jobs open at the time of your interview—but situations change, and a reasonable persistence could lead to a staff job months—or even years—later. An editor who is especially impressed by your ability might also recommend you to another magazine that is looking for a new staff writer or editor.

Second Approach

Apply for *any* entry-level job on the staff of any magazine. At this stage, indicate your willingness to work as a mail clerk, as a manuscript typist, as a proofreader, as a secretary, or as a junior researcher.

Once you are in that job, volunteer to help some overworked member of the staff. Watch especially for any chance to write a few captions, to carry out some research, or to read proofs.

Try to come up with strong article ideas regularly. If the first three ideas are turned down, find out why, and then come up with a fourth. Here again, intelligent persistence is important.

Be very alert to any chance to move up, even a notch. Recognize that if you are an extremely efficient mailroom clerk or secretary and seem contented with your lot, you might remain in that position indefinitely. Without neglecting the job you have, look around for a more demanding one.

Keep writing, either for the magazine you are working for or for other publications. While watching for possible editorial openings on your own magazine, also observe what is happening on other magazines. Moving from one magazine to another is characteristic of many successful magazine careers. Remaining too long in a subordinate job on the first magazine you join may turn out to be a mistake.

Many magazine staff writers and editors have created their own careers. If you read the autobiography of Herbert Mayes, one of the most successful twentieth-century editors, you will realize that nothing but his own determination led him to the editorships of *Good Housekeeping, Cosmopolitan,* and *McCall's.*

If you feel that you would like magazine staff work more than any alternative career, you should set out singlemindedly to achieve that objective.

WHAT DO STAFF MEMBERS DO?

The entry-level jobs on magazines may require little explanation. A mailroom clerk or a manuscript typist ordinarily concentrates on jobs as routine and limited as those carried out by mail clerks and typists at IBM, although the surroundings are often livelier on magazines.

If you have a chance to become secretary to a magazine editor, you should consider this an unusual opportunity.

Secretaries in an editorial office of a magazine learn as much (or as little) as they wish to learn about editing. The secretary opens the mail and decides what is urgent, what is important, and what is routine. When the telephone rings, a secretary often decides which calls must go through to the editor immediately and which can be rerouted or delayed to avoid interrupting the editor's urgent current work. The secretary takes dictation, and here can absorb a great deal by noticing the suggestions the editor makes to a writer about the development of an article or the revisions needed in a manuscript.

Some secretaries find this work satisfying and remain in the same job for 40 years. Others see this as the ideal introductory job, giving them a clear idea of the varied possibilities on a magazine staff.

If you are a very good secretary but want to be something more than that, you should indicate that after a reasonable time. Many editors—not all—will recognize your ambitions and will encourage you to move on to a job as a researcher or as a junior editor.

A researcher often works in gathering information that will be used by staff writers, and also checks every word in the manuscripts of both staff writers and free-lancers. Researchers read articles with great suspicion, assuming that any name might be misspelled, any date misstated, any quote distorted. The researcher's job is to go back to original sources to double-check every statement.

Although researching is an essential and often an absorbing job, most people who go to work for magazines have as their goal either staff-writing or editing. It may be worth examining these positions.

THE LIFE OF A STAFF WRITER

A staff writer enjoys many of the benefits that attract people to free-lancing but faces little of the financial uncertainty that makes free-lancing hazardous.

Staff writers may earn as little as $15,000 (on a small magazine) or as much as $50,000 (on a *few* national magazines). They also ordinarily receive the same benefits that are available to other editorial employees (health insurance, disability insurance, paid vacations, company pensions).

Staff writers are paid to write, and the magazine offers them far more assistance than most free-lancers can afford. Writers are provided with an office, a word processor, unlimited use of a telephone, and in many cases secretarial services.

If the writer has to fly to London or Rio or Hong Kong for a story, a secretary arranges for the tickets and makes reservations at hotels the writer probably couldn't afford if he or she were paying for the room. When telephoning a senator's office or a television star's home, the writer is often treated with deference because the magazine he or she is writing for is important to people who depend on publicity.

Staff writers can drop by the offices of the editors to discuss their story ideas and sometimes can get quick approval if the ideas they suggest are strong and perishable. If the editors are unenthusiastic about the writer's current batch of ideas, they may suggest some alternatives.

The staff writer's workload will vary from magazine to magazine. Many staff writers on news magazines may be expected to write two or three stories a week. On some other publications (such as *National Geographic*), a staff writer may spend weeks or even months on a major project, especially one requiring extensive travel.

For many who have endured the uncertainties of free-lancing, staff-writing sounds ideal. Yet periodically some very successful staff writers sacrifice the salary and the secretary and the expense account and the health insurance and the company pension plan to return to free-lancing. Why?

Some become bored by the routine they discover in their staff-writing jobs. If you are working for *Time,* for example, you are likely to spend most of your time in an office tapping away at stories in a single area: national affairs, or foreign news, or sports, or business, or religion. These are very broad areas, but after 10 years you could begin to feel that you were repeating yourself.

On other magazines, staff writers may become specialists in medicine or travel or science or entertainment, and will then be expected to come up with fresh ideas for articles in those fields month after month.

For many writers, such assignments are completely satisfactory. For others any form of repetition becomes boring, and working for a single magazine seems too restrictive. These writers want to write an article for *McCall's* one month, conduct an interview for *Playboy* the next, and then work on an essay for *The Atlantic* or a piece for *The Nation.* They want to regain the freedom they remember from their free-lance days.

Others may wish to experiment with a play or a television series, or to take time off to complete a novel.

This reaction is most common among writers who find themselves working on articles that are of more interest to their editors than to themselves. Whereas some staff writers have considerable freedom in selecting the specific stories they wish to write, others do not. If those decisions are being made by editors, a staff writer may begin to feel that he or she is just a highly paid technician, using carefully developed skills in a way that may be satisfactory to the magazine but not to the writer. This is compounded when writers find themselves in basic disagreement with their magazine's editorial viewpoint.

If you make a strong enough impression on an editor to be offered a staff-writing job, you should try it for at least a few months. You will then discover whether the benefits—assured income, travel expenses, secretarial help, assistance from researchers, easy access to editors—compensate you for some loss of freedom.

THE LIFE OF AN EDITOR

The entry-level job on many editorial staffs usually involves reading unsolicited article memos and query letters.

The first reader (now usually called "assistant to the editors") reads hundreds of letters and manuscripts week after week, searching for the few that are worth sending along to other editors for further consideration. One editorial assistant said, "It's like shucking a thousand oysters, hoping that one of them contains a pearl."

If you can go back to that search each day without becoming bored, this examination of unsolicited mail can be very revealing. You will begin to see what makes those occasional unheralded queries catch your attention. You will also learn a great deal by observing the reactions of experienced editors to the ideas you send along for further consideration.

It is very easy to get stuck in your first magazine job if you are both conscientious and undemanding. But after a few months—certainly no more than a year or two—you should look for a chance to prove that you are a potential editor, not just a reader.

When you move from first reader to assistant editor, you can begin to demonstrate the qualities that are of major importance in magazine editing. These include:

1. Ability to recognize promising article ideas. Much of any editor's life is spent in separating the best article ideas from those which are just fairly good. (Very weak ideas often have obvious flaws that are easy to detect. It is the idea that is just all right, but not really outstanding, that is more likely to slip past an inexperienced editor. And magazines need *exceptional* ideas.)

2. Ability to analyze. An editor should see quickly what improvements are needed in a manuscript, and how those improvements can be achieved. Vague directions to a writer about possible changes are of little value, can waste the writer's time, and lead to final rejection of a promising article idea.

3. Ability to work with writers. A certain amount of diplomatic skill is needed when dealing with writers. Some changes—minor or major—are required in many articles. Occasionally a magazine will have to ask a writer to cut a well-written 3,500-word article to 2,000 words because of the limited space available. It is sometimes necessary to persuade (rather than force) a famous writer to cut a favorite passage or to revise a lead. An editor who lacks empathy for writers and skill in dealing with them will probably have limited success.

4. A visual imagination. Most editors must have some understanding of the importance of illustrations in modern magazines. Although you would have the services of an art director and an art department on any major magazine, you would ordinarily be expected to contribute ideas and to react to layout designs.

5. Ability to "see" an issue that is taking shape. While some magazines have fairly static organization of contents issue after issue, others do not. It is important that you develop the ability to visualize the best way of presenting articles in an issue. What would be the strongest lead? Which articles should be given dramatic display? Should a service article be trimmed and presented in a single page? Although it is sometimes possible to experiment with the makeup of an issue, a very good editor can put material together in the most effective order without waiting to see the article layouts.

6. Ability to work with other staff members. Magazine editing requires close collaboration. An editor who cannot work harmoniously with staff writers, photographers, layout artists, researchers, fellow editors, circulation directors, advertising sales reps, and dozens of other specialists is unlikely to move into a higher editorial post.

There are some other obvious requirements: intelligence, wide background knowledge, appreciation of talent, a feeling for style, curiosity, and imagination.

An editor who possesses or develops all these qualities is probably destined to rise from assistant editor to associate editor to senior editor to assistant managing editor. (The titles differ on different magazines.) He or she might end up as managing editor, editor, executive director, or editor-in-chief.

16

Advice from Eight Editors

Editors of a wide range of national magazines offer specific suggestions to beginning free-lance writers and describe the kinds of articles that are most likely to interest them.

I asked the editors of eight national magazines these questions:

Do beginning free-lancers have a chance of selling articles to you?
If that is a possibility, what kind of article should a writer try for your magazine?
Are there some articles you publish that only staff writers or experienced free-lancers should attempt?
What general advice would you offer to beginning free-lancers? What are the most common errors made by inexperienced magazine writers in approaching you?

Each of the eight editors whose suggestions are offered here tried to give advice that would be as applicable in 1999 as in 1992. Of course, editors change and magazines change, and it is essential that you study recent issues of any magazine before trying to write for it. But the following comments will remind you that it is possible for you to achieve publication in a wide range of magazines if your approach is imaginative, professional, and persistent.

ROBERTA ANNE MYERS
ARTICLES EDITOR
SEVENTEEN

If you're going to write for *Seventeen,* you must learn to think like a teenager.

For example, you must keep in mind that the teenager's calendar is different from the one most of us follow. August means last days at the beach. September is back to school, or on to college. December is Christmas parties. April or May is prom time, and June is graduation. Then it's back to the beach, or summer internships, or jobs.

If you're writing seasonal pieces for *Seventeen,* you should anticipate those dates on the teenage calendar. We have a three-month lead time for our issues, and we need some time to edit articles and arrange for illustrations. That means that a piece about getting a great summer job planned for our May issue should be in our office in January. We can move more quickly when that is essential, but generally we prefer to see pieces at least four or five months before the ideal publication date.

Before you offer an idea to *Seventeen,* I would urge you to buy at least three copies and read each of them thoroughly and analytically. Every major article you see in those issues was written by a free-lancer. We do use staff writers for our fashion and beauty pieces, but we depend heavily on free-lancers for a major portion of every issue.

The best way for a beginning free-lancer to get a start here is to take a close look at our shorter features—especially the "Talk" pieces. As you'll see, most of these run about 150 to 200 words, and we pay approximately $1 a word for them. As good examples of the kind of thing we particularly like in these departments, you might read "Going for Broke" in the June, 1991, issue, and "Trashy Behavior" in the July, 1991, issue. Those were written by two free-lance writers who keep up with contemporary issues and understand *Seventeen*'s readers.

For longer articles, two that might serve as models for a free-lancer who has not previously written for us are "Sex and the Prom" by Judith Newman (May, 1991) and "Ads in Movies" by Nina Killham (August, 1991). These worked out well for us because they both explored an aspect of teenagers' lives in a way that was neither condescending nor preachy.

Incidentally, we get a lot of article proposals from people who are ready to tell us, "Teenagers are having sex." That's true, but the next question is, What do these writers have to tell us that's new? Judith Newman selected an angle for dealing with that subject that would interest our readers and offer them useful advice.

Once you have settled on an idea that seems right for us, we prefer that you send us a one-page query letter that sketches it out. It's not necessary to tell us how you plan to structure it, paragraph by paragraph. We read those query letters closely, and we're looking both at the idea itself and some sign of liveliness in the writing.

It's also good to send along clips of anything you've published. This gives us some idea of your writing skill, and it tells us that you've worked with an editor before and understand what is involved in preparing a piece for publication.

It's almost always a waste of time to send us a complete manuscript. We prefer to work with the writer to shape the piece to the needs of our magazine. (One of the rare exceptions would be a complete quiz—for example, "How Much Do You Know about Valentine's Day?".)

When we feel enthusiastic about an idea and have confidence in the writer's ability, we usually discuss the article possibility first by telephone, and then offer the writer a contract. We also send the writer a detailed assignment letter. We do not try to tell the writer *how* to write the piece or what structure to use, but we do want to have a good understanding of what the article will cover, and we suggest a word limit—say 1,500 to 2,000 words for a major piece.

Once we receive the manuscript, we will be ready to go through many revisions with the writer if we think there is something there. When the article is accepted, our payments range from $1 to $2 a word. (The higher rates go to established writers who deal with more complex material.) If the piece shows no promise at all of working out (usually after a second try), we pay the writer a kill fee—25 percent of the agreed-on price. About 75 percent of the pieces for which we offer contracts are accepted and published.

When you are preparing to write for *Seventeen*, I would *emphasize* the importance of examining the three most recent issues. But along with your own close reading of those issues, this list of some broad classifications and titles of some recent pieces might give you an idea of the kind of articles we are looking for:

> Relationships: "How a Guy Knows When He Is in Love," by Steve Friedman (October, 1991)
> Current Events: "We Are the World," by River Phoenix (April, 1990)
> School Issues: "Reality Check" (Careers)—(August, 1991)
> Getting Ready for College: Special College Section (September, 1991)

Of course, you don't have to confine yourself to ideas that fit neatly into these categories. Again my advice would be to shift your mind to about five months ahead of the date on which you're reading this—and think about what's on a teenager's mind.

* * *

PHILIP BARRY OSBORNE
ASSISTANT MANAGING EDITOR
READER'S DIGEST

The only kind of writing E. B. White said he could accomplish with minimum effort was about the small things in his day. In many ways this also produces some of our best writing, because it touches readers right where they live.

Consider Martha Sweeney, whose first article was published in *Reader's Digest*. Not long ago, Martha was in a coin laundry outside her hometown of Stonewall, Texas, when half a dozen young motorcyclists roared up to a gas station next door. They were all a boisterous, rough-looking lot, and one of them—younger than the others, no more than 17—was the loudest and roughest-acting of the bunch. Then something about this older woman observing him, something about this small, rural town in which he found himself—something caused the boy to hesitate. After his friends had gassed up their cycles, he told them his starter was on the blink and to go on without him. He said he would catch up. After the others went roaring off, the boy brought some dirty clothes into the laundry and glanced at Martha.

"His shoulders sagged as if he were terribly weary," Martha later wrote. "Dust and grease and sweat stained his shirt and jeans. A beginning beard faintly shadowed his chin and lean cheeks. He turned, and briefly our eyes met. Emotion flickered across his face— doubt, longing, pain?"

The boy ran his clothes through the washer and dryer, and then disappeared into the men's room. When he emerged ten minutes later, he was wearing clean pants and shirt, and he had shaved his scraggly beard, scrubbed his hands and face, and combed his hair. He grinned in Martha's direction and, jumping on his motorcycle, zoomed away. Not following the others, but going back the way he had come.

This type of writing, an inspirational narrative, falls into the broad category we call art-of-living. Also in this category are inspirational articles on faith and religion, and self-help articles. As a group, art-of-living articles are a staple of general interest magazines— and represent the widest open market for new writers.

All it takes to be an art-of-living writer is uncovering some uncommon experience or concern that touches all of our lives and emotions in a special way—and the discipline to get it down on paper.

You don't have to be a best-selling poet or author to write such a piece for us. All of us have these everyday experiences, if we just learn to turn on our mental Geiger counters.

The secret of these articles is their personal immediacy. Self-help articles help us deal with the world around us by showing us how to improve ourselves and grow in new ways and directions. Inspirational articles deal more with our inner world of personal feelings; this kind of writing tends to surprise us with the familiar, revealing old, some-times forgotten truths in a fresh, vivid way. It's been said that the obvious is that which is never seen until someone expresses it simply. And so it is with inspirational articles. The writer must startle us with what we often know and, in Stendhal's words, be "a mirror walking along the main road"—a "life watcher."

If you would like to experiment with the art-of-living article, let me offer five suggestions:

1. Guard against overwriting. There's a natural tendency among art-of-living writers to get too exquisite and ornamental in their prose. These writers ignore the fact that the best art-of-living pieces deal with the small concerns and verities of life—and that you don't need fancy words for them. So think more in terms of creating a small, delicate watercolor rather than a giant oil painting.

2. Steep yourself in what you're writing about. Many writers mistakenly feel that the simple themes of art-of-living require only simple, superficial research. Trying to write like that is like trying to go swimming without getting wet. If you're writing a narrative or essay about the power of faith, read widely on this experience. That will give your writing depth and a tone of authority.

Tone is basically your attitude toward your material—and toward your audience. Our pet peeve at *Reader's Digest* is the art-of-living writer who scants on research simply because he or she feels superior to the subject and the reader. That always filters through the tone of the writing.

3. Pinpoint your lesson or message. Why do so many writers neglect this fundamental requirement of every art-of-living article? Why are they content to wander through the garden and sniff every flower—without ever picking one?

An editor of *Reader's Digest* tells the following story about one of the magazine's top writers. The writer offered us an inspirational narrative about a man whose heart had stopped eight times during a protracted medical crisis. Though most of the story elements were there, the article still lacked a message or theme or "takeaway," as we call it. So for days the writer stuck with the people he had been interviewing—until one afternoon, the patient's doctor told the writer that during the third day of massaging the man's heart, another doctor had said, "Why don't you let him go? He's ready to die. This is wrong to keep him going."

Suddenly, the writer had the lesson or message for his article. "For now," as the editor relates the story, "a legitimate conflict could be focused between the doctor who wanted to save his patient and the other, faceless doctors (and maybe all of us readers, as well) who were saying, 'Let the poor guy die.' In the end, the patient could say, as he did say, 'I'm so glad he didn't let me go.' And there you've got it. Without some lesson, a piece becomes impenetrable—a sphinx without a riddle."

4. Sharpen your eye for the telling anecdote. Because art-of-living articles are about people, you need plenty of "people" anecdotes. That sounds painfully obvious. Yet art-of-living writers often skimp on anecdotes.

Every anecdote should almost stand by itself as a good story. It should be affecting, educating, and illuminating. By studying art-of-living pieces in recent issues of *Reader's Digest,* you will see how important this element is.

5. Don't be afraid of ghosting. Art-of-living articles tend to work best as first-person accounts, especially inspirational narratives. Yet many art-of-living writers are leery about writing under someone else's name. They shouldn't be.

John Allen, a former assistant managing editor at *Reader's Digest,* explains it well: "I've heard people speak against ghosting and argue the morality of it. Frankly, I disagree. I just feel there are so many experts out there: psychiatrists, doctors, ministers, people who have some very good ideas but who can't write a line. If you can help them communicate their value, you're doing everybody a favor, including yourself. So search out that person who has the authority, the expertise, the story, the art-of-living message. He or she has done all the work and has lived it; that person's gone through school, gotten the credentials. No, don't eschew the ghosting of an article."

Whether you're ghosting an article, doing your own first-person piece, or writing a straight, journalistic third-person story, there's a common vein we want to see running through every one of our articles. We want pieces that are memorable, quotable, and of lasting—rather than passing—interest. We want stories that touch the hearts and minds of every one of our readers—stories that affect them, that move them, that change them for the better. Above all, stories that make us all more deeply aware of the world around us, and the world within. In short, we want *impact*.

A few years ago, we ran an article called "Rescue on the Freeway." This was the story of a California man who had saved the lives of two women after others had ignored them as they lay injured on a busy freeway. Soon after reading the article, James Oostyke, a young branch bank manager in Ada, Michigan, was driving to work when he spotted two men clinging to a floundering boat in the Thornapple River. Though the fishermen were clearly in trouble, other cars were speeding past without stopping.

"Suddenly," Oostyke wrote us, "the story of the freeway rescue flashed through my mind, and I knew that I, too, had to become involved." He stopped, removed some of his clothes, and—though not a particularly good swimmer—thrashed out to the boat and dragged the two men back to shore.

With *Reader's Digest,* this kind of impact is felt not just in this country, but around the world. With our start-up of Russian and Hungarian editions in 1991, we now have 41 editions in 17 languages and more than 100 million readers.

The magazine's global impact was nowhere more evident than when we published an original article called "The Murder of Robbie Wayne, Age Six." This was the true, horrifying tale of a victim of child abuse—a little boy who was starved, beaten, tortured, and finally murdered by his 245-pound stepfather. This article won a National Magazine Award. Yet something we prize even more was the incredible worldwide reaction we received.

One of our Asian editions received a sympathy card signed by 30 Pakistanis and filled with personal messages from all of them. Asking that the card be placed on Robbie's grave, they wrote that they had observed two-minute silences for the boy ten times on different occasions and in different places. This touched us, as it would touch anyone. Thousands of miles away from a series of sordid events, a group of Pakistanis pray for a child they've never seen and never will. That's the kind of impact we want for the magazine—and for the writers we publish.

* * *

HAL WINGO
ASSISTANT MANAGING EDITOR
PEOPLE

As a free-lancer, you would have your best chance at *People* by offering us a suggestion about someone we haven't heard of—an unknown. Many writers don't realize that, because they haven't taken the time to analyze several complete issues of the magazine—they've just looked at the covers.

Approximately 60 percent of an issue is given over to noncelebrities. Sometimes it is 70 percent.

We give a lot of space to teachers, doctors, clerics, individuals who have achieved something or who are involved in some dramatic situation. Of course, these can't be just local achievers. The people must be unusual enough to interest readers across the country.

We are always receptive to stories about doctors who have pioneered something, for instance, or those who have tried new techniques. Or you can try us with something as obvious as doctors whose patients are celebrities. (Sometimes I think we've done every dentist and orthodontist in California.)

Of course, there should be a timeliness to the piece—some kind of news peg. We look for that in every article we publish.

What you should avoid is offering us *obvious* ideas. Too many free-lancers write us, "I really think you should have a story on Barbra Streisand and I would like to do that for you." Sooner or later, of course, we will have a story on Barbra Streisand—but it must be a *story,* and since she is a highly visible public figure the editors are likely to recognize the possibility rather quickly and the story will probably be in the works before a free-lancer suggests it. But those who had written earlier think they have a claim on Barbra. Some of them will write and ask, "How dare you take my idea?"

When you do have a good idea, please don't try to tell us about it over the telephone. For one thing, I'm on the phone many times each day, talking to our own correspondents and stringers across the country. I can't avoid those calls, and that doesn't leave me much time to accept calls that are unessential.

Besides, telephoning is an inefficient way to present ideas to *People,* as I suspect it is to most magazines. I need something to show to editors in several departments. An idea might be worth considering for three or four different sections of the magazine. If the writer doesn't send me something I can send around to department editors, I'm going to have to type it up myself—and I just don't have time to do that.

I don't think I've ever given anyone an assignment on the basis of a telephone call alone. Even if the proposal is something exceptional, I would still say, "That really sounds good. Now send me a letter right away, so I'll have the details in writing."

There could always be an exception, I suppose. If someone called me this morning and said, "I'm standing about 50 feet from a falling bridge, and one man is holding it up with his bare arms," I'd probably say, "Grab a photographer and do something for us." And if Paul Newman were the man holding up the bridge, wow!

The best possible way to approach us is with a brief query letter. And I emphasize brief. No more than four paragraphs—and three would be even better.

All the writer has to tell us is this: "Here's the person I want to do a story about. Here's what I have to say about him. Here's my access to this person." (Incidentally, when a writer says, "This person I want to write about is a close personal friend," that is usually the kiss of death for that assignment. We're looking for objective reporting, not a series of biased remarks about someone.)

If the writer has some particular qualifications—has written for newspapers or other magazines, for example—he or she should mention that in a sentence or two.

Once we see that a story has possibilities for us—because it is bizarre, perhaps, or funny, or tragic, but in any case is a story the rest of us can relate to—we generally buy a file from the free-lancer. It should be as well-written as possible, but ordinarily we do not expect it to be ready to rush into print. It should be packed with information, and it should have a beginning, a middle, and an end. If the idea is going to be developed into a two- or three-page piece, as many as three or four editors could be involved in writing, rewriting, and editing it. What we are buying is information—lots of information—presented as clearly as the writer can present it. Ordinarily we like to see about 2,000 or 2,500 tightly packed words, which gives us plenty of material to choose from. If necessary, we can go back to the writer for any additional details. But the free-lancers who have the strongest chance here are those who know how to ask probing questions. They are serving as field reporters for us.

Our payment for a two-page or three-page story would ordinarily be around $750. A cover story will usually bring the writer $850.

One last word to free-lancers: You should keep in mind that an editorial decision is a very subjective thing. Sometimes we're right, sometimes we're wrong. But somebody must make those decisions.

I'd hate to think that a negative decision here discouraged anybody from trying again—trying us and other magazines. That's why every writer who offers us an idea receives a personal note. I don't know whether we can keep that up indefinitely, but that's what we do now.

It's a way of saying, "Thank you for offering this." And we mean it. It's a tough life, being a free-lancer. And being receptive to ideas from all over keeps a magazine from becoming ingrown. *People* and all other magazines need that sense of openness.

* * *

ROBERTA ASHLEY
EXECUTIVE EDITOR
COSMOPOLITAN

If I were a free-lancer living in Iowa City, Iowa, and I wanted to write an article for *Cosmopolitan,* I would not just dash something off and rush it into the mail. I would know that anything written quickly and casually would be rejected just as quickly.

Before I thought of choosing an idea for the magazine, I would go to the library and find the six most recent issues. I would read them closely—every article in them—trying to get a real feeling of what the editors were looking for.

As a result of my study, I hope I would begin to recognize some obvious facts about *Cosmo.* I'd see that every article was chosen to appeal to young women—those 18 to 35 or so. I would notice that there were no feature articles chosen specifically to appeal to men.

By being very analytical, I might begin to observe that certain elements were present in most of the issues I read. I would see that there was often a medical piece, a man–woman piece, a straight emotional piece, a sex piece, and a profile.

I would also notice the lengths of the various articles. Some run around 2,500 words, I would realize, and as a beginning free-lancer I would begin by trying to come up with an idea that could be developed effectively in that shorter length.

After this study, I would begin writing down every article possibility that occurred to me. I would discard most of them, but I would do some research on the ones that seemed both fresh and provocative. (If I didn't feel genuinely enthusiastic about at least one of the ideas, I wouldn't waste my time by just going through the motions and sending off an article suggestion. I would wait until I had come up with an idea that seemed to be as good as any the magazine had ever published.)

Then I would write a letter (or an article memo) describing my proposed piece as vividly as possible. And I would keep it brief: I would recognize that two skillfully written paragraphs would be more effective than six or seven loosely written ones.

I would know there was something wrong with my idea if I had to go on for two or three pages to make it clear.

Then I would look at the masthead and pick an editor who seemed logical for the submission I had in mind. I would make a point of finding a *current* editor, which is simple enough, since the editors are listed in every issue. I would know of the common mistake made by many writers—addressing letters to editors who haven't been with the magazine for 15 years.

And I would double-check to make sure I had the editor's name and title right. I would realize that any editor might feel that a writer who cannot copy down her name and title correctly is going to have trouble writing 3,000 words.

I wouldn't send a batch of ideas at one time, but I might send two at once, or even three, if I thought they were very good.

In my letter I would say that I would be willing to write the piece on speculation if the magazine were interested. I would be taking a gamble, of course, but I would understand from the beginning that magazine writing is a gamble on both sides.

If the editors responded by expressing interest in my idea, I would pay close attention to any suggestions they offered. If they said the article should include several anecdotes, I would include several anecdotes. If they said I should quote at least three authorities in a medical piece, I would quote at least three authorities. If they suggested that I try to hold the story to 2,500 words, the manuscript they received would not be 3,500 words long or 4,000 words long. It would be very close to 2,500.

We are always looking for new writers simply because the established writers do move on. Many excellent writers are now concentrating on writing plays or film scripts or books. If an inexperienced writer offers us a story that I sense is from the heart, there's usually enough energy in that for us to encourage the writer to send us the piece on speculation. If it is 60 percent right, we will work with the writer to make it publishable. We do not casually discard a writer's work.

*   *   *

IAN LEDGERWOOD
EDITOR-AT-LARGE
MODERN MATURITY

We are looking for writers who understand our magazine and its audience. They must produce articles that will appeal to readers over 50 and present a positive image of aging. We are particularly interested in stories about very active people in our age group—not necessarily retired.

We have always published articles about personal finances and investment, but we are now emphasizing these subjects; they might be good areas for a free-lancer to consider. The stories should offer specific, practical advice to people who are planning their retirement or those who have already retired.

We also like human-interest articles. Many of these focus on well-known people in such fields as science, art, or education, but we are also receptive to articles about people who have accomplished a great deal but are not widely known.

For many years we limited our travel articles to places in the United States, but surveys have confirmed our belief that our readers travel widely in all parts of the world. Even those who don't travel like to read about other places. We've published articles on Mexico, Scotland, Ireland, Italy, Portugal, and Hawaii. Any place that might appeal to travelers 50 and older could be a possible subject for us. While we have our own travel editor, we do buy material from other writers.

We have a regular department that tells our readers how to keep well, but we also run additional health pieces, some of them written by free-lancers. These require thorough, careful research, and the writer should quote recognized experts in the field. It is also helpful if the writer has a special angle. For example, one of our recent health articles was entitled "Wrapping the Human Package." It took a look inside—and outside—the vast and complex network that is our skin.

We are sometimes receptive to how-to and craft articles, and we also like informational stories on science and technology. These should give a clear indication of the effects of new discoveries or developments on living conditions, both now and in the future.

A common error free-lancers make in approaching us is to offer us ideas about people who are too young. However, if the young people are doing something directly related to older people, we could be interested. For example, we published an article called "Adopt-a-Grandparent," which described a program in Santa Monica, California, that brings together people in their seventies and eighties with youngsters 12 through 17. Sixteen students participate in the program and receive school credit for the activity. It made a bright and lively four-color contribution to the magazine.

Because we are a national magazine, with a current circulation of about 22½ million, we would not be likely to publish a story about a purely local art show or something of that type. But we do feature articles about traveling exhibitions, or about long-term or permanent exhibits in cities that many people visit each year—Washington, D.C., or New York, or San Francisco.

I know some editors prefer that writers offering an idea send along no more than a paragraph or two. In approaching *Modern Maturity*, it is all right to present a couple of pages. We want to have a clear indication of just what your idea is.

While there is no set form to follow, I think it's a good idea to include a suggested lead paragraph. This gives us an indication of your writing style. Then you can go into some detail about your story, the sources of your information, and your previous published material.

Even after we have been intrigued by an article idea, we end up turning down about one article out of every four. Usually these are rejected because of poor writing or inadequate research. We do pay a kill fee in such cases—25 percent of the amount we would have paid if the article had been accepted.

But that means we do accept about three-fourths of the stories we've asked writers to complete for us, and we have recently increased our rates for the material we buy. For a major article (2,000 to 2,500 words), our payment is $2,000 to $4,000. For 500 to 750 words, we pay $1,000. And for short-shorts (150 words), we pay $400.

A point to remember: While our magazine is produced for people aged 50 and older, they do not consider themselves to be in a special group and they have the same interests and aspirations as the rest of the population. At *Modern Maturity,* we subscribe to this same philosophy.

* * *

TOM SHEALEY
MANAGING EDITOR
BACKPACKER

If I were a beginning free-lancer, I would start by concentrating on the shorter pieces that many magazines publish—some of them no more than 150 or 200 words. By coming up with an unusual idea, doing good research on it, and then writing it with some skill, you can prove your value to an editor before you attempt to convince him or her that you are ready to take on a major article.

Most magazines have these brief sections. You'll find them in publications such as *Omni,* and all up and down the scale. Some of these departments are written by staff writers, but if they're done by free-lancers this is usually the best place to break into a magazine.

At *Backpacker,* I'd suggest that an unknown writer begin by studying our "Footnotes" section, and then come up with something fresh and unusual for it. A recent example of a particularly good free-lance submission told about the destruction of California's Mono Lake (June, 1991). Another was about The Adirondack Council, fighting to preserve New York's mountain park (August, 1991). These free-lancers provided us with something that we might not have managed to find on our own.

A writer who begins instead by offering a major feature to *Backpacker* is going against heavy odds. It is very difficult for a free-lancer I've never dealt with before to sell us a major article. That doesn't mean it's impossible: During the past four years we have published maybe four major pieces written by relatively inexperienced free-lancers. They just came up with very good ideas, or very unusual angles on more traditional magazine ideas, and their query letters were lively enough to convince me that they'd be able to handle the assignments. One of the pieces was "Almost Killed by Galen Powell" by Ronald Sawyer (February, 1991). He obviously understood what our readers are hoping to find when they open a new issue, and he also handled the article with enough skill so there was no long struggle getting it into shape. I am always ready to go through some rewrites on a piece if that's necessary, but there is a learning curve in magazine writing, and a completely inexperienced writer can eat up more of my time than I can spare. This is basically a one-man operation when it comes to putting an issue together, and there are limits on the number of hours I can give to any single article.

I do wish beginners would spend more time studying *Backpacker* and other magazines they want to write for. I spend about an hour or an hour and a half each morning looking through my mail, and 95 percent of the query letters are automatic rejects.

It should be obvious to anyone who has seen even one issue of *Backpacker* that this is a magazine for active, self-propelled people who like to spend their free time in the wilderness. Yet I was offered an article about the best RV sites in some part of the country. Another writer offered me a guide for couples who want to drive from inn to inn in Vermont. And somebody else wanted to do an article for us covering the best hotels in the country. Our readers would think I was crazy if we published any of those pieces.

In addition to offering ideas that are so far off-target, some beginners show no imagination at all in their query letters. As soon as I see a letter beginning "I am a free-lance writer and I would like to write for *Backpacker*," I stamp it "Reject." The first couple of sentences often tell me whether or not it's worth reading any further. I sometimes reject an article suggestion without even taking the letter all the way out of the envelope, pulling it out just far enough to read the first sentence or two. If those few early words are dull, there's no point in going any further. That may sound unreasonable, but the writer's first job is to grab my attention, and if he fails with me, he'll fail with my readers.

I am surprised also by those writers who send me one hopeless idea after another. They have no clue to what the magazine is about. I'm sometimes tempted to come up with two different rejection letters. The first one would be the usual—"Thank you for letting us see your article suggestion. Unfortunately it does not meet our current requirements." The other one, which I would reserve for those hopeless, persistent free-lancers who waste every editor's time, would say, "Don't ever dare to send me this kind of junk again. If you do, I'm going to put the federal authorities on your trail."

It's not that I'm expecting Ernest Hemingway when I open an envelope. We can't afford Hemingway. But I am looking for people who have an unusual way of looking at things, and who know how to put sentences together.

One paragraph from a promising writer is usually enough to convince me that he or she has a good idea and knows how to handle it. Half a page, single spaced, should be enough to present *any* idea to us. If I need more than that, I'll ask for it once I've reacted to the basic proposal.

What I'm looking for is some sign the writer is interested in the magazine, understands it, and likes it. Otherwise, there'd be no reason for him or her to write for us, or for me to spend time reading what he or she has to say.

If I were a beginning free-lancer, and I'd made up my mind to write for *Backpacker*, I'd take a chance and go ahead and write the 150 or 200 words for a "Footnotes" piece, and send them in. And just before I closed the envelope, I'd take another look at the very first sentence, and make sure it would grab an editor's attention. If I had any doubt about that, I'd revise it.

When a good query letter reaches me, even if I decide not to take the piece, I'll take the time to send the writer a personal note. It'll be brief. It might say, "Thanks for your story. It didn't quite measure up because . . . but please send me more ideas." And that note means something: I don't write it unless I want to hear from the writer again.

When a writer has proved himself or herself by sending us three or four really good short pieces, I'll be ready to take a look at his or her ideas for a major piece. It will have to measure up to those we get from other professionals, and, as I say, the odds are pretty high. But if it strikes me as a possibility, I'll sit here and bang out some specific notes about what I'm expecting. I always try to give clear directions, so I won't waste the writer's time and he or she won't waste mine.

But realistically, if I were you I'd begin with the brief articles that give you a chance to prove what you can do, and which won't eat up a lot of your time. Remember—the idea is the thing that will impress me, but the way you present it is what will make it stand out in the morning mail. For the short pieces we accept, the payments range from $100 to $200. Our payments on the major features begin at $200 and can go as high as $2,000.

* * *

ANDREA THOMPSON
ARTICLES EDITOR
McCALL'S

I would suggest that beginning writers start submitting article ideas to smaller magazines before they approach the major national magazines.

We prefer to work with free-lancers who have first demonstrated their ability by being published in several other magazines before they offer an idea to *McCall's*. We need some clear indication of achievement before we feel ready to make an article assignment.

Once you have a number of credits, please study several issues of *McCall's* closely and analytically, and try to come up with an idea that is just right for us. An idea that might appeal strongly to the editors of *Parents* would not necessarily work out for *McCall's,* which targets a much broader audience. (And, of course, an idea we like might not appeal to the editors of other magazines.)

When you have an idea you think is right for us, write a query letter rather than submitting a complete manuscript. Most magazines prefer to receive a query first, except in certain categories, such as essays, that cannot really be judged without seeing the completed manuscript. Editors frequently wish to give writers advice on such matters as length and tone, and sometimes will be able to suggest sources for research that might not occur to the writer.

Your query letter should be just long enough to present your idea effectively. That might be one page, a page and a half, or even two pages—anything longer than that will lose the editor's attention.

What we are watching for when we open the mail is something fresh, something novel. It seems at times that a particular idea is floating in the air out there, because suddenly ten letters will suggest the same article possibility.

We look closely at the letter itself. A good, strong, vital letter suggests that the writer is really interested in the topic and will be ready to handle it with enthusiasm. The writer should outline the idea, tell us any particular interests or background that qualify him or her to handle the story, describe any resources he or she plans to use, such as experts in the field, and estimate the length of the finished piece.

One writer we hear from about every three months sends us a letter asking, "Do any of the following five topics interest you?" And she then gives us her list, with a brief summary of each of her ideas. One surmises that the same proposals are reaching two dozen other editors at the same time. This is the volume approach to trying to place an article—send lots of ideas to lots of editors and maybe one of them will land somewhere. Of course, this kind of routine query letter leads to automatic rejection.

Professionals focus their attention on one strong idea that is right for us, rather than giving us a menu to order from. I'm impressed when writers give specific evidence in their letters of being familiar with our editorial content, by referring to particular articles or features we have published.

When you do approach us, it's a good idea to list your most recent work. We also like to see tearsheets—especially of pieces that show your ability to handle the particular kind of article you are proposing. For example, if you are offering us a human interest article, I would like to see a published human interest piece or two. If you are proposing a medical piece, then one or two published medical articles will prove that you know how to find good sources in that field and know how to carry out the necessary research, in depth.

If we decide we do want to take on a proposed article, we generally call the writer to discuss it and then send an assignment letter, which is usually quite detailed. We indicate the amount we are ready to pay for a successful piece (generally from $1,500 to $3,000 for a feature article), and the length we prefer—usually 2,500 to 3,000 words. We also set a time for delivery, ordinarily a month or so from the date of the assignment. (In some cases, by mutual agreement, a deadline might be two or three months in the future.)

As you will know if you look closely at *McCall's,* we publish many celebrity pieces. Most are written by writers who concentrate in that area, and unless a free-lancer has special qualifications or access, he or she probably should not venture into that area for *McCall's.*

As a beginning free-lancer, you might want to consider the possibility of carving out a specialty in magazine writing. Some editors prefer to assign pieces to writers who have gained recognition as specialists—in the field of health, for example, or entertainment, or travel.

If you do plan to offer an idea to *McCall's,* you might find it helpful to study closely three articles by established free-lancers we published in 1991.

In our February, 1991, issue, we featured "Women & Heart Disease," by Sandra Blakeslee, a writer who specializes in health. This article tells us exactly what *women* should know about heart disease. It's up-to-date and provocative.

In our September, 1991, issue, we published "The Sexual Passages of a Marriage," by Debra Kent, a free-lance writer who specializes in relationship and sexuality issues. The article is well-structured and supported with expert opinion and research, which is especially important for a broad topic like this.

In our August, 1991, issue we featured "How to Let More Pleasure into Your Life," by Laura Miller. The lead is particularly good—it draws the reader in immediately:

> It had just rained. And like every other rush-hour traveler, all I could think about was how the sudden storm had snarled traffic. And messed up my clean car. And made me late, again, for my baby-sitter, who charges by the minute the moment the clock strikes 5. I leaned forward in my seat, clutching the wheel anxiously as I strained to see what the holdup ahead of me was. The digital dashboard clock flipped to 5:02. And another ten cents.

Eight minutes later, safely in my driveway, I grabbed my briefcase and empty lunch container and hurriedly stepped out of the car. And that's when I saw it: the sky. It was a beautiful royal blue, and right in the middle was an enormous rainbow, perched above the house across the street, looking like a brilliant billboard for household paints.

The sight was so marvelous, so spectacular, so out-of-place on my quiet, sleepy street that I found myself collapsing in my plastic raincoat on the front porch, right between the two pots of geraniums, simply to stare. What an astonishingly peaceful few moments: the air was crisp and cool; the grass looked extra green; and the rainbow just shimmered before me, like a flying saucer or the last page in a fairy tale.

Sitting there, calm and happy and enchanted—despite the fact that the baby-sitter meter was running—it dawned on me how infrequently I allowed myself totally carefree moments. Little time-outs. Simple pleasures. . . .

The article offers concrete strategies for letting more pleasure into our life and uses scientific studies and experts to tell us why this is important.

*   *   *

DOUGLAS FOSTER
EDITOR
MOTHER JONES

If I were a beginning writer who wanted to write for *Mother Jones,* I would start by taking a close look at two sections of the magazine. One is called "Outfront," and the other is "Previews"—where we cover the arts, music, books, and movies. In both of these sections freelancers we have never heard of before have a good chance of weighing in.

With these short pieces the best approach might be to go ahead and write the article and send it in, since you are not risking much time. (I would never suggest that a writer do that on a long feature.)

If you offer us an acceptable short item, you will be reasonably paid for your work.

All our payments, for short and long pieces, are determined by our contract with the National Writers Union. They begin at 75 cents a word, but we pay up to a dollar a word for a longer investigative piece that requires heavy research.

I realize that some beginning free-lancers would prefer to skip the try-out stage on short pieces and begin by writing major articles. At *Mother Jones,* that is unrealistic. You shouldn't count on getting a major assignment here until you have proved your ability by doing two or three shorter pieces for us or by getting your work published in some other magazines.

When you have gained some experience and are ready to approach us with an article suggestion, it is an immediate turn-off if you query letter indicates that you haven't read the magazine for years. One obvious sign is the failure to take the time to look at the masthead and pick a current name from the list of staff members when you make your submission.

It is obvious to us that some writers have a dim memory of the magazine from the past, but haven't kept up with it. This shows up if they submit a query to a section or department that's no longer in the magazine, or if they query on a topic that overlaps a recent cover story, for example.

Mother Jones, like all magazines, changes with the passage of the years, and if you don't read it regularly you probably shouldn't try to write for it. Write instead for the magazines you *do* read.

When you've reached the point where you're ready to submit an idea for a longer article, you should write us a brief letter—usually no more than a page—presenting the central idea clearly, and indicating just how you plan to research it and write it. Please be sure to send along some clips. (Incidentally, those clips do not have to come from big-name magazines. In fact, we realize that something that comes from a smaller magazine or a campus newspaper may be better evidence of your style and ability, since it is less likely that you received much help from an editor. Those clips tell us what you can do, unaided.)

We don't want a batch of material, but a few clips of your very best work can give us an indication of your skill. We wouldn't ordinarily read more than one or two examples, but we would scan the others. The important thing is to select material that shows your distinctive style and your ability as a researcher and writer. If the examples you send have some kind of relationship to the idea you are proposing, that's an advantage.

I suggest keeping the query letter down to a page for a reason. If the idea is clear in your mind, you won't need more space than that to make it clear to us.

If I were you, I'd address the letter to a senior editor or an associate editor. Two mailbags a day come in here with my name on them, and because I am tied up with other things I see very little of it.

It is perfectly acceptable if you are pitching to a certain department to call here and ask the receptionist, "Who edits _____ section?" But it is not a good idea to try to pitch the idea itself over the phone.

One young free-lancer who started in a small way with us and then came up with strong features was Ethan Watters. His first major articles for us focused on "The Devil in Mr. Ingram" (July/August 1991) and on a Washington state child abuse case.

I will repeat one bit of advice I'm sure other editors will also endorse. *Read the magazine.* Absorb it. Understand why readers respond to it, month after month, and then try to come up with an idea that can be handled in a small space that is aimed directly at those readers.

When you do that, we'll notice. A writer with good ideas who shows full understanding of a magazine is welcome anywhere, any time.

Experiments in Magazine Writing

In this section you will find much of the material you will need to write two magazine articles, and an outline for a third article.

You will want to supplement the notes that follow by carrying out additional library research and by conducting at least five interviews for each of the articles. Keep in mind that you need anecdotes and lively quotes to bring a magazine article to life.

You might want to work on these projects in two stages.

First: Select specific magazines that you think would be receptive to each of these articles and prepare article memos that you believe would arouse the interest of the editors of those magazines.

Second: Assume that those editors have responded favorably to your memos, and write the complete articles.

Remember that these articles are for you to practice on—not to submit for publication. After you have experimented with them, you will be ready to come up with your own article ideas and to offer those ideas to the magazines that are most likely to be receptive.

ARTICLE WRITING EXPERIMENT NO. 1: THE MYSTERIOUS COMPUTER-USER'S SYNDROME

Assume that you are a friend of David Carter, a reporter on the local newspaper. You visit him one morning at the newsroom and notice that he has white pads wrapped around his wrists.

"What happened to you?" you ask, thinking that he must have had a bad fall and strained both wrists.

"The doctor says I've been using the computer too much. Three weeks ago I woke up with a sharp pain in my elbow and a tingling feeling in my fingers. Same thing the next morning, and every morning since. And then I began noticing it during the day. . . ."

David nods toward an editor who is sitting at a terminal about 15 feet away. The editor has similar pads around his wrists.

"Same problem," David says. "And two other reporters are worried, almost sure they have the same thing."

"What is it?"

"Carpal tunnel syndrome, the doctor called it. And I hear it's showing up in newsrooms across the country."

* * *

After you talk a bit longer to David, you decide that this is a subject worth writing about. You realize that it might have already been covered by a lot of magazines, so you go to the university library and look up "carpal tunnel syndrome" in *Reader's Guide to Periodical Literature.*

You start with the 1986 volume. One article—in *McCall's.* 1987—one article. 1988—two. 1989—four. 1990—four. 1991—at least three.

The magazines in which these pieces appeared include *Science News, Prevention, Glamour, Better Homes & Gardens, Good Housekeeping, Nation's Business, People,* and *American Health.*

This indicates that the subject is of interest to a broad range of readers but has not yet been so widely reported that most editors would think that their readers had read about it. (Incidentally, many editors would assume that the articles published three or four years ago would not be remembered by most readers.)

Your next step will be to look up some of those articles. This will give you background information about carpal tunnel syndrome and also remind you what is already known by some readers (and some editors).

In *American Health* (July/August 1991) you will find an informative article by Ronald E. Roel. It begins,

> Lydia Ruiz was in top form. An ace telephone operator for Southern Bell in Orlando, Fla., she could sit at her computer terminal all day and, speeding her fingers across the keyboard, handle 1,300 directory-assistance calls—a third more than the average. Then one morning three years ago, she woke up feeling as if her hands were aflame. "The pain came on so suddenly," she said.
>
> She was baffled, of course, but the orthopedic surgeon's diagnosis didn't sound all that bad: She had carpal tunnel syndrome, a disorder involving the carpal tendons that control hand and finger movements. The tendons pass through the wrist in a narrow, tunnel-like enclosure, and with chronic overwork or excessive twisting they can become inflamed, swell, and pinch the adjacent median nerve. Typically, this results in aches, numbness, tingling or burning pain. . . .

As you read on, you realize that carpal tunnel syndrome is certainly not limited to newspaper offices. It affects thousands of Americans, working on a wide range of jobs.

You also find the names of some experts who have studied this problem. These can be useful when you're ready to do your own detailed research.

One thing you might notice: Roel makes very effective use of anecdotes and direct quotes. You obviously should not borrow these, but you should be determined to watch for both when you are conducting interviews for your article.

* * *

As you consult this and other articles, you begin making notes of some useful background material. For example,

Reported VDT trauma injuries (including carpal tunnel syndrome):

1982—23,000
1989—147,000

You write a note to yourself: "Check Bureau of Labor Statistics for any later figures." You find out that 75 reporters and editors at the *San Francisco Chronicle* have reported problems with carpal tunnel syndrome or similar injuries caused by repetitious motion. You write, "What other trades or businesses are affected?"

* * *

After reading several of the articles you've located through *Reader's Guide to Periodical Literature,* you are ready to use your library's databases for some further research. If the library happens to offer you a chance to use InfoTrac, for example, you could call up the "General Business File" and look especially for the abstracts of articles about carpal tunnel syndrome. You might find a brief summary of an article called "Keystroker's Cramp" from *PC Magazine,* December 12, 1989:

The incidence of carpal tunnel syndrome, a recently identified and potentially crippling wrist disorder linked to keyboard use, is increasing as computers become more common in offices. Carpal tunnel syndrome is known medically as a nerve entrapment disorder. The tendons connecting the fingers to arm muscles pass through a tiny opening in the wrist and are surrounded by "synovial sheaths," thin fluid-filled sacs which swell when the tendons are overused. This tends to squeeze the median nerve, which provides sensation to the entire hand, against the wrist bones or the carpal ligament. Users can reduce the risk of nerve-entrapment disorders by adjusting desk equipment to the most comfortable position and by keeping the wrists straight while typing. A padded, contoured wrist rest can be attached to the front of most keyboards.

This article seems likely to give you a few additional details about the nature of the problem and some suggestions on prevention. With the help of a research librarian, you track down the complete article.

InfoTrac also reminds you of articles in many specialized publications. You go down the long list and select those that seem most useful.

* * *

Once you begin focusing on any subject, you become aware of how much is being published about it in newspapers. A professor who was troubled by carpal tunnel syndrome tells you, "I have seen—I'm sure I'm not exaggerating—at least 50 stories of some size. One paper recently devoted four full pages to the subject." He also comments, "I suspect that there has always been carpal tunnel. Meat cutters have had hand problems for years (a surgeon in Omaha has been doing 1,000 wrists a year since he can't remember when—all those guys using knives in the cold rooms of the meat packers). Barbers . . . dental technicians . . . it was carpal tunnel, but it was sometimes called something else. It wasn't long before women who work the check-out counters at supermarkets were showing up in splints. And then with surgical scars on their wrists. . . ."

You make note of some points to check:

What other names have been used in the past for similar problems?
Does the state Industrial Insurance system recognize this as a major industrial disease?
How is it treated?
How expensive is the operation on the wrists—and how successful?

* * *

You also run across a column by Jake Highton, a journalism professor at the University of Nevada, Reno:

When video display terminals first appeared in newspaper offices in the early 1970s, reporters joked that working with the VDT's called for hazardous-duty pay and automatic retirement after 10 years.

Bawdy jokesters even said the machines caused sterility.

Two decades later VDT's are no laughing matter. Computer diseases have reached epidemic proportions. A marvelous tool has become a peril.

Prolonged use of desktop computers has caused painful inflammations of the wrist known as carpal tunnel syndrome. The tendonitis has struck secretaries, data-entry clerks, journalists, and any of the 10 million American workers who use computer terminals.

Repetitive movements have caused severe neck and back strain, impaired vision, and damaged hands and fingers.

* * *

You now have plenty of material for your article memo. Please plan it for a *specific* magazine. (It is also a good idea to have three or four alternative possibilities in mind, and that is usually not difficult for a medical article dealing with a problem of very wide concern.)

A few suggestions for when you turn from your memo to the article itself:

Read enough background material to prepare you to ask a series of intelligent questions when you interview experts.
Choose nationally recognized experts. Even the best-qualified general practitioner may have little experience with this problem.

Be sure that those experts answer your questions in words that readers will understand. Avoid the use of medical jargon.

Interview at least three people who have suffered from carpal tunnel syndrome. Ask each of them many questions. Watch for revealing quotes and anecdotes.

Consider the possibility of using an opening anecdote to catch the reader's attention. You might select a summarizing quote to end the article.

Test your completed article on two or three people who will give you an honest reaction and helpful suggestions.

Double-check every detail.

* * *

ARTICLE WRITING EXPERIMENT NO. 2: ONE WAY TO MAKE MONEY

A friend tells you that the United States government is about to call in all hundred dollar bills now in circulation and replace them with new bills. The reason, he says, is that counterfeiters have been using laser printers to print fake $100 bills that even bankers find hard to detect.

You drop by your bank and talk to a vice president named Doug Winters. When you ask him about your friend's statement, he laughs.

"That rumor pops up ever so often," he said. "If they were about to do that, they wouldn't say anything in advance, but once they actually began calling them in, thousands of people would be involved in handling the change. There's no way they could keep it secret."

"But what about the laser printers? Are they so good now that a counterfeiter could use one without any danger of someone recognizing a bill was phony?"

"We've had very good printers for fifty years," the banker says. "The big problem counterfeiters have had is with the paper. It's specially manufactured, the paper used in printing money, and they keep a very close watch over it. No other paper has the same characteristics. Banks and the Secret Service would be pretty quick to catch any bills printed on any other kind of paper."

Winters has a special interest in counterfeiters and counterfeiting, and since it's a dull morning at the bank he keeps talking.

"You know the real problem?" he asks you. "Most people never take a look at their money. If they did, they'd find it fairly easy to recognize most of the counterfeits that are floating around now. One thing they should do is take a close look at the eyes. Those engravers the mint uses know what they're doing. Even the bags under the eyes look real. And, here, take a look at the shadow under Alexander Hamilton's nose on the ten. You know most people wouldn't remember that genuine tens have that shadow? And on the twenties—look at Andy Jackson's hair. My wife's hair doesn't look that good. It's beautiful stuff, our money, but most people just accept it—put it into their wallets or their purses without ever bothering to take a look. I've seen a few counterfeits here over the last ten years, and some of them you wouldn't believe could fool a five-year-old. The paper didn't even feel right."

Winters tells you about a farmer in New Jersey who used pen, ink, and a camel's hair brush to draw the portraits on $20 bills. Then he would go over to New York City and pass them in small stores. "That went on for 17 years," he says. "The counterfeiter was finally caught because a grocery store clerk took one of the twenties when his hands were wet. That smeared some of the lines on the bill."

* * *

On the way home you begin to wonder if you've accidentally happened on a subject for a magazine article. Winters's stories about counterfeiters interested you, and if you gathered more of them and some information about how to detect a counterfeit bill, and how much is in circulation now, would that have possibilities for a magazine? If so, what magazine?

As a first step you drop by the university library and take a look at *Reader's Guide to Periodical Literature*. You notice two things: In every volume you glance at you find six, seven, or eight articles about counterfeiters and counterfeiting. The magazines that have published those articles since 1980 include *Reader's Digest, Discover, Newsweek, American History Illustrated, Harper's, The New Yorker, People, Forbes, Travel/Holiday, Time, Nation's Business, Changing Times, Antiques and Collecting Hobbies*, and *American Heritage*. Obviously other people are also interested in the subject.

You decide to begin with some library research. From your first sources you discover that counterfeiting started almost as soon as money was invented, and that the early rulers showed considerable imagination in coming up with what they considered appropriate sentences.

In England back in the 1500s and 1600s, a counterfeiter was punished by being "hanged by the neck and then cut down alive." Then, the law provided, "his entrails [are] to be taken out and burned while he was yet alive; . . . his head [to] be cut off and his body divided into four parts, and . . . his head and quarters [to] be at the king's disposal."

You find this grisly information in *Counterfeiting in Colonial America,* by Kenneth Scott, published in 1957 by Oxford University Press.

You also run across a series in *The New Yorker* which indicates that the Romans were as determined as the Britons to discourage counterfeiting—and perhaps even more imaginative. St. Clair McKelway offers the details:

Some of the earliest counterfeiters laboriously clipped coins around the edges and passed the clipped coins on to their fellow citizens. Then they manufactured counterfeit coins, using the valuable metal they had clipped to make a thin coating for them. To discourage this kind of thing, some of the sound-money men laboriously clipped counterfeiters, beginning with their ears and going on from there. . . . Later the noses of Roman counterfeiters [were trimmed] along with their ears. . . . By the time the Roman civilization reached its apex, the hands, feet, noses, ears and citizenship rights were clipped away and the same counterfeiters were then forthrightly castrated. . . . What was left of them was thrown into an arena full of hungry lions. Unclipped and uneaten counterfeiters do not seem to have been deterred by the threat of these penalties.

For more information about home-grown counterfeiters, you also take a look at

Counterfeiting in America, by Lynn Glaser (Crown), and discover this description of one hard-working early craftsman:

> To make his counterfeits Emanuel Ninger bought Crane bond paper, which except for the absence of the blue and red fibers was quite similar to that used in regular United States bills. He then cut the paper to size and immersed it in a jar filled with weak coffee.
>
> After soaking for an hour the paper would have the appearance of having passed through many hands. While it was still wet, Ninger placed it over the face of a genuine note. On a makeshift table he would trace the details of the note onto the new paper with a pencil. He then went over the tracings with pen and ink. A camel's hair brush was used to color the note, and silk threads were imitated with red and blue ink. . . . Ninger did not attempt to reproduce the fine lathework exactly. He only suggested it, but he did this so skillfully that it is hard to distinguish his work from the Treasury's.

You need some current information on the subject, and by typing in "Counterfeiting" and then "Counterfeiters" on your library's database you come up with the titles and publication dates of some recent stories:

> "Bill gets new look: hard-to-copy style . . . Treasury adds strip, words too tiny to duplicate to stymie counterfeiters. ($100 bill)."

That story, by Paul Duke, Jr., is in the *Wall Street Journal,* July 26, 1991. *The New York Times* also offers a report on the same date:

> "U.S. bets $100 you can't copy this bill (Slightly changed bills should prevent counterfeiting)."

Time, on May 27, 1991, publishes "Foiling the Fakers—preventing high tech counterfeiting."

You also find stories about a demand for a new detector to spot high-tech counterfeit bills, and about the secrecy bank note printers are required to maintain about their methods and operations.

You now recognize that there should be plenty of new material for an article about counterfeiters.

You are now prepared to

1. Choose a specific magazine that may be receptive to this article.
2. Settle on an angle.
3. Write an article memo.

Then, because this is an experiment, it would be useful to complete your research and write the article.

Keep in mind that you will need to set up some interviews—with a banker, a clerk who handles a lot of money, and someone from the U.S. Secret Service, for example. It might be a good idea to carry out a small-scale survey to discover how many people can tell you whose portrait appears on a $1, $5, $10, $50, and $100 bill. You may be surprised by the results, and so may your readers.

* * *

ARTICLE WRITING EXPERIMENT NO. 3: AFTER THE ACCIDENT

In this third experiment, you will have a chance to make any revisions you wish on this detailed article memo, and then write an article based on your revised version.

Possible Title

Seven experts tell what you should do
AFTER THE ACCIDENT

Possible Lead to the Article Memo

You are rushing to the airport to meet a friend's plane. You are already twenty minutes late, and you decide to edge past the slow-moving car in front of you. For just a few seconds you speed up to 55 in a 45-mile-an-hour zone.

Then, suddenly . . .

Crash!

Where did that blue Plymouth come from?

You didn't see it emerging from your right while you were concentrating on passing on your left. And evidently the man driving the Plymouth didn't see you.

The right door of your car is smashed, the right fender crumpled, and both of the windows on that side are shattered. But the blue Plymouth is in much worse shape. It may be totalled.

And not just the car. You see a stream of blood pouring from a bad cut in the driver's head, and he seems to be having trouble breathing.

Then you notice a sharp pain in your shoulder and neck.

Extended Capsule Statement (in the Form of Questions)

What do you do? Stay in your car and wait for the highway patrol to arrive? Rush over to the Plymouth and offer aid? Look for a phone somewhere to get word to your friend that you won't be there to pick him up at the airport? Call your doctor, because of the increasing pain in your shoulder? Begin making notes about what just happened, knowing you may have to testify in court? Take the camera you happen to have in the back seat and start taking some photos to record the scene?

Note About Sources

In researching this article, I plan to interview

Highway patrol officers
Paramedics
Physicians assigned to hospital emergency rooms
Attorneys who concentrate on automobile accident cases
An automobile insurance executive

The American Automobile Association
Experts on the diagnosis and treatment of automobile accident victims

Based on the information and anecdotal material I gather from these experts, I believe I can write a useful article that will tell readers of (name of magazine) what to do after an accident—in the first five minutes, the first hour, and the first 24 hours.

Brief Note About Your Background and Qualifications

* * *

Consider these questions when preparing your article memo:

1. What magazine might be receptive to this article?
2. Is this memo appropriate for that magazine? For example, if you were planning to submit this to a woman's magazine, you might wish to indicate clearly that the driver in the opening anecdote is a woman. If you were sending this to *Seventeen,* it would probably be a good idea to indicate that the driver is a teenager.
3. Is this the best article title for the magazine you've chosen? Do the editors show a preference for some other kind of title?
4. Is the opening anecdote too long? Could it be shortened and still be effective?
5. Can you think of a better anecdote, or a different kind of lead that would attract the attention of the audience you have in mind?
6. Do you need to interview all the people mentioned in the "Sources" section of your article memo? If you would eliminate some of them, which ones? Why?
7. If the editor of the magazine you have in mind emphasizes his or her preference for short memos, how could you present this idea in a page, or at most a page and a quarter?

And Now—The Next Step

When you have considered all these questions and have made any necessary revisions in the memo, you will be ready to conduct the necessary interviews and write your article.

Keep in mind that readers take articles such as this one seriously. As the writer, you need to remember the importance of offering completely reliable advice from experts you yourself would trust.

A Look
at the
New Journalism

What is the New Journalism? How much influence has it had on American magazines? Here you will find a summary of the advocates' and the critics' views of this widely discussed movement in magazine writing.

A young feature writer named Tom Wolfe returned to New York from California one day in 1963 with many notes for an article about custom-built cars—and no idea of how to put them together into a piece for *Esquire*.

Wolfe "sat around worrying over the thing," he recalled later. As the hours and then the days passed, *Esquire* became impatient. The editors had already scheduled the piece, and because they had "locked in" a two-page color illustration, it was impossible to reschedule it for a later issue.

When Wolfe seemed unable to make a start on the article, Byron Dobell, an experienced and sympathetic editor, offered a suggestion. Wolfe could just type up his notes, telling Dobell what he had seen and heard and observed, and drop these pages off at the *Esquire* offices. Dobell would give this material to an experienced magazine writer, who could then turn the notes into a publishable piece.

"So about 8 o'clock that night I started typing the notes out in the form of a memorandum that began, 'Dear Byron,'" Wolfe recalled later. "I started typing away, starting right with the first time I saw any custom cars in California. I just started recording it all, and inside a couple of hours, typing along like a madman, I could tell that something was beginning to happen. . . ."

By midnight, Wolfe's memo was 20 pages long and he still had many more impressions to pass along to the writer who would create an article from these rough notes. Finally, at 6:15 the next morning, he stopped typing. He now had 49 pages.

He knew there wouldn't be anyone at the *Esquire* offices at that hour, but around 9:30 he took the notes over to the magazine and left them for Dobell.

Around four that afternoon, he received a call from Dobell.

"He told me they were striking out the 'Dear Byron' at the top of the memorandum and running the rest of it in the magazine," Wolfe wrote later.

Dobell had recognized what Wolfe had accomplished once he had broken his paralyzing "writer's block." His memorandum, although unorthodox and somewhat shapeless, gave a vivid impression of the strange world occupied by those whose lives are centered around "customized" cars.

The article—"There Goes (Varoom! Varoom!) That Kandy-Kolored (Thphhhhhh!) Tangerine-Flake Streamline Baby (Rahghhh!) Around the Bend (Brummmmmmmmmmmmmmmmmm) . . ."—marked the beginning of a noteworthy career in recent magazine history.

Some writers and critics see Wolfe as an innovator who has encouraged many younger writers to break away from the gray, lifeless writing that is found in many traditional magazine pieces. Other writers and critics denounce him as someone who has debased magazine journalism by introducing elements that do not belong in nonfiction writing.

Both those who like his work and those who dislike it recognize Wolfe as a pioneer in the New Journalism. That label now seems permanent, although neither Wolfe nor his critics find it very satisfactory.

Before dealing with the controversy that has surrounded Wolfe and other New Journalists, it may be useful to answer a basic question:

Exactly what is the New Journalism?

THE FOUR CHARACTERISTICS OF THE NEW JOURNALISM

In his book, *The New Journalism,* Wolfe responds to that question by listing four characteristics:

1. Scene-by-scene construction. In the New Journalism the writer simply moves from scene to scene, recording what he or she sees, hears, and observes. The writer does not try to extract information from a variety of sources and then shape all that material into a traditional magazine article. Rather than concentrating on a few important questions and answers, the writer should serve as a witness to the ordinary, day-to-day lives of those being written about.

2. Fully recorded dialogue. Wolfe is convinced that realistic dialogue, fully reported, "involves the reader more completely than any other single device." He believes it "establishes and defines character more quickly and effectively than any other single device."

3. Presenting scenes through the eyes of someone in the article, rather than through

the eyes of the writer. This gives the reader "the feeling of being inside the character's mind and experiencing the emotional reality of the scene as he or she experiences it."

4. Recording many of the details that some traditional magazine writers may consider insignificant. Wolfe lists some of these: "everyday gestures, habits, manners, customs, styles of furniture, clothing, decoration, styles of traveling, eating, keeping house, modes of behaving toward children, servants, superiors, inferiors, peers, plus the various looks, poses, styles of walking and other symbolic details that might exist within a scene." These, he says, are symbolic of people's "status life." By that he means "the entire pattern of behavior and possessions through which people express their position in the world or what they think it is or what they hope it is."

Scene-by-Scene Construction

In "The Kentucky Derby Is Decadent and Depraved," one of the famous early examples of the New Journalism, Hunter S. Thompson begins by describing his arrival in Louisville:

> I got off the plane around midnight and no one spoke as I crossed the dark runway to the terminal. The air was thick and hot, like wandering into a steam bath. Inside, people hugged each other and shook hands . . . big grins and a whoop here and there: "By God! You old *bastard! Good* to see you, boy! *Damn* good . . . and I mean it."
>
> In the air-conditioned lounge I met a man from Houston who said his name was something or other—"but just call me Jimbo"—and he was here to get it on. "I'm ready for *anything,* by God! Anything at all. Yeah, what are you drinkin?" I ordered a Margarita with ice, but he wouldn't hear of it: "Naw, naw . . . what the hell kind of drink is that for Kentucky Derby time? What's *wrong* with you, boy?" He grinned and winked at the bartender. "Goddam, we gotta educate this boy. Get him some good *whiskey*. . . ."

Thompson moves restlessly from scene to scene, sketching some of them in no more than four or five lines, lingering over others—especially those in various Louisville bars. The reader follows him as he goes looking for Ralph Steadman, an English artist who is supposed to be arriving from London. Steadman has agreed to do some drawings of the Derby that will be used by *Scanlan's Monthly* to illustrate Thompson's article. From the beginning, Thompson worries about the Englishman's ability to adjust to the Louisville atmosphere:

> All I knew about him was that this was his first visit to the United States. And the more I pondered that fact, the more it gave me fear. Would he bear up under the heinous culture shock of being lifted out of London and plunged into the drunken mob scene at the Kentucky Derby?

Finally, shortly before the Derby weekend begins, Steadman arrives. Thompson warns him:

> "Just keep in mind for the next few days that we're in Louisville, Kentucky. Not London. Not even New York. This is a weird place. . . . Just pretend that you're in a huge outdoor loony bin. If the inmates get out of control we'll soak them down with Mace."

Although the relationship between Thompson and the English illustrator remains fairly easy during their first meetings, strains begin to show up, and before Derby Day begins they are completely alienated:

> . . . the weekend became a vicious, drunken nightmare. We both went completely to pieces. The main problem was my prior attachment to Louisville, which naturally led to meetings with old friends, relatives, etc., many of whom were in the process of falling apart, going mad, plotting divorces, cracking up under the strain of terrible debts or recovering from bad accidents. Right in the middle of the whole frenzied Derby action, a member of my own family had to be institutionalized. This added a certain amount of strain to the situation, and since poor Steadman had no choice but to take whatever came his way, he was subjected to shock after shock.
>
> Another problem was his habit of sketching people he met in the various social situations I dragged him into, then giving them the sketches. The results were always unfortunate. I warned him several times about letting the subjects see his foul renderings, but for some perverse reason he kept doing it. Consequently, he was regarded with fear and loathing by nearly everyone who'd seen or even heard about his work.

Later Thompson offers a close-up view of the English illustrator at work:

> I left Steadman sketching in the Paddock bar and went off to place our bets on the sixth race. When I came back he was staring intently at a group of young men at a table not far away. "Jesus, look at the corruption in that face!" he whispered. "Look at the madness, the fear, the greed!" I looked. . . . The face he'd picked out to draw was the face of an old friend of mine. . . .

From the moment of Steadman's arrival in Louisville, the focus of Thompson's article shifts abruptly. While he devotes some paragraphs to the pre-Derby activities and about 25 lines to the "big race," the English illustrator has become the center of the piece. On the Monday after the race, Steadman appears at Thompson's motel room:

> Steadman was mumbling about sickness and terrible heat; I . . . tried to focus on him as he moved around the room in a very distracted way for a few moments, then suddenly darted over to the beer bucket and seized a Colt .45. "Christ," I said. "You're getting out of control."
>
> He nodded . . . taking a long drink. "You know, this is really awful," he said finally. "I must get out of this place. . . ." He shook his head nervously. "The plane leaves at 3:30, but I don't know if I'll make it."

Finally Thompson warns Steadman to stop drinking ("They'll zip you in a strait-jacket and . . . beat you on the kidneys with big sticks until you straighten out"). Then he drives him out to the airport ("nearly naked after taking off most of his clothing . . . his body racked with fits of coughing and wild choking sobs"), shoves him out of the car, and snarls "Bug off, you worthless faggot!" as the poor illustrator heads for his plane.

Wolfe comments that Thompson has developed "a manic, highly adrenal first-person style in which Thompson's own emotions continually dominate the story."

Some critics agree with that comment, but feel that the highly personal style is a fault in magazine writing.

Use of Fully Recorded Dialogue

Tom Wolfe's "The First Tycoon of Teen" opens with a scene on a plane that is moving along a runway, revving up for takeoff. He focuses on one of the passengers—Phil Spector, the 23-year-old president of a record company:

> "Miss!" says Phil Spector.
> "Yes?"
> "I, like I have to get off the plane."
> [The stewardess] stops there beside his seat with her legs bent slightly, at a 25-degree angle to her ischium.
> She laughs with her mouth, yes, yes, but there is no no in her eyes, you little bearded creep. . . .
> "Sir?"
> "I, you know, I have to get off," says Phil Spector. "I don't want to *fly* on this plane. Let me—" . . . She is standing there hoping this is a joke. "—uh, I'm not putting you on, I'm not putting you down, I'm not anything, all I want is—you know?—just open door and let me off. I'll walk back. The rest—everybody—I mean, go ahead, *fly*."
> "Sir, we're already in a pattern. There are seven aircraft, seven jet aircraft, behind us waiting for the runway—"

Spector persists, and others join in:

> "Yeah, we wanna get off. There's something wiggy or something about this plane."
> "Yeah!"
> "Yeah!"

The stewardess runs to the pilot's cabin, tells him what is happening in the cabin. He breaks up the takeoff pattern on the runway, turns the plane around, stops it, and discharges all the passengers.

Presenting Scenes Through the Eyes of Someone in the Article (or Book)

Wolfe and some other New Journalists have experimented with the idea of creating "the illusion of seeing the action through the eyes of someone who was actually on the scene and involved in it, rather than a narrator."

This has been one of the most widely criticized techniques used by the New Journalists, but it was employed very effectively by Truman Capote in his remarkable book, *In Cold Blood*.

There are two tests for scenes presented in this way:

Has the writer interviewed the viewpoint character intensively and in depth?
Is the reader convinced that this is exactly the way this scene appeared to the viewpoint character?

In the case of *In Cold Blood*, Capote's research was intensive and prolonged. And many, many readers apparently accepted such scenes as an accurate reflection of the thoughts and feelings of the people he focused on.

Recording Details Symbolic of "Status Life"

While many traditional journalists limit their descriptions of people in their articles to a few factual details (age, height, hair color, occupation, and so forth), Wolfe and other New Journalists often include many additional details about dress, personal appearance, behavior, and possessions.

In "Las Vegas (What?) Las Vegas (Can't hear you! Too noisy) Las Vegas!!!" Wolfe offers characterizing details about various people and also about the city itself:

> . . . one of the indelible images of Las Vegas is that of the old babes at the row upon row of slot machines. There they are at six o'clock Sunday morning no less than at three o'clock Tuesday afternoon. Some of them pack their old hummocky shanks into Capri pants, but many of them just put on the old print dress, the same one day after day, and the old hob-heeled shoes, looking like they might be going out to buy eggs in Tupelo, Mississippi. They have a Dixie Cup full of nickles or dimes in the left hand and an Iron Boy work glove on the right hand to keep the callouses from getting sore.

> . . . I am watching . . . men at a green-topped card table playing poker. They are sliding their Bee-brand cards into their hands and squinting at the pips with a set to the lips like Conrad Veidt in a tunic collar studying a code message from S.S. headquarters. Big Sid Wyman, the old Big Time gambler from St. Louis, is there, with his eyes looking like two poached eggs engraved with a road map of West Virginia after all night at the poker table. Sixty-year-old Chicago Tommy Hargan is there with his topknot of white hair pulled back over his little pink skull and a mountain of chips in front of his old caved-in sternum. Sixty-two year-old Dallas Maxie Welch is there, fat and phlegmatic as an Indian Ocean potentate.

As these excerpts indicate, the "symbolic details" some New Journalists choose to record sometimes give an impression that is closer to a caricature than to a photograph.

THE DEBATE OVER THE NEW JOURNALISM

None of the techniques used by the New Journalists is really new, of course. Wolfe himself lists some rather ancient New Journalists in his book about the phenomenon. He writes,

> . . . one can go back into literary history and find examples of nonfiction written by reporters . . . showing many of the characteristics of the New Journalism. For a start, [James] Boswell.

He then adds the names of other very old New Journalists: Charles Dickens, Mark Twain, Anton Chekhov, Stephen Crane, John Reed, and George Orwell.

Still, the debate over these techniques has focused on the current group of New Journalists, and especially on the work of Wolfe himself.

The critics offer these objections:

> The reporting is not objective. Readers are not given the information they need to reach their own conclusions about the subject, but instead are presented with the writer's subjective judgment.

The writer often insists on being the focus of his or her own work. Sometimes what starts out as an article about something else ends up being a fragment of the writer's autobiography.

The reader is asked to believe that the writer can present accurately a scene as it appears to a character in the article. Many critics believe that this is impossible, and that the writer who uses this device has become a short-story writer rather than an article writer.

The subjects chosen by many New Journalists are of ephemeral interest anyway and do not deserve either the writer's or the reader's attention.

Some New Journalists are not as careful as they should be about verifying facts.

The tricks used by some New Journalists to attract and hold readers are cheap and circusy, and will make much of their work seem faddish and outdated within a few years after it first appears.

Defenders of the New Journalism would respond:

Objectivity is a myth. All reporting is limited and subjective, and the New Journalists do not try to disguise this.

In some articles, the writer is the natural focus of interest. Hunter S. Thompson was reporting his own intensely personal reaction to Louisville, the Kentucky Derby, and to the English illustrator who became the center of interest later in the article. In much other New Journalism, the writer is rarely visible—and in some, does not appear at all.

If a writer interviews a character at length and with skill, he or she *can* re-create what was going through the person's mind at a particular instance. Writers who spend enough time with a subject can begin to understand him or her well enough to begin to see the world through the character's eyes.

The subjects of many magazine articles are of ephemeral interest. If the observation and the presentation is exceptional, the fact that the writer deals with subjects of passing interest will not prevent the work from being read long after first publication. A great deal of New Journalism is being preserved in book form, whereas most of the more traditional journalism in magazines quickly disappears.

Although New Journalists have occasionally failed to check facts with sufficient care, that has also been a failing of some traditional journalists over the years.

About the use of tricks (such as reproducing sounds in type, or repeating the word "hernia" 57 times in the lead to his article about Las Vegas) Wolfe writes, "I never felt the slightest hesitation about trying any device that might conceivably grab the reader for a few seconds longer. I tried to yell right in his ear: *Stick around!*"

The argument will obviously continue as long as the New Journalism attracts those who wish to experiment with magazine writing and repels those who find some of the experiments a move away from responsible reporting.

Three of the four techniques described by Wolfe seem to me of great value in some types of magazine writing:

Scene-by-scene construction
Extensive use of fully recorded dialogue
Inclusion of details of "status life"

While these should not be introduced in an arbitrary way, they could be used effectively in many articles, particularly in personality pieces. Of course, a writer should guard against overuse of any of them. A long, aimless monologue or dialogue could become so tedious that a reader would give up and turn to another article. Too many details of "status life" could become a bore.

I have some reservations about the fourth technique: presenting scenes through the minds of the characters. This requires saturation reporting and enormous skill. When it is both accurate and successful, it is a substantial achievement—but it should not be undertaken lightly.

Appendix A: Checklist for a Magazine Article

"A writer must learn to look at his or her manuscript the way an editor looks at it," said an editor of *Esquire*.

The 15-point checklist that follows should help you test your article manuscript before you mail it.

1. DO I HAVE A GOOD WORKING TITLE?

Some writers do not worry much about this because they know that magazines frequently discard the writer's working title and substitute one worked out by the editors. Nevertheless, your working title serves a purpose. It can renew the editor's interest in your article. (You should keep in mind that the editor has seen many other manuscripts in the weeks between the approval of your article proposal and the arrival of your completed manuscript.) A weak title can give an editor a negative initial impression.

2. HAVE I CHOSEN THE BEST POSSIBLE LEAD?

If you have any doubt about the effectiveness of your lead, you should revise it. It is impossible to exaggerate the importance of these opening paragraphs. You might want to take another look at Chapter 9, "The First Hundred Words," to remind yourself of the methods used by successful free-lancers to gain the reader's immediate attention.

3. HAVE I INCLUDED A CLEAR CAPSULE STATEMENT?

The editor (and the reader) should be told early in your manuscript exactly what the article is about. This may be stated directly or implied, but the reader should not be left in doubt.

4. HAVE I DONE ENOUGH RESEARCH?

As you reread your article, try to think of any question a reader might ask that you have left unanswered in your article. "You can tell immediately when a writer tries to stretch insufficient research far enough to provide material for a full-length article," one editor commented. "If we published those pieces, the reader would feel cheated. Writers should know more than they write, and should be discarding chunks of research rather than stretching it out." If you feel your research is thin, you should remedy this fault before submitting a manuscript.

5. HAVE I USED ENOUGH ANECDOTES?

While there is no set number of anecdotes that a writer should use in a magazine article, you should be aware of the value of these stories in gaining and holding the reader's attention. Often an anecdote is the most effective method of revealing personal characteristics or making a point.

6. HAVE I USED ONLY THOSE STATISTICS THAT ARE ESSENTIAL?

Some writers who make insufficient use of anecdotes tend to *overuse* statistics. Although statistics are essential in some articles, you should realize that the eyes of many readers glaze over when they are confronted by a series of numbers. When statistics must be used, you should always attempt to present them dramatically.

7. HAVE I VARIED MY PRESENTATION?

In the course of a single 2,500-word article, experienced free-lancers will often make use of direct quotes, anecdotes, brief expository passages, surprising statements, a striking comparison, and one or two dramatically presented statistics. They are always conscious of the danger of boring the reader, and they recognize that one method of holding reader interest is the use of a variety of techniques in presenting material.

8. HAVE I AVOIDED OVERUSING THE PASSIVE VOICE?

"The habitual use of the active voice . . . makes for forcible writing," William Strunk, Jr., wrote in *The Elements of Style*. "This is true not only in narrative concerned principally with action but in writing of any kind." While it is natural at times to use the passive voice, this should always be a conscious choice, and the use should be limited.

9. HAVE I KEPT THE SAME TONE THROUGHOUT THE ARTICLE?

It is usually a mistake to begin a serious article with a light anecdote, or a light piece with a solemn anecdote. It is also distracting to introduce a satirical remark in a straightforward, informational article. Most editors suggest that the tone of a magazine article should be set in the opening paragraph and maintained consistently.

10. HAVE I ELIMINATED ALL CLICHÉS?

Manuscripts received by magazines often include such trite expressions as "just the tip of the iceberg," "the name of the game," "a political football," and "at this point in time." Editors are puzzled why anyone who writes so lazily expects a magazine to be receptive to his or her work. When you have any question in your mind about whether a particular expression would be considered a cliché, eliminate it. Substitute another phrase about which you have no doubts.

11. HAVE I AVOIDED REPEATING ANY POINT UNINTENTIONALLY?

Writers sometimes make the same point two or three times in a 2,500-word article. This is sometimes deliberate, but it usually is a mistake. You should make the point as emphatically as possible the first time and then assume that the reader has absorbed it.

12. HAVE I CONVINCED THE READER THAT THE INFORMATION I AM OFFERING IS RELIABLE?

It is important for the reader to have complete confidence in your sources. You should establish clearly the qualifications of those you quote.

13. DOES THE ARTICLE FLOW SMOOTHLY?

Because you have assembled material from a variety of sources, there could be a certain bumpiness in your completed manuscript. Often the insertion of a few transitional phrases will remedy this problem. Some professional writers read their articles aloud to themselves or to others to test the smoothness of the flow.

14. IS THE ARTICLE LOGICALLY ORGANIZED?

"The structure of an article may not be visible to the casual reader," said a *Cosmopolitan* editor, "but it must be there." It is the *absence* of a logical structure that will make at least some readers feel vaguely dissatisfied. The logic of your organization should be clear to you, and it should also be apparent to an editor, who is accustomed to looking at manuscripts critically.

15. IS THE ENDING AS CAREFULLY CHOSEN AS THE LEAD?

A surprising number of manuscripts simply limp to a conclusion. Others end abruptly, as though someone had suddenly pulled the plug on the writer's electric typewriter. This is far too important a section of your article to be written casually. The closing segment of your article—especially the last two or three paragraphs—should be carefully planned in advance. A close analysis of a dozen or two dozen skillfully written articles will remind you of the wide variety of techniques used by professionals to end their articles. Some offer a fresh restatement of the central point. Some look ahead to future developments. Many select a very good quote or a revealing anecdote that will leave a final vivid impression in the reader's mind.

* * *

A manuscript that can pass this 15-point test should have a strong chance for acceptance.

You may still wonder whether it is worthwhile going to all this trouble over a magazine article. These statements from two *Reader's Digest* editors may convince you that it is:

We need roughly 360 ideas a year for the 12 issues of the *Digest*. No group of editors is creative enough to come up with 360 excellent ideas year after year. That's why we depend heavily upon contributions from free-lance writers.

And

Whenever I open a letter containing an article proposal, or whenever I pick up a manuscript, I hope I will be able to say yes.

Appendix B: Information on Mechanics

FORMAT FOR A MAGAZINE ARTICLE

Many professional writers offer these suggestions about the proper form for presenting your material to a magazine editor:

Type your name, address, and telephone number in the top left-hand corner of the first page.

Type the title of the article in capital letters about one-fourth of the way down the page. Center the title.

Type your byline exactly as you would like it to appear in the magazine. Use upper- and lowercase letters. Center the byline.

Skip down at least four lines, and then begin your lead.

Double-space your manuscript. *Never* submit a single-spaced manuscript to a magazine. It cannot be read with ease, and it probably will not be read at all.

Do not type the word *more* at the bottom of a magazine manuscript page.

At the top of page 2 and all subsequent pages, type the title of your article and your name. Pages can become separated when being circulated in a magazine office.

Number each page at the top, far right, where the number can be seen easily. Do not follow the common newspaper practice of writing *add-1*, *add-2*, etc. Page 2 should be numbered simply 2.

Do not crowd too many words on your pages. Leave *at least* 10 spaces on the left-hand and right-hand sides of each page. Some writers leave 15. Leave *at least* eight lines at the bottom of each page.

A FEW REMINDERS ABOUT MANUSCRIPT PREPARATION

The appearance of a magazine manuscript is very important. Editors who must spend hours each day (or night) reading article proposals and complete manuscripts may form an immediately negative opinion of any writer who is careless or sloppy in presenting his or her work.

Here are a few basic suggestions, made by 25 editors:

Use a good 20-pound bond paper for the final draft of an article memo or a magazine article. Such paper is expensive, but it holds up better than a lighter-weight paper when it is passed from hand to hand in an editorial office.

If you are submitting a manuscript produced on a word processor, use a *laser* printer. Many editors will not consider a manuscript printed on a dot matrix printer.

If you type your manuscript, use a good, fresh, black ribbon or a film cartridge. Never submit a manuscript that is too faint to be read comfortably.

Keep in mind that professionals never submit a manuscript containing a single visible correction. In magazine writing, *neatness counts*.

HOW TO MAIL A MANUSCRIPT

These suggestions were made by successful free-lance writers and magazine editors:

Mail your manuscript flat. Use a cardboard stiffener in a 9 × 12 or 10 × 13 envelope.

Never cram a manuscript into an ordinary business-sized envelope. When a manuscript is handled this way, it often arrives looking messy and uninviting.

Always include a self-addressed, stamped envelope (SASE) with every submission. Magazines receive thousands of article ideas and manuscripts every year—some receive hundreds of thousands—and it is unfair to expect them to bear the cost of the return postage on unsolicited, unacceptable material.

If you do not want your manuscript to be folded, provide a return envelope that is large enough for it to be returned flat. You can send your manuscript in a 10 × 13 envelope and enclose an unfolded 9 × 12 envelope for the return journey.

An important reminder: Do not bind your manuscript. Editors prefer to deal with loose pages. A bound manuscript is seen by many editors as the sure mark of the amateur.

HOW TO HELP EDITORS ILLUSTRATE YOUR ARTICLES

If you are a very skillful photographer, or if you have access to professional-quality photographs that could be used to illustrate your articles, you should always indicate that in your article memos or query letters.

This is particularly important when you are writing for medium-sized or small magazines. The staffs of these magazines are always overworked, and the editors will appreciate your assistance in obtaining (or providing) illustrations.

Obviously, it would be helpful to these editors if most of their free-lance contributors were expert photographers. Relatively few free-lancers are equally good writers and photographers, however, and editors recognize this. If you have limited skill as a photographer, you should never submit amateurish work to a magazine. Instead, you should experiment with three other methods of providing illustrations when offering your work to small magazines.

Collaborating with a Photographer

Notice the published work of photographers in your city or region. When you observe that one photographer is unusually imaginative and professional, discuss with him or her the possibility of collaborating on a few magazine articles.

The photographer will be taking a gamble, just as you are. If the articles (with the accompanying photographs) are accepted, you will both benefit. If the articles are rejected, both you and the photographer should take an objective look at the submissions and try to discover why the editors said no.

You may wish to work out a simple letter of agreement with the photographer. It could be as brief as this one:

> I, James Wallace, agree to provide at least 12 8 × 10 glossy black-and-white prints to illustrate the article "How to Build a Tool-Shed," now being written by Tom Edmunds.
>
> I will complete this assignment within four weeks.
>
> If a magazine accepts both Mr. Edmunds's article and my photographs, and makes separate payments for text and illustrations, I will accept the amount paid for the photographs as payment in full for my services. If an editor makes a lump-sum payment for both text and photographs, I will accept one-third (33$\frac{1}{3}$%) of the total payment as compensation for my work. If the editor accepts Mr. Edmunds's article but rejects my photographs, I will receive no payment.
>
> If the article is not sold within 24 months after I complete this assignment, upon my request Mr. Edmunds agrees to return my prints. I will be free to use my work in any way I wish, and will receive no payment.

You could, of course, have a more complex agreement drawn up by a lawyer. But this brief letter covers the most likely contingencies.

In searching for a collaborator, you should watch newspapers in your region, but you might also take a close look at the work of members of the local photography clubs.

Working with Public Relations Offices

If you are writing an article about fire dangers or fire prevention, you can probably obtain the photographs you need by getting in touch with the public relations departments of major fire insurance companies or The National Board of Fire Underwriters.

If you are writing about Alaska or Hawaii or Arizona or Texas, you can obtain all the photographs you can use by writing to their state tourist offices.

Sometimes these public relations departments or tourist offices will agree to arrange special shootings if they believe your article will be particularly valuable to them.

You run into a more complex question when you ask for similar assistance from a department representing some other enterprises—an oil company, say, or a drug manufacturer, or a major utility. These departments would probably be helpful and might also volunteer to set up a special photographic assignment at no cost to you. But some writers (and some editors) feel uncomfortable about accepting such assistance. Even though the article is completely objective, they believe there is always the danger that the illustrations may appear staged and may in some subtle way distort the story and make a point beneficial to those who are paying for the photographs.

Obviously, you should be cautious when accepting any free service. At the same time, there is no need to become paranoid about the activities of public relations people. Many have backgrounds in news reporting and understand the difference between propaganda and straightforward presentation of information. Some can be quite candid about the shortcomings of the businesses they represent.

In any case, you (and the editor) have the freedom to discard any photographs that seem to you biased or misleading.

One reminder: Always be candid in telling an editor the sources of the photographs you submit. Most editors will then pass along that information to their readers by crediting "Exxon" or "British Airways" or "Reno Chamber of Commerce" when they use photographs provided by these companies or organizations.

Using "Stock" Photos

Hundreds of thousands of photographs can be obtained from photo agencies, the wire services, and libraries. A research librarian can help you locate those you need.

There is a major limitation to these photographs. They were not taken to illustrate your article, and that will often be apparent even to the most obtuse reader. If you are writing an article describing your experiences in building a prefabricated house, a "stock" photo of someone else's prefab will not fool—or satisfy—the reader. On the other hand, if you are writing about a holiday in the Basque country, it is possible that one of the agencies could supply you with some photographs that have not been overused and are far superior to your own snapshots.

Fees for the publication of these photographs are usually moderate and are paid by the magazine. You will help the editor by doing some research and calling his or her attention to the photos that could enhance your article.

A Checklist for Photos

Whatever source you use, you should take a critical look at every photograph before you offer it to an editor.

This checklist might help:

1. Is the photo technically perfect? (If you are uncertain about this, ask a very critical professional photographer to examine the photos with you.)
2. Does it illustrate a major point in your article?
3. Does it have a single, dominant point of interest?

4. Is there anything in the background that would distract the reader from that central point? (If so, the photograph should not be submitted.)
5. If the magazine you are writing for obviously prefers to have people in every photo, does your photo have people in it? (If not, you should probably eliminate it and substitute a photo that meets the magazine's requirements.)
6. Does the photo compare favorably with the illustrations used in recent issues of the magazine? (If not, it should be discarded. You do not wish to offer illustrations the editor would consider marginal or inferior.)

Mailing Your Photos

The following suggestions come from an editor who has handled photos submitted by thousands of free-lance writers and photographers:

1. If you send prints, put them between two pieces of corrugated cardboard. Use a rubber band—one carefully chosen so it will not bend the prints—to hold the boards together.
2. If you send transparencies, package them in individual slide sleeves.
3. Stamp or write your name, address, and telephone number on each print, slide, or slide sleeve.
4. Always include a note that indicates exactly how many prints, slides, and transparencies you are submitting.
5. Provide clear identification and background information with each photo.
6. If you have obtained model releases from the people shown in your photos, enclose copies. If you have not obtained releases, explain why they will not be needed.
7. Number every print, slide, or transparency.
8. Always include a self-addressed, stamped envelope for return of your photos, slides, or transparencies.
9. Pack your photos with special care, and write "Photos—Please Do Not Bend" on the envelope or package. Assume that the package may be roughly handled in the mails.

WHAT HAPPENS WHEN YOUR MEMO REACHES A MAGAZINE?

When you submit an article idea to a magazine, you may have several questions in your mind:

Who will read the memo first?
How many editors will read it before a decision is reached?
What factors will influence that decision?
How long will it take?
If the editors like the idea, will they suggest it be written on speculation?
If the draft submitted is unacceptable, will the editors give you a second chance?
If the article is accepted, how long will you have to wait before you see it in print?

Because wide differences exist in the way various magazines are edited, and because the size of magazine staffs can range from one lone editor to a staff of several hundred, no single set of answers can be given to these questions. But on the basis of a close study of many magazines, large and small, some general responses to these questions can be offered.

Who will read the memo first?

If you mail your memo to a specific editor by name, there is a good chance that editor will take the time to read it. If he or she does not have time to consider it, that editor will at least feel some responsibility for passing it along to someone else on the staff.

The decision made by that first editor to read your memo will depend of course on the strength of your idea and the skill of your memo. But by addressing it to a specific senior editor or articles editor or assistant managing editor by name, you will keep your idea from being treated too routinely.

If, on the other hand, you address your article memo to "The Editor" (by title or by name) or "The Editors," your proposal will be lumped in with the hundreds or even thousands of other pieces of mail that reach the magazine that week. After waiting its turn, it will then be read by a first reader.

This is likely to be a younger member of the staff, with a limited amount of editorial experience. First readers are almost always conscientious and competent, but their principal assignment is to protect other editors from the ceaseless flow of amateurish and unpublishable manuscripts that flood into every editorial office. A very good first reader will recognize work of exceptional promise and may present it effectively to other editors, who can then serve as advocates before the editorial board. Unfortunately, not all first readers have developed the self-confidence that is needed to call attention to the occasional nugget found in the slush pile.

By failing to address your article memo to a specific editor by name, you subject your work to an unnecessary preliminary examination by someone who plays no major role in the magazine's decisions.

How many editors will read it before a decision is reached?

On a very small magazine, the editor may make one-person decisions. On somewhat larger magazines, three or four editors may consider your ideas. On major magazines, as many as a dozen people may be involved: the editor, the managing editor, one or two assistant managing editors, one or two articles editors, two or three assistant articles editors, an art director, a picture editor, and perhaps two or three departmental editors. This group makes up the editorial board.

What factors will influence that decision?

The two major factors are the appeal of your idea and the professionalism of your memo.

The chance for a favorable decision is increased if the editor who presents your proposal to the editorial board is genuinely enthusiastic. But some other factors will be considered:

1. Does the magazine have a large inventory of unpublished articles? If so, the tendency of some editorial boards is to say no to almost all new proposals until some of the backlog is cleared away.
2. Do all of the editors believe you can write an acceptable piece? Unless you've written for the magazine before, the editors' opinions about your ability will be based chiefly on the one-page or page-and-a-half memo that is usually copied and distributed before the editorial board meeting.
3. Is the idea perishable? Some ideas that might be strong if published within three months would seem dated if publication were delayed six months or nine months. Unless the editors feel enthusiastic enough to clear space for early publication of your article, they may hesitate to encourage you to write it.
4. Is the idea exceptionally good? Editors who feel that your idea is all right but no more than that will tend to vote no. They know that *fairly good* ideas are easy to find. Your value as a contributor will depend on your ability to offer fresher, stronger ideas than the members of the editorial board can come up with on their own.
5. Can the article be effectively illustrated? For some magazines this is a major concern. Especially on smaller magazines, your own offer to assist in providing illustrations can be crucial.
6. Are the authorities cited in the article memo impressive? This is particularly important in articles dealing with medicine, science, economics, and human behavior.

How long will it take?

Because of the number of people involved in reaching a decision, it is not unusual for a writer to have to wait from four to six weeks before learning whether an article idea has been accepted or rejected. This can be explained by the number of ideas that reach major magazines month after month. Considering these article proposals is only one of the responsibilities of each member of the editorial board. They must also plan and schedule issues, choose covers, edit articles, confer with staff writers, attend numerous staff meetings, lunch with regular free-lance contributors, work out contracts, read final proofs, and fit in a dozen other activities during an ordinary week.

If you have not received a decision within six weeks after you submit an idea, you are justified in writing a polite, nonaccusatory letter to the editor. It is a good practice to include a copy of your article memo in case the original has gotten lost in the magazine office.

If the editors like the idea, will they suggest it be written on speculation?

Unless you have written for the magazine before, the answer is usually yes. After you have had three or four articles published by some magazines, you will be offered a guaranteed kill fee—a portion of the agreed-on payment that you will receive even if the article is not accepted. If an accepted article would bring a payment of $750, the kill fee might be $200 or $250.

Incidentally, even if you are asked to write an article on speculation, the editors obviously hope that the piece will justify acceptance. It would be a foolish waste of time for editors to encourage writers to spend time on articles they did not expect to publish.

If the draft submitted is unacceptable, will the editors give you a second chance?

In almost all cases, the answer is yes. A few impatient editors may lose confidence in you if you send them an unacceptable manuscript, but ordinarily an editor will give you specific suggestions and will hope that your second submission is acceptable.

If the article is accepted, how long will you have to wait before you see it in print?

There are wide variations in the period of time between acceptance and publication.

Some writers are astonished by the speed with which their work is rushed into print. The idea happens to reach the magazine at exactly the right time, the manuscript is quickly completed and accepted, and the editors schedule it immediately.

This is a rare experience for most free-lancers. Often the writer must wait four months, six months, or a year before the article appears. Sometimes this waiting period can stretch out to 18 months, two years, even three years.

Some editors feel more comfortable with a large inventory, and as a result a piece they accept this month may not be scheduled until many earlier manuscripts have been published.

Other factors also influence the time of publication. Editors may hold your article for months, waiting until they find the right illustration for it. A magazine may see your piece as fitting more naturally into a spring or summer or fall issue, and hold it back for that reason. If the article is longer than most, the editor might wait for enough space to open up in a large issue before scheduling it.

Once your article is accepted, you should relax and wait until the editor tells you it has been scheduled. But if a year goes by and your work has still not appeared, again you are justified in inquiring. Your note should be brief, specific, and carefully written.

If an article is accepted but not published, you can request that the editors return it to you for submission to other magazines. Some editors will send it back without conditions; others will ask that you repay their payment to you if you sell the piece to another magazine.

Acknowledgments

CHAPTER FOUR

pp. 32–33:   Analysis of *Ghost Town Quarterly* quoted by permission of Sherril Steele-Carlin.

pp. 33–34:   Analysis of *Backpacker* quoted by permission of Charles Plueddeman.

CHAPTER FIVE

pp. 40–45:   Query letters and article memos quoted by permission of Margaret Davidson, Celia Scully, Richard D. Rothschild, and Bob Oliver.

CHAPTER NINE

p. 78:   "The 'Problem' Child" by Julius Segal, Ph.D., and Herbert Yahres reprinted from *Family Health*, May 1981, by special permission. Copyright © 1981 by Family Media, Inc. All rights reserved.

pp. 82–83:   Excerpts from "Out of the Rough and into the Slammer" by Kathleen Maxa quoted by permission of the author and *Esquire* Magazine. Copyright © 1980 by *Esquire* Magazine.

pp. 81–82:   Excerpts from "Warts, Brains, and Other Astonishments" by Lewis Thomas, reprinted by permission. From *The Medusa and the Snail, More Notes of a Biology Watcher* by Lewis Thomas. Copyright © 1974, 1975, 1976, 1978, 1979 by Lewis Thomas. Reprinted by Permission of Viking Penguin, Inc.

CHAPTER TEN

pp. 89–90:   Excerpts from "Walking Tall with Michael J. Fox" by Chris Chase, quoted by permission of *Cosmopolitan*. Copyright © 1991 by Cosmopolitan.

p. 91:   Excerpts from "Games Restaurants Play" by James Villas, originally published in *Esquire*, quoted by permission of the author.

CHAPTER ELEVEN

pp. 95:   Excerpts from *The Elements of Style*, Third Edition, by William Strunk, Jr. and E. B. White, reprinted by permission of Macmillan Publishing Company. Copyright © 1979 by Macmillan Publishing Company.

CHAPTER TWELVE

pp. 102–103:   Excerpts from "What Will You Do?" by Joseph Anthony, reprinted from "Money" column in March/April 1990 issue of *National Geographic Traveler,* by permission.

pp. 103–104:   Excerpts from "Savior on the Streets" by Mark Stuart Gill reprinted with permission of the author from the July 1991, issue of *Reader's Digest.* Copyright © 1991 by Mark Stuart Gill.

pp. 104–105:   Excerpts from "Those Mysterious, Maddening Allergies" by Maxine Abrams reprinted from *Cosmopolitan* by permission. Copyright © 1991 by *Cosmopolitan.*

pp. 105–106:   Excerpts from "A Fraud That Shook the World of Science" by Morton Hunt. Copyright © 1981 by The New York Times Company, reprinted by permission.

pp. 107–109:   Excerpts from "Portrait of Hemingway," by Lillian Ross, originally published in *The New Yorker,* quoted by permission of the author and the Robert Lantz-Joy Harris Literary Agency.

CHAPTER FOURTEEN

pp. 126–134:   Quotations from Fulton Oursler, Jr., Albert Rosenfeld, John G. Stewart, Roger Rappaport, Margaret Davidson, Linda Stewart, Philip B. Osborne, John Frook, Robert Laxalt, Richard Matthews, Hal Wingo, and Roberta Ashley used by permission.

CHAPTER FIFTEEN

pp. 137–138:   Letter from Teresa Gibbs quoted by permission of the author.

CHAPTER SIXTEEN

pp. 146–161:   These first-person statements from editors were prepared especially for this book. This material is used with the permission of Roberta Anne Myers, Articles Editor of *Seventeen*; Philip Barry Osborne, Assistant Managing Editor of *Reader's Digest*; Hal Wingo, Assistant Managing Editor of *People*; Roberta Ashley, Executive Editor of *Cosmopolitan*; Ian Ledgerwood, Editor-at-Large of *Modern Maturity*; Tom Shealey, Managing Editor of *Backpacker*; Andrea Thompson, Articles Editor of *McCall's*; and Douglas Foster, Editor of *Mother Jones.* (A portion of the statement by Philip Barry Osborne was published previously by *Writer's Digest.*)

A LOOK AT THE NEW JOURNALISM

pp. 173–174:   Excerpts from "The Kentucky Derby is Decadent and Depraved" by Hunter S. Thompson quoted by permission of the author and the Gonzo Foundation for Smarter Journalism.

pp. 175–176:   Excerpts from "The Kandy-Kolored Tangerine-Flake Streamline Baby" by Tom Wolfe reprinted by permission of Farrar, Straus & Giroux, Inc. Copyright © 1963, 1964, 1965 by Tom Wolfe.

Index